PANGEA

PANGEA

Lori,

enjoy the Book

Peter DeChristopher

Peter DeChristopher

Library of Congress Control Number: 2022907573
ISBN: Hardcover   978-1-6698-1991-2
                 Softcover   978-1-6698-1990-5
                 eBook   978-1-6698-1989-9

Print information available on the last page.

Rev. date: 06/08/2022

To order additional copies of this book, contact:
Xlibris
844-714-8691
www.Xlibris.com
Orders@Xlibris.com
840468

CONTENTS

In the Beginning ix
A Prelude to an Untamed World.. xiii

Chapter 1   As the Night Sky Speaks to Us 1
Chapter 2   The Awakening of Isolde 13
Chapter 3   Kill 'Em All...29
Chapter 4   The Journey Northward of the Five................................35
Chapter 5   Unlikely Alliances 41
Chapter 6   Into the Darkness..54
Chapter 7   The Dark Tower..81
Chapter 8   The Journey Back..97
Chapter 9   Evil's Far Reach..103
Chapter 10   The Penance of Queen Lazuli....................................... 117
Chapter 11   The Best Laid Plans..127
Chapter 12   The Forgotten Warriors 133
Chapter 13   The Tale and Its Consequences....................................148
Chapter 14   The Daughters of Shayla 155
Chapter 15   The Hunt for Answers 166
Chapter 16   The March to the Gathering 177
Chapter 17   Ravens Rock...188
Chapter 18   An Endless Wasteland of Water and Ice.......................197
Chapter 19   The Gathering of the Kingdoms.................................. 208
Chapter 20   A March to War..214
Chapter 21   The March through the Valley of Lost Souls 231
Chapter 22   The Great Chamber.. 240
Chapter 23   The Longest Day 251
Chapter 24   The Aftermath..260

Creatures, Places, and Things...267

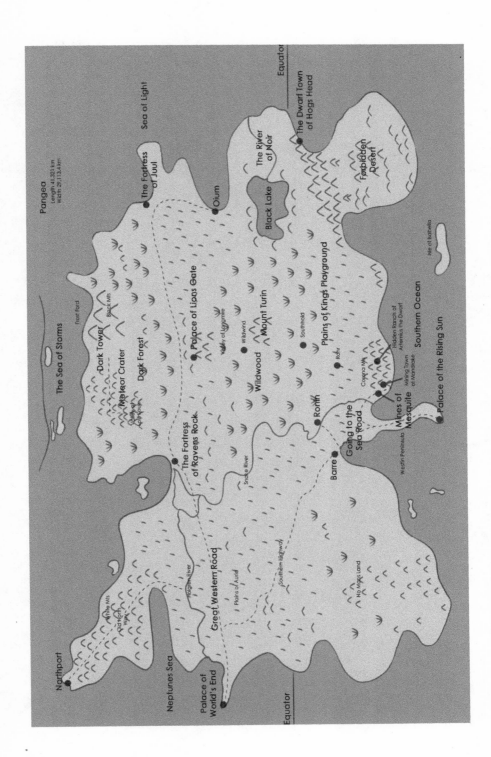

In the Beginning

In a galaxy created in the infancy of the celestial universe over thirteen billion years ago at the beginning of time and space, the Sombrero Galaxy was born of gas and rock with millions of solar systems in its constellation. One such solar system settled with eight planets revolving around its sun—a dwarf sun of enormous size, adorning its satellites with a radiance of a scarlet hue projecting from its core. One such planet—the fourth planet in this solar system—was positioned to have the ability to set forth the seeds of creation and overseen by the creator of all that is—the *Ancient of Days*—who, through his wisdom, also created the *Guardians* to oversee all aspects of his creations and to monitor all life that would evolve in every form. These spiritual entities created by the *deity* are not only of spirit but are also of flesh and blood. Though they were given the powers of the seers, they were tasked to watch over all living entities as the planet evolved from an uninhabitable ball of molten rock to a planet able to evolve life of both fauna and flora.

After billions of years of meteoric bombardment and tectonic movement the planet began to settle into a stable orbit. Then after many more billions of years of evolution, it evolved an atmosphere capable of sustaining life. Oxygen saturation, once stabilized, settled at a level of 45% of the gases in the atmosphere; thus, contributing to extremely long lifespans which began to emerge from the seas more than seven billion years ago. The oxygen saturation has also attributed to many species obtaining the ability to grow to enormous sizes, such as spiders three meters round and scorpions four meters long.

Life in its varied forms settled throughout the world in its many continents which were divided by rising sea levels. The waters over many millions of years became abundant with many aquatic species which ranged in size from the microscopic bacteria to the largest predators roaming the world. Dinosaurs, as long as forty-five meters, to this day dominate the land, while the megalodon shark, the Kronosaurus, and the long-necked plesiosaurs dominate the seas. Eventually, many species crawled out of the seas and adapted to life on firm land. Through tectonic movement and after billions of years, the continents converged to form a single *supercontinent* known in the Modern Age as *Pangea*.

Though as life crawled out of the seas, many species adapted to living on firm land in its varied forms and adapted their lives to its many climates. One species which emerged, then divided into two distinct races, this species became known as the *Tehrans*. Their aquatic selves settled in the *Lemurian Archipelago*, a thousand kilometers off the eastern coast of the supercontinent. Though this subspecies of *Tehran* does venture on land to eat and breed, they remain ancient in physiology and appearance, with very pale skin tone and webbed feet and hands allowing them to navigate easily in the warm waters of the *Sea of Light*, one thousand kilometers off the eastern coast of the supercontinent. The species settled within an island chain known in the modern day as the Lemurian Archipelago. This species settled on its largest island known as the *Isle of Andalusia*, thus naming this a subspecies the *Andalusians*.

The terrestrial Tehrans inhabit the *supercontinent*. After many millennia of fighting among themselves, the most barbaric and dominate Tehrans claimed leadership over their weaker selves and settled into clans to rule over designated areas of the *supercontinent*. This became known in their history as the beginning of the *First Age* of Pangea. As the clans grew in number and clashed with one another over many millions of years, many lives were lost in numerous battles. It was decided among the leaders of the three dominant clans to create a *peace treaty* to coexist with one another. The three clans divided the supercontinent into three distinct realms—the *Northern Realm*, the *Southern Realm*, and the *Western Realm*. The clan leadership put forth in the treaty to rule within those boundaries only. This became known as the beginning of the *Second Age* of Pangea.

As time evolved the race of Tehrans became the dominant species on the *supercontinent*. The clans agreed to live by the *Laws of Life* set forth and inscribed by the *Ancient of Days*, which are overseen and enforced by the Guardians.

Millions of years before the beginning of the First Age, as the continents were still separated and was each its own, a child was born, sired by Limrath—the first of the Guardians Order who impregnated his companion, Mira. A daughter was brought forth by their union; she was named by the Ancient of Days *Isolde*, meaning, in the ancient tongue of the creator, "she who is gazed upon;" for she was born with great beauty and majesty.

Isolde was taken to the Lemurian Archipelago as an infant by her parents. She was given to the *Alicorn* queen, *Elisheba*, to raise as her own, for it is her destiny to wander the planet to council the kings of Pangea in times of uncertainty and to lead their armies against all who wish to do harm to the planet and its inhabitants. It is Isolde's destiny to defend the *righteous* and the *meek*. As a consequence of being the only child conceived by the Guardians, Isolde was taught the ways and the sorcery of the *Alicorns* to assist her in her future travels, as she is blessed with the vision of the Guardians and the magic of the Alicorns.

With the dwarf sun emanating its rays in a dimly lit fashion radiating a *scarlet hue* known as the *twilight*, most species on Pangea, through evolution, have developed extremely large eyes which cover about one-third of their facial features. This has given them the ability to see clearly in the *twilight* of day, as well as in the *dimindark* of night. They have conquered the known world through their barbaric way of life and their warmongering nature; thus, in their cruelty have become the rulers as well as the taskmasters of the realms, enslaving the variety of dwarf species to assist in their mining of gems and gold, along with the primitive race smaller than the Tehrans which stand about 152 centimeters in height called the *Neanderthals*. *Tehran* males stand almost four meters in height, while the females are smaller, usually less than three meters tall. Pangea is primitive in nature due to the large amount and varied species of known predators, which are both prehistoric and modern that dominate the wilds.

The landscape consists mostly of forest and plains, with the *Forbidden Desert* located in the southeastern region of the *supercontinent*. This region is dominated by the large worms that live under the desert sand called the *louse worms*, which are twenty-five meters in length and contain thousands of needle-like teeth a meter long used for penetrating its victim and releasing their fluids which are then consumed. Once they have drained their victim's bodies of all their fluids, they reject their flesh or what is left of it. The worm's leatherlike skin allows them to live under the scorching sand; thus, it protects them from the desert heat which can reach as much as 333.2 kelvins.

In the *frozen zone* atop the *Black Mountains* of the Northern Realm resides a species known as the *Centaurs*. This half-man half-horse species lives in isolation in the caves which are prevalent throughout the mountaintops and its slopes above the winter storm that has been ongoing since the beginning of time in this *evil* realm. They have lived in this fashion for millions of seasons. Some of this species, which have longed for a different life in a somewhat warmer climate, have formed smaller clans and live a nomadic life, wandering throughout the supercontinent.

In the center of the supercontinent there is the uncharted wilderness known as *Wildwood*. The Tehran kings in their peace treaty have agreed not to trespass within its borders due to its topography and massive number of predators that exist within it. The *Warrows*, who dwell within it are one meter tall elves that have built their villages on the treetops of this uncharted forest. Their population, according to their estimates, is in the thousands between the two clans. In the Northern Wildwood is the city is known as *Wildwind*, while in the Southern Wildwood, the city is known as *Southold*. The distinction between the two clans is the color of their hair. the Northern Warrows have a distinct *jet-black hair*, while the Warrows of the Southern Wildwood have *golden hair*. They have resided in this hostile environment as far back as the First Age of existence and rarely leave the confines of this untamed place.

But as cruel as the Tehrans are, there is another species that dwell in the *Dark Forest* known as the *Malakai*. This cyclops species roams the wilds of Pangea and it stands about 7.62 meters tall and are troll-like in appearance. They are mute and dumb in their intelligence but are insatiable in appetite. They are known to leave the Dark Forest from time to time and roam the wilds of the supercontinent, especially in the *winter season* when their food sources are scarce. They travel in small tribes using their nail-laden clubs to do their bidding.

The world has not advanced technologically due to the number of predators who dominate the wilderness. Many predators, like most species, are just trying to survive from day to day; therefore, the world has been stalled in a medieval lifestyle.

As they enter into to Fourth Age of their existence, time is beginning to unfold from a great evil once encountered at the end of the Second Age that all thought was asleep, which now seems destined to awaken.

This is that story.

———

A Prelude to an Untamed World

As the two exiled Tehrans struggle to elude their pursuers through the unchartered terrain of the Southern Wildwood, gasping for air as they glance behind them for they neither could not identify their assailants even as the dwarf sun sits at its zenith. The scarlet hues emanating from its star is as bright as dusk; thus, it does not have the radiance to penetrate the thick canopy of - Wildwood. Both Tehrans can sense that their fate is just moments from its conclusion if they cannot outrun their assailants or find a hidden enclave to hide in which to evade the oncoming slaughter if they continue to scamper out in the open. Brambles as sharp as a megalodon's teeth have cut them hundreds of times, leaving a bloody trail for their hunters to follow. Fatigued and injured from the pursuit through the dense forest, the two stumble and falter down a steep ravine about ten meters deep; both hit the bottom with a loud thud.

Dazed and confused, the two Tehrans lay semiconscious at the washes bottom, not able to move from exhaustion and pain.

One of the Tehrans asks the other, "Are we dead yet?"

Wondering if the hunters pursuing them are still on the chase, the other Tehran moves his large eyes, unable to move his body, and answers his companion, "I think we will be!" as he raises his large eyes in front of him.

Standing alongside the two is a large pterosaur staring down at them, not two meters from where they lay. The beast extends its wings, which spread ten meters wide, and begins to flap them back and forth, sending a whirlwind of air and stirring up the fragments left on the floor of the basin. The beast then pulls its head back and lets out a shrieking scream so loud that the surrounding trees shake with a vengeance; with a breath so hot and powerful that it blows like a hurricane at its full force. Then slowly the beast lowers its head as it gazes at the two incapacitated Tehrans for a brief moment; saliva dripping from its 150-millimeter-long fangs which number too many to conceive. Then suddenly the beast leans forward and grabs the nearest Tehran in its large jaws above his waist, then raises its huge head above its body and bites down on its prey, cutting the Tehran in half and crunching his bones, leaving his lower extremities to plunge to the ground in a bloody clump. The other Tehran watches in horror. He attempts to get up and run from the carnage, but his movements are met with a ferocious bite which engulfs his body with one mouthful. The pterosaur then swallows its second victim and screams for moments on end in satisfaction of consuming its prey.

The beast then gazes to and fro to scope out the sky above it and contemplate if it is safe to take to the air, for its screams might have alerted many nearby predators of its whereabouts. Then after a few moments of calm, satisfied that no other predators are near, the beast takes to the air and, in mere seconds, it is out of sight from where the carnage has just occurred.

Watching from the safety of the dimly lit canopy high atop the forest floor are the hunters who were pursuing the two Tehrans through - Wildwood. They lay witness to the cycle of life and death in this untamed land; thus, they contemplate that the nature of Pangea will always be that

"The strong will survive and the weak shall perish."

Satisfied by the outcome which they have just witnessed, the seven golden-haired Warrows of the Southern Wildwood who were pursuing the two Tehrans will now return to the Warrow village of Southold that sits high atop the canopy of the Southern Wildwood.

CHAPTER I

As the Night Sky Speaks to Us

"For the skies will burn and the seas will boil, for when evil reveals itself the world will fall into shadow, which will be the beginning of the end of times."

—Isolde, The White Witch

The Dwarfs settle in for the evening in the mining village of Mandrake is located deep within the mountain chain known as the Corona Mountains, which abound the warm waters of the Southern Ocean. They labor by mining gems and gold from the dawn of twilight until the sun fades into the dimindark. They labor each and every day of their lives, for time is meaningless to these slaves. Those that are incapable of completing their daily tasks are quickly put to death, then quickly replaced by other Dwarfs as ordered by their queen. The Dwarfs have labored over this duty for millions of seasons in the enslavement of the empress, *Queen Lazuli*, ruler of the Southern Realm who has ruled over this realm for millions of seasons and dwells in the castle known as the *Palace of the Rising Sun*. She is their taskmaster who rules without conscience or empathy for any other than herself; for her only desires are of gems, power, and the sexual gratification others can bestow on her. The Dwarfs are supervised by the soldiers of this evil queen who also dwell in the village beside the Dwarfs and the Neanderthals themselves. The Dwarfs live with their families in small cottages constructed by their ancestors millions of seasons ago and reside with generation upon generation, as they have always done; thus, some families reside with as many as six generations in their household.

"Grandpa, tell us a bedtime story," asks Tommy, for he and his twin brother Julian share a room in their family's cottage in the dwarf village of Mandrake. The twins are five full seasons in age and stand about thirty-eight centimeters in height, which is tall for their age, considering that they are dwarfs. By the time they reach thirteen full seasons of age, they will be thrust into—with their fathers and grandfathers to work alongside them both—the *Mines of Mesquite*, deep below the Corona Mountains, digging for gems and gold, for as slaves of the queen, that has been their destiny from generation after generation.

"Okay, you two, hop into bed," requests their grandfather.

"Grandfather, tell us the story about the evil being that lived in the *Dark Tower*," asks Julian.

"The Necromancer? Why do you want to hear about him, Julian?" asks Grandpa.

"'Cause that's my favorite story."

Grandfather lets out a big sigh. "Okay, then . . . a long, long time ago a giant rock fell from the sky and crashed in the Dark Forest. It made a hole so deep that it took days for many Tehrans to climb down inside it. When they finally reached the bottom, they found some kind of being who was five meters tall."

"Wow, he was a big one, Grandpa," remarks Tommy.

"Yes, he was, Tommy. Anyway, this being said, he came from the stars to rule over the world, for he proclaimed himself as the king of the world, and everyone who lived on the planet was his slave."

"Like we are to Queen Lazuli?" questions Julian.

Grandfather gives a glum look at his grandchildren and says, "Yes, children, but he then became enraged at the Tehrans who were not sure if they should accept him as their king, for they worshiped the Ancient of Days as their creator. The Necromancer became enraged. He then shot flames out of his fingertips with a fire so hot it incinerated many Tehrans for refusing to kneel to him and call him king. He then became known as the Necromancer, the *Demon of Fire*."

"How did he live, Grandpa?"

"Well, he sucked the souls out of the Tehrans, taking away their ability to think for themselves, and they became his zombie army. Like we eat food, he ate their souls."

"That's not very tasty," remarks Tommy.

"I'd rather have swine sausage. Now that's tasty," says Julian,

"Aha!" remarks Tommy.

Grandpa then chuckles at Julian's remark. "After that, many Tehrans began to disappear."

"Were they ever found, Grandpa?"

"Well, the missing Tehrans became part of the Necromancer's army, along with many Malakai and Neanderthals, who were weak-willed to begin with and easy to manipulate their actions. Thus, with them under his spells, he tried to conquer all of Pangea."

"Did he succeed, Grandpa?"

"No, Julian, he did not. He was vanquished to the *Underworld*. In the end, it was Isolde, the *White Witch* who is pure of heart, who slayed him. She was riding atop of Elisheba, Queen of the Alicorns, who raised Isolde from a baby. Thus, she slayed him with her sword crafted by the Warrows of Wildwind which was made of pure gold."

"So she killed him?" asks Julian

"Well, my boy, she did slay him, but legends say he was vanquished to the Underworld, but he swore that one day he would return."

"Can he do that, Grandfather?" asks Tommy.

"Well, children, evil will always find a way to return," concludes Grandpa.

"Okay, story completed. Now it is time to go to bed . . . Good night, Tommy. Good night, Julian."

The children say goodnight to their grandfather. He then blows out the candle, which was lighting their room, and as he leaves, he then shuts the door behind him.

The twins' father, who was listening from the other room, says to his father, "If they only knew that was a true story."

Grandfather then says, "It should always be a fairytale to them."

"We can only hope," answers the twins' father.

As the dimindark wears on, the illumination of the twin full moons lights up the night sky. Queen Lazuli's soldiers are sitting outside their sleeping quarters in the town of Mandrake, as the dwarfs have settled in for the evening in their cottages. thus, the Neanderthals are nestled in their caves just on the outskirts of town with their fires glowing, lighting up the eastern edge of the mining village. The smell of the sea air fills their nostrils, as the village is only ten kilometers from the Southern Ocean. In this tropical climate the temperature does not vary much, as the daytime temperature year-round is about 302 Kelvins. In the evenings, the temperature drops to about 294 Kelvins. The soldiers drink wheat ale and tell the tales of their fathers and their fathers' fathers of the Great War which ended the Second Age, for they fear that history will repeat itself especially with all the activity they have been witnessing lately with the many streaks of light which have been propelling daily across the night sky.

"Lieutenant, look! There's another one," says a private, as he points to the southern sky. "They are always heading north . . . always," says the private.

"You're right, private, they all seem to follow the same path," answers Lieutenant *Liam Collinsworth*, who is in command of the squad of soldiers and responsible for the production of gold and gems found in the Mines of Mesquite.

"Do you think history will repeat itself, lieutenant?" asks the private.

"Well, private, the night sky sure is talking to us, but what is it saying, that is the question," remarks the lieutenant.

"Maybe it's saying we're all in deep shit," remarks Sergeant *Roland March*. Then the company of men laugh at his remark.

"Well, if history does indeed repeat itself, as the private alluded to, we all may be in deeper shit than we think," answers the lieutenant.

Again the company laughs, but their laugh is one of concern, for in the back of their minds this is how it all played out last time, which led to the Great War of the Second Age when the Necromancer set the world ablaze in his bid to conquer all that dwelt in the world.

"There have been rumors of Malakai roaming the Northern and Western Realms and killing many a bison and elk to feed on," says another private.

"Are you sure?" asks Sergeant March.

"Well, that's what I heard from my cousin who is a captain on *General Levi's* staff. The general was told that by General *Harlee Antonia* of the *Daughters of Shayla* in a private meeting," answers the private.

"An assassin of the queen told the general that?" remarks Sergeant March. "That's what my cousin told me," answers the private.

"Harlee Antonia . . . The Daughters of Shayla, huh? They are usually very resourceful," remarks the lieutenant. He goes on, "They are very secretive and move about like the wind, unseen and deadly, and are the queen's most trusted warriors."

"Then you believe that story?" asks the sergeant.

"Well, let's say that I believe that if the Daughters of Shayla are telling the General that I would be concerned," says Lieutenant Collinsworth.

"What do we do?" asks another private.

"Do? Nothing. The Northern Realm is on the other side of the continent, and the Western Realm is too far away from us to worry about it . . . for now," says the lieutenant.

"As long as the Malakai stay there, we have nothing to worry about," remarks Sergeant March.

"But when and if they move about and somehow make it to the Southern Realm, we will have a problem," answers the lieutenant.

"When and if are the questions at hand," remarks the sergeant.

"It sure is," concludes the lieutenant.

Meanwhile, in the Northern Realm . . .

In the Northern Realm in the king's city of *Lions Gate*, *King Galen Emor* stands atop the citadel's highest tower overlooking the city below. The king gazes out upon the Dark Forest which commences less than ten kilometers from the citadel to its north. Alongside the king is *Giselle the Sorceress;* the king's advisor and seer of all things in the present, but she only has the ability to see fragments and shadows of the future. She has been by the king's side for the last two million seasons as his spiritual and policy advisor. Her age is undetermined, for the king has always remembered her in the service of the crown as she was his father's advisor before him. As beautiful as she is, with her long flowing red hair falling into the small of her back, the potency of her spells and potions are legendary throughout the supercontinent; for with them she has the ability to change the course of the present.

As the two watch the night sky and the activity going on high above their heads, Giselle feels an uneasiness in her bones, a premonition of a feeling she felt just once before millions of seasons ago. Since the Great War, which ended the Second Age, the Northern Realm and the realm's primary city of Lions Gate has always been on high alert, thus building the fortresses of *Ravens Rock* on the western border and *Juul* to the east—both borders of the Dark Forest. These fortresses were built to protect against any invasions coming out of that dark realm and from the tribes of Malakai and Neanderthals, who dwell primarily in the "Dark Forest and who regularly cross over into the Northern Realm with the purpose of invading the small villages along its border to forage on their livestock to satisfy their hunger. The fortresses were built after the Great War two million seasons ago.

The meteoric activity this evening is very active.

"These streaks of light appear to be falling directly into the Dark Forest, Your Highness," surmises Giselle.

"Is it a warning or just coincidence?" King Galen turns and looks toward the sorceress.

"I have felt an uneasiness, like the presence of an evil spirit, stirring in the Dark Forest, building and building like a volcano getting ready for a pyroclastic eruption which can destroy and incinerate everything it touches," answers Giselle.

"Incinerate like a *demon of fire*, sorceress?" proclaims the king.

"Yes, Your Highness, exactly like that!" Giselle answers, as she stares directly out into the darkness of the realm.

"I will double the guards around Lions Gate. I will send a patrol to navigate the dark realm's border as the first line of defense against anything coming out of the forest itself," the king announces to Giselle.

At the dawn of twilight, King Galen will send the field commander of his army, *Captain William*, and his squad of twelve soldiers to patrol the realm's border with the Dark Forest.

The squad leaves the citadel just before the dawn of twilight as the morning dew still covers the ground. They ride clustered together as the visibility is still nonexistent. The terrain is hilly with tall grasses standing about a meter in height which can hide many a predator, so their pace is slow and cautious, with few trees to block one's view in which one can see for many kilometers through to the horizon. This terrain, known as the *Grassy Plains*, continues south of the citadel leading up to - Wildwood in which this makes the historical range of the large wild bison standing three meters tall and the tiny *plains raptor* dinosaurs, which stand about thirty-eight centimeters high that hunt in packs who roam this part of the continent in the warmer weather of the *Season of Summer*, then recede south as the *Season of Harvest* approaches.

The fortresses of Ravens Rock and Juul have regular patrols along the border, and report regularly any types of sightings they encounter directly to the king. It is a short sprint to the border from Lions Gate, thus there are no trails leading up to the Dark Forest, for this is wild country and not well traveled because of the abundance of predators that roam here. As the squad of soldiers reach near the border, they stop on top of a hill overlooking the landscape. As they look ahead, the tree line appears like a wall seemingly impossible to penetrate. With the twilight barely able to permeate its canopy, it appears gloomy and bleak; one can only wonder what kinds of beasts roam this foul land.

{The Dark Forest, as far back as anyone can remember, has had storm clouds which continuously swirl below the peaks of the Black Mountains. This mountain chain surrounds the castle known as the Dark Tower and the *Great Meteor Crater*. The woods are said to be crawling with beasts never before encountered out of this realm, while the castle is said to be protected by the Malakai, the cyclops beasts who were controlled by the Necromancer who, through his actions, initiated the Great War of the Second Age.}

"What do you think, captain?" asks Sergeant *Billy Zane*.

"I think we need to be extremely careful, stay together if we can, and watch each other's backs," answers the captain.

As the troop descends the sloping hill, they hold their steeds to a slow walk, treading carefully as they inch closer to fulfill the king's orders of guarding against any and all beasts that dare to exit this foul realm. As the troop approaches the tree line, a cold swirling wind encompasses their being.

"The temperature seems like it has dropped significantly, captain," says the sergeant.

"Evil has a way of sending chills down your spine, sergeant. This forest is very, very old, for it is guarded by the puppets of calamity. What dwells in it is as old as time itself, and as malevolent as the foulest beasts that roam the planet," answers the captain.

The trees are very tall, some as tall as ninety meters, and all seem to be deformed in shape from the nefarious nature of this forest. As the soldiers stand before its prominence, one of the privates states, "It has a foul smell to it. Like the smell of death."

The soldiers look toward one another; each with a reluctant look in their eyes with a hint of fear. The captain breaks the silence. "Come on now, boys, we have a job to do."

So for hours they walk their steeds along the forest's edge, inspecting upward into the canopy, then downward along the forest floor. There are no sounds or any movement of the beasts that roam here that they have heard, only a cold stillness permeating the surrounding air.

As the twilight begins to fade, the captain orders the soldiers to make camp for the night. "The dimindark will soon encompass the realm. Surround the camp with fires large enough for us to see out into the dimindark and, sergeant, post guards at the camps boundaries."

Sergeant Zane nods his head in acknowledgment.

As the dimindark settles in, the hearths are simmering with mutton stew, abounding its aroma throughout the camp which overtakes the foulness of the surrounding air.

"Smells good, private," says the sergeant.

"Mutton stew with just a hint of red pepper. I don't know about you, sarge, but I'm starving," says the private.

"I think we all are. The morning meal was the last time we have eaten," replies the sergeant.

As the evening wears on, there appears to be movement in the surrounding woodlands; for what was once a stillness now appears to be a stirring, just beyond the glow of the firelight.

"Sounds like there is something moving about in the tree branches," remarks the sergeant.

As the troop looks upward, they notice the glow of red eyeshine filling the lower branches of what seems to be hundreds of pairs of eyes staring back of them.

"What the—" remarks a private.

"Antler bats!" yells the captain.

{Antler bats are bats that are huge, about one meter in length, with antlers fifteen centimeters long. They have pointed teeth fifty millimeters long. They attack in mass numbers and leave only their victim's skeletons as evidence of their barrage. Their primary habitat is the treetops encompassing the Dark Forest.}

The bats start to screech and flap their wings in excitement.

Captain William then remarks, "Don't make any sudden moves. Slowly . . . move toward the fires. They cannot see well in the brightness of light."

"Where are the torches?" asks Sergeant Zane. "Over there in a pile," remarks a private.

"I'll get them," answers another private.

"No, don't move!" orders the captain. "Slowly move toward the fires. If you move away from the light, they will attack."

"Fuck it, I'm gonna get them," insists another private.

Before the captain can stop him, the private begins to slowly crawl over to the pile of unlit torches. Everyone in the squad holds their breath in anticipation. But as he gets about halfway to the torches, the swarm of bats leave their branches and take to the air. Like a swarm of killer bees, they swoop down toward the private and begin to forge toward him; thus, hundreds of bats encircle his body like the vicious swirl of a tornado, then their entire colony race to attack him.

The swarm attack the private in mass, sending the swarm into a feeding frenzy. Piece by piece, they begin to tear his body apart, ripping his flesh and sending streams of blood high into the air. They cover his body like a blanket on a cold winter's night.

Once the bats have ripped apart chunks of their prey, they fly back up into the tree branches with pieces of his flesh and organs in their fangs. As one bats leaves, another takes its place. The soldier's screams are deafening but only last for a moment, for within seconds all that was left of the private was his skeleton stretched out in the middle of the campsite, lying in a pool of his own blood. The antler bats have devoured every inch of his being.

The watching soldiers are left aghast, some are in shock. The captain rallies to grab the torches. Then in their clump, he lunges them into the nearest fire, lighting up the campsite as bright as a volcano exploding in the dimindark, exposing the full ire of the colony of bats. With the illumination of the many torches, the colony of bats take to the air; this time, flying up high into the sky to avoid the brightness of the lit torches. Within moments the trees are bare of the beasts, and the stillness of the night is once again resumed; only the chill of the night air signifies where the carnage had just instilled.

"Each one of you grab a torch and hold it high above your heads," commands the captain.

So each of them do as they are ordered.

"How can they be so barbaric? They left nothing but bones," says a private.

"Barbaric? They're bats. All they do is eat, shit, and make little bats. Well, not so little in this case," answers Sergeant Zane.

"He never had a chance. Once they start the feeding frenzy, there is no stopping them until they have devoured all that there is," remarks the captain.

"The Dark Forest is infested with many colonies of them spread throughout the realm," Sergeant Zane remarks.

"At the dawn of twilight, we will bury what is left of the private. Understand, sergeant?" "Yes, sir," he replies.

"Keep all of the torches lit throughout the night and double the sentries. All we need now is a tribe of Malakai to show themselves," remarks Captain William.

"Then I'm going home," replies the sergeant.

As the dawn of twilight rises from the east, the company buries the skeleton of the private in the tall grasses right before the border of the Dark Forest where he was slain.

"His soul, will it ascend to the Spirit Realm by his bones being buried and not doing the ritual of the *Rising Ceremony*, captain?" asks one of the other privates.

"Well, I don't rightly know, private, but there was no flesh left to burn just bones, so I hope his soul ascended as he lost his life," prophesies the captain.

After the burial, one of the privates who was wandering just outside the campground wanders back to the campsite with two arms full of small eggs.

"What have you got there, private?" asks the captain.

"Eggs, captain, lots of 'em," remarks the private who seems so pleased with himself.

"Let me have a look at them—raptor eggs!" says the captain in a highly alerted state.

"I hate raptors," says the sergeant.

"But their eggs *are* tasty," the captain says, smiling.

"Yeah, they are, but where are the little buggers?" asks the sergeant.

"Good question. We need to stay alert. Remember where we are, sergeant," insists the captain.

The private, who is designated as their cook, asks, "How do we want the eggs cooked, looking at you or scrambled?"

"Mix them up, private. But right now I need a cup of tea. A strong cup of tea," remarks the sergeant.

The soldiers sit down for their meal and chat about the one they are leaving behind and recount the memories that they all shared together as a crew. A somber mood has come over the patrol as they reminisce of past stories about their fallen comrade and stroll down memory lane.

Once the morning meal is completed and the cooking pans are put away back in the cook's pack, the squad mounts their steeds and begin the day's patrol along the border of the Dark Forest. They will need to proceed with extreme caution so as to not repeat the past evening's events. While losses are part of living in this extreme environment, it is never acceptable to the captain to lose even one of his men, for they are as close as a family can be.

The captain has reiterated may times to his men that "Blood only means one is related, but loyalty is what makes one family."

CHAPTER II

The Awakening of Isolde

Isolde is standing on a porch just outside the meeting room of the wood carved castle of *King Leo the Just*, who is the ruler of the Warrows of the Northern Wildwood. He rules over the city of Wildwind in which he has ruled over for the past two million seasons. Isolde gazes out onto the wilderness of this untamed realm, as she is some two hundred meters above the forest floor in this tree village of the Northern Warrow clan.

As it is told, Wildwind was built at the beginning of the Second Age by King Leo's father, King Leo II, before the Great War of the Second Age. The city is built high atop the forest floor in the canopy of the Redwood Forest. The city was built purposely in the treetops to protect its inhabitants from the onslaught of predators that roam throughout this wild and untamed realm. It is a city made of hardwood. Its houses and walkways are as ornate as the statues in the catacombs of the Palace of the Rising Sun that Isolde vaguely remembers as those burial tombs have been infested with the large *black scorpions* since before the Great War of the Second Age. Not a soul has ventured into the dark tomb except the condemned that Queen Lazuli has sentenced to death in those hallows.

Wildwind's walkways are adorned with wooden carvings of the heroes of old whose lives were extinguished in that Great War. They are as wide as the streets of *World's End*. The city has many levels and many staircases, as the population has expanded over the many seasons since it was first erected. Its expanse wanders out as far as one's large eyes can see.

As the king enters his private porch adjoining his quarters, he is accompanied by six Warrow warriors, his personal guards. He smiles as he catches a glimpse of Isolde. As he approaches her, he embraces her as an old friend; one that he has known since the king was a *Warling* born unto this world over two and a half million seasons past.

"What brings you here, my lady?" asks King Leo, as he gazes up into the large eyes of the White Witch.

"Come, sit. Let us whisper to each other on the comings and goings of the world outside of this realm, my lady."

The King's Guard brings a chair large enough for a Tehran to sit on. As they both sit at the large rectangular table in the middle of the porch, Isolde says to the king, "I have forgotten just how beautiful Wildwood is, your majesty."

"Yes, beautiful but unforgiving. It seems like more and more beasts roam the forest floor every season, especially in the Season of the Harvest, though we are quite safe high above it, except for an occasional serpent which slithers inside the city. In which case, it does make for a splendid meal," replies the king.

Both laugh at the king's remark.

{Isolde's age is undetermined, as she was taken to Pangea by her parents *Limrak* and *Mira*, who were two of the Guardians of the world, to be raised by Elisheba, Queen of the Alicorns. At about one thousand seasons of age, which was millions and millions of seasons ago, she was destined to and appointed by the Ancient of Days to wander the land as a council for its leaders, and a warrior of the deity to right the wrongs as established by the deity, as well as enforcing *Alicorn Law*. She has wandered the world as far back as anyone can recall and has seen the world's entire history even before the continents converged firsthand. She is pure of heart and soul and as wise as many in the Spirit World. She is thin with salt and pepper hair which flows below her shoulders, and her attire is one of a wandering nomad whose clothes are worn and tattered. She is assisted by a walking stick or her staff, which is rumored to carry magical and healing powers—the magic of the Alicorns. By her side, which hangs in its sheath, is her golden sword named *Casabel*, as named by King Leo II. It was crafted and then forged specifically for the White Witch to aid her in the Great War of the Second Age by the Warrow swordsmiths. Casabel, translated

from the Warrow language of *Wathra*, means "demon kill
Necromancer to his demise into the Underworld.}

"Have you seen the streaks of light in the night sky,
Isolde asks King Leo.

"The Wiki have informed my soldiers of such happe̶n̶̶̶̶. ̶T̶h̶e̶ ̶t̶r̶e̶e
canopy covers much of the sky so it is difficult to see through it or above
the tree line. What do you think it means, my lady?" the king asks.

"You were just a warling when the Great War was fought, but before
the war and prior to the Necromancer showing himself to the world, there
were many steaks of light in the sky reminiscent of what is happening today.
Then the great meteor strike happened in the Dark Forest. It was after that
the Necromancer showed himself and committed many harrowing deeds
upon the world," says Isolde.

"Do you think that history is going to repeat itself or just maybe the
gods of the Spirit World are trying to tell us something?" remarks the king.

"I have a feeling it is a bit of both, your majesty, for I have felt a
presence . . . an evil presence like a dark shadow hovering over the world,
biding its time to show itself," answers Isolde.

"What do we do then, my lady?" inquires the king.

"I have to know for sure for if our enemy has returned. We will need
to prepare for his rebirth. I will travel to the Dark Tower to see for myself.
It is the only way to know for certain if we will bear a second coming of
the evil Necromancer," remarks Isolde.

"No, my lady, it is much too dangerous to travel there. I implore of you
not to go, for evil lurks throughout the realm, not just in the tower itself,"
insists the king.

"I have faced evil before and sent it to the Underworld, I am not afraid
for myself, but for the generations of what is yet to come. What I do, your
majesty, I am compelled to do!" Isolde speaks firmly.

"It is not a matter of fear but of prudence," insists the king.

Then the king pauses for a moment and says to Isolde, "If you are
to travel to the dark realm, at least let a squad of my most accomplished
warriors accompany you as your guard, my lady, for that is the prudent
solution."

Isolde sits back in her chair and thinks for a moment.

King Leo continues.

"We are small in stature and can blend into the forest without being
seen," surmises the king.

"Alright then, I understand your logic. I will take two of your warriors with me as companions, not as protectors. Do you agree with that, your majesty?" concludes Isolde.

Before the king can reply, a Warrow guard speaks up, "Your majesty, I would like to volunteer to accompany Isolde as her companion."

Then another personal guard speaks up, "Me, also, your majesty."

The king turns and faces the two volunteers, then turns back to Isolde. He then points to one of his Warrow guards and says, "Turak, sergeant of my guard." He then points to the other guard, "Philo, one of my best archers."

Isolde then stands and bows to the two Warrows. "It will be a pleasure to have you both accompany me on this adventure."

Then the two Warrows bow back at Isolde.

"We will depart at the dawn of twilight, Master Warrows," Isolde concludes.

The evenings in the Summer Season are short, thus the twilight gives forth its glow much longer than during the solstice of winter. As the dawn begins to rise in the east, Isolde readies herself to leave the tree city of Wildwind. She stands one last time on the porch just outside her guest quarters and gazes at the forest in all its magnificence. As she sips her morning cup of tea, she watches as the Wiki abound with their offspring, teaching them how to play and to survive in the treetops. As the music of many songbirds fills the air with their beautiful melodies, she wonders if this may be the last time her large eyes will gaze upon such a sight, for the future is uncertain even with her ability to see glimpses into it. In this case, her vision is clouded. Isolde then says goodbye to the beauty that surrounds her and heads toward the castle exit. In the hallway just outside her room, she is met by her two Warrow companions.

"Good morning, Turak. Good morning, Philo. Are you ready for our adventure?"

Both nod their heads yes.

"Good. Then let us be on our way, for it is a long journey in which we are about to embark."

The three then walk out the main doors of the wooden castle and head about one hundred and fifty meters to the west to where one of the many hidden staircases that leads down to the forest floor is located. The staircases are invisible to the naked eye and will reveal themselves only to the trained eye once they cite the *Words of Revelation*. The *revealing spell* was the genius of the Warrows at the beginning of Second Age as Wildwind's construction was near completion. The spell was derived to protect the Warrow population. By speaking the spell, it will reveal the hidden staircases as an entrance to the city from the forest floor or as an escape from any and all unwanted visitors should the city become overrun by their enemies. There are only a few outside the Warrows who have knowledge of their whereabouts, and less than a handful who know the words to speak to reveal them, Isolde being one of the chosen few.

As Isolde and the two Warrows approach the hidden staircase, they stop in front of an empty space between two giant redwood trees.

Isolde waves her hand in front of her face and speaks in the ancient Warrow language of Wathra the revelation spell, "Un ama rathier dal a la gosh (translated in the modern tongue meaning "among the treetops")."

Then suddenly the staircase appears out of thin air. It is an ornate spiral staircase made of hardwood two meters wide positioned in between two giant redwood trees two hundred fifty meters tall, thus it descends the two hundred meters to the forest floor of Wildwood.

As the three begin their descent down the winding staircase, Philo says to Isolde, "You speak Wathran as if you were born unto it, my lady."

"I have had millions of seasons of practice, Master Warrow," Isolde replies.

The staircase winds between the two giant redwoods. It is an exhausting descent numbering more than five thousand steps in total. As they continue their descent to the forest floor, Isolde notices a Wiki flying through the air, then landing on the nearby branches, following them as they continue their descent. He is keeping the three companions in its sight.

Isolde turns to Turak, "A friend of yours?"

Turak looks up toward the arthropod, then says to Isolde, "He is *Amolo*, a Wiki friend and a great Warrow scout."

{The Wiki are the four-armed arthropods about the height of the Warrows with wings two meters long. They are the scouts of the Warrows and can soar in the air among and above the forest. They have adapted the large eyes common throughout all the species of the realms to see in the twilight as well in the dimindark. The Warrows and the Wiki have lived among one another in peace for a thousand seasons, as the arthropods dwell in the treetops of - Wildwood. Their offspring play and are raised together with the Warlings in the city of Wildwind. The two species share in the spoils of their hunts; the Wiki forewarn the Warrows on the comings and goings-on throughout Wildwood and beyond, thus they are their loyal companions.}

"Will he be joining us on our journey, Turak?"

"Well, my lady, he and I have had many adventures together over the seasons which have taken us throughout Wildwood and beyond."

"Then I will take that as a yes," concludes Isolde.

Turak then calls out to Amolo in a call that the Warrows use when they want to have the Wiki come to them. The call sounds similar to a raven's caw. Amolo swoops down from in between the large branches of the redwood trees and lands on a branch next to Isolde. She then turns in his direction and looks him up and down.

"My Lady, this is Amolo, Turak says.

"Amolo, it's a pleasure to meet you," Isolde says to the Wiki.

Amolo bows his head in respect, then Isolde turns to the Warrows and asks, "Do either of you speak in the language of the Wiki?"

"No, but they understand our language," answers Philo.

"Their language consists mostly of awkward sounds which is only familiar to other Wiki," answers Turak.

"Okay good, then we should be all set," as Isolde rolls her eyes.

"He will be *our* scout, my lady. He will be able to warn us of any danger that we may not be aware of, for with his ability to fly among the trees, he can see far ahead, much farther than any of us," concludes Philo.

"Yes, you may be right, Master Warrow. We just might have an advantage with him scouting for us," Isolde answers.

As the four reach the bottom of the hidden staircase, they step off onto the ground of Wildwood. The staircase then suddenly disappears behind them; the magic of the Warrows has fulfilled its task.

Turak says to Isolde, "We need to head north and keep silent in every way possible, for there are many predators looking for a morning meal, my lady. It is a four-day journey to Lions Gate by foot, two days through - Wildwood till we reach the Grassy Plains. After that, we are out in the open and vulnerable."

"I understand, Turak. Then let us be on our way, and may the spirits guide our journey and protect us from dangers," concludes Isolde.

Amolo takes to the air and darts between the large branches of the redwood trees. Large pterosaurs flying above the tree line peer down on the forest in search of a meal, thus a Wiki is the perfect snack.

Along their journey, suddenly, large footsteps can be heard in the distance. They appear to be getting louder with each step, so the three linger in the shadows alongside the large redwood tree trunks. They stay very still, hoping to blend into the surrounding forest. Then moments later, a pride of large two-legged large-eyed dinosaurs called *tyrannosaurs*, which hunt in packs, pass alongside the three but are unaware of their presence, for they hunt by sight not by scent. They stand ten meters tall with their heads measuring two meters long in which their huge jaws are filled with hundreds of sharp fangs which can be as long as sixteen centimeters. Their ferocious appetites make them the most feared dinosaur to roam this untamed realm. They will head to the Southern Wildwood come the Season of Harvest, for the temperatures further south remain warmer come the winter season. Thus, the Warrows of the southern city of "Southold" will have to contend with their presence then. The presence of the four go unnoticed by the large beasts, so they stay hidden until the dinosaurs are out of their line of vision to continue on their journey.

Philo whispers out loud, "Whew, that was a close call."

Isolde and Turak shake their heads in agreement.

"I know of a cave system in which we need to reach before the twilight fades into the dimindark. If not, we will be at a great risk roaming the forest at night," whispers Turak.

The four continue on their way, but it is a slow arduous walk, with them trying to stay in the shadows to blend into the landscape and out of the jaws of the many predators roaming the realm.

Wildwood is thick with many brambles, thus encountering them can leave many deep cuts and scrapes on their thin skin, which can leave traces on the forest floor and a bloody trail for predators to follow and ambush them along their route. The golden swords of the Warrows are used as a machete to clear their paths as they move forward. The journey is slow as they cautiously move through the uncharted realm. Hours later as the twilight is fading, they reach the system of caves that Turak had mentioned at the beginning of their adventure. Amolo has been up by the treetops and moving about as he has been scouting ahead of the three.

He has now come down to relay information to his companions. He appears to be agitated as he stands in front of Turak. Amolo is pointing toward the caves, grunting in a low whisper.

"What's wrong?" whispers Isolde.

"I'm not sure. Wait here. I will go and see what Amolo is trying to warn us about," whispers Turak.

"Be careful," remarks Philo.

Turak sprints ahead in silence; the Warrows are called the *Ninjas of Wildwood*, for they move, attack, and strike in stealth. Turak inches closer to the cave system and notices movement in and around the caves. He lunges up into the branches of the redwoods and leaps from branch to branch and from tree to tree until he is overhead of the upcoming hills with the caves carved into their slopes. His large eyes peer to and fro as he looks down. He sees bodies moving about the forest floor. These creatures have much hair covering their entire bodies and are bipedal, smaller than Tehrans but not much bigger than Warrows . . . Neanderthals.

These primitive beasts have taken refuge in the caves. For how long they have dwelled here is not known. Turak was last here about ten seasons ago, and the caves were empty at that time. He becomes uneasy, for these beasts are barbaric in nature. They are known to dwell in the Dark Forest, and for them to be this far south means something has driven them away from their homeland. Turak sits about twenty meters above the forest floor, watching the movements of the primitive beasts. There seem to be about twenty of them in total; a small tribe for Neanderthals which usually number at least one hundred per tribe. He notices males and females but no offspring. Were the little ones eaten by predators? In his mind, that seems the only thing to make sense and the reason for such a small tribe, which most would have likely become prey to the large beasts that roam the forest floor and the skies above. The cave system is about two kilometers wide. The caves stretch up into the surrounding hillsides, some as high as twenty meters. There must be close to a hundred individual caves in total; some are connected to one another, but the majority are not.

The dimindark brings out the nocturnal beasts, including the large serpents—the constrictors—which are twenty meters in length and as round as two meters, thus they can devour a beast the size of a large bison whole. These serpents roam the entirety of the supercontinent south of the Grassy Plains and are abundant throughout Wildwood. They are called the *Silent Death* and have been suspect in many disappearances throughout the land for many a megaannum. Turak has now put himself in a precarious position, but the four have no choice but to move forward, but how? Do they go around the beasts? Confront them in battle? Or just wait it out till the dawn rises to move around them, for the Neanderthals are basically nocturnal?

The dwarf sun is now just above the western horizon, and the scarlet hue of the twilight, which barley penetrates the forest floor, is fading into the dimindark, which is now starting to creep over the land. Turak must make a mad dash back to his companions and inform them of what lies ahead before the full obscurity of the dimindark overtakes them. Turak uses the large branches of the redwoods to scurry back to his companions. In just a few moments of moving among the branches, he arrives back by the three.

"I see what got Amolo in such a huff . . . Neanderthals . . . about twenty of them taking up refuge in the cave system we are headed for," Turak reports.

"Neanderthals . . . H-how did they get h-here? This is crazy, there are no Neanderthals in Wildwood," whispers Philo.

Turak turns to Philo. "Philo, I know what I saw and I saw Neanderthals. Yes, here in Wildwood!"

Both turn to Isolde. Both look confused not knowing how to proceed.

"What do we do, my lady?" asks Turak.

"Well, we can't stay here. It is too dangerous. There is much that crawls and slithers which can devour us for dinner. We need to keep moving," answers Isolde.

Turak scratches his head.

"Wait a minute, I just remembered, the last cave on the far west is cut straight through the hills and comes out on the other side facing north. It is the only cave to do so, once through it, it would be a straight shot out to the Grassy Plains from there," analyzes Turak.

"Are you sure, Turak?" whispers Isolde.

"I am. I have used it may times, sort of like a short cut instead of climbing over the hills. It is safer than being out in the open," answers Turak in a whisper.

"Then let us hope the Neanderthals are not living in that one," whispers Isolde.

Turak then looks at Philo and whispers, "What?"

Philo looks up, then to his companions. "The branches. We can use the branches as walkways to avoid the forest floor and stay out of the line of vision of the Neanderthals. Use them like the walkways of Wildwind until we reach the cave system. The branches are wide enough to walk across. They will never look up toward the branches. They are not that smart."

Isolde smiles at Philo and whispers, "You are very cunning, Philo. I like the way you think."

Philo smiles and whispers to Isolde, "Thank you, my lady."

The four then climb the trunk of the nearest redwood. One by one, they ascend onto the lower lying branches of the huge tree still about ten meters into the air, then slowly and cautiously begin to walk across the branches, which are about a meter wide, trying to keep as silent as possible. They pass over the tribe of the prehistoric beasts trying not to make a sound, hoping none will look up. Slowly, they are making progress. Turak is leading the four from branch to branch and from tree to tree. Then Turak stops, he turns to his companions, and motions to the three to stop and stay very still for he sees something moving just outside the campfires of the Neanderthal camp—two large yellow eyes which are radiating in the bleakness of the dimindark.

The yellow eyeshine appears to be coming from the forest floor, but they seem to be moving toward the camp very, very slowly. The four moving on the thick branches are now more than halfway to their destination. The two large yellow eyes move up to the camp and sits right behind one of the campfires, camouflaging itself with the glow of the flames. Turak realizes it is a *serpent*. It must be fourteen meters long. It sits in silence as still as a large boulder as it waits for its prey to come into its striking range.

Then a Neanderthal carrying wood logs in his arms walks toward the fire to keep its flames burning. The fire is right behind where the serpent waits in silence. As the Neanderthal adds the logs to the fire, the serpent lunges through the flames and grabs the beast in its huge fang-filled jaws. The serpent has engulfed the beast from its head to its waist. Not a sound was made by either, for the *Silent Death* has made its first kill. The only sound that was decipherable was the bones of the Neanderthal being crushed and ground under the tremendous pressure of the serpent's jaws. The serpent then slowly pulls itself and his prey back behind the crackling flames and begins to consume the Neanderthal whole, as he slowly forces the beast down its large throat.

No one in the tribe is aware of the carnage that just commenced basically right in front of them. The four remain perfectly still in the branches above the camp so as to not draw the attention of the serpent as they are in its striking range. The serpent settles back behind the fire after consuming the Neanderthal which takes just a moment. Thus, it waits for another victim to enter its striking range. Then a female Neanderthal wandering around the campsite starts to make calling sounds; it is as if she is looking for another in the tribe. She spots a few logs thrown on the ground near the fire where the serpent is waiting behind. She draws the attention of the other Neanderthals in the tribe, then a few more begin to call out. The female Neanderthal begins to walk over to the scattered logs and continues making calling sounds. As she approaches the fire, she screams as she spots the large serpent. Then all at once the serpent lunges through the fire and grabs the female Neanderthal from atop her head down to her shoulders, crushing her and ending her life immediately. This alerts the attention of the rest of the tribe, and many of them run toward the serpent, some with their wooden spears in their hands. The serpent with the female Neanderthal in his powerful jaws begins to withdraw, as to back away from the campsite to finish its meal in the bleakness of the dimindark.

The Neanderthals are in a panic mode as they have lost two of their clan to the beasts that roam the wilds of this untamed land. With all the chaos going on beneath them, the four rushes over the branches of the redwoods and climb down the closest tree nearest the last cave on the western edge.

The four then hide behind a large redwood tree about five meters from the cave entrance, waiting for the right moment to flee for the safety of the cave. Then after a few moments, Isolde is the first run for the cover of safety. She arrives safely at the cave opening and stands just inside its entrance. She then begins to call to the others.

Amolo is the next to venture across to the cave entrance. He sprints into the air and, in a flash, is by Isolde's side.

Turak turns to Philo, as says, "We go together."

Philo nods his head in agreement, then the two sprint across the field and as they do one of the Neanderthals catches a glimpse of them moving toward the caves. He turns, and as he does, both Warrows, bows in hand, each let go an arrow; thus, two arrows strike the Neanderthal in between his large eyes, killing him instantly. He then falls to the ground, dead. The four have made it safely into the cave entrance. The four stand just inside the cave, trying to catch their breath. Then after a few moments of calm, they begin to move deep into the cave to move away from the prehistoric beasts.

Isolde turns to Amolo and says to him, "Amolo, at the dawn of twilight, fly back to Wildwind. I will give you a note to give to the king. He needs to know of the Neanderthals living in the caves of Wildwood and where they are living. Once you have completed this task, come back to us."

Amolo nods his head up and down in approval.

Turak then turns to Philo. "Wait a moment, Philo. We killed a Neanderthal, then left his body lying on the ground with our arrows stuck in his head, and he is out in the open."

"I know. You have to admit it was good shooting on our part," answers Philo.

"No no no, the Neanderthals will see the arrows sticking out of his head and come looking for us," answers Turak.

"Oh, I never thought of that. What do you want to do, Turak?" asks Philo.

"We need to drag his body in here with us so they don't come looking for us," remarks Turak.

The Warrows then slink up to the cave entrance and peek outside into the Neanderthal's campsite. The distant fires glowing keep the Neanderthals' visibility of where the four intruders are located to a minimum. The beasts are still in disarray, running all over the campsite, while some of the Neanderthals have followed the serpent, having pursued it into the bleakness of the dimindark. The two Warrows quickly move out into the campsite, and both grab ahold of the dead Neanderthal by his legs and drag him over the ground quickly back into the cave to hide his body from the rest of its tribe. Once inside the cave, the four can breathe a sigh of relief and take a moment to figure out the next move.

"Take the body with us into the middle of the cave just in case some of the tribe come looking for him. Hopefully, they won't suspect that he is in this particular cave," Isolde requests.

"Okay, good idea," remarks Turak.

As the four trek deeper into the bowels of the cave, dragging the dead Neanderthal behind them. The companions travel without any torches to keep their presence a secret for their own safety, though they are concerned for the cave is completely dark and the four cannot, even with their large eyes, scan the path ahead. Their worry is if any other beasts, other than themselves, is lurking inside the cave. Their footsteps in the empty stillness of the cave echo with every step they take, so the four try to walk as nimbly as they can. In the darkness it would be the perfect ambush in the perfect location for the many predators that take refuge in the sanctuary of these caves to attack unnoticed.

As the four cautiously tread deeper into the cave, they hear the shuffling of feet ahead of them. Then all at once it is silent again. The Warrows have drawn their bows, and both bows are loaded with two arrows each. The Warrows are now in the lead position of the small group. Then once again they hear the shuffling of feet and the four witness the red glow of two eyes piercing through the darkness looking toward them.

"Damn, this is what I was hoping we'd avoid," whispers Turak.

Then a low long growl accompanies the eye shine, which is continuing to stare in their direction.

"That doesn't sound good," whispers Philo.

Amolo keeps looking over his shoulder, making sure that they are not followed by the Neanderthals which would trap the four with foes in front as well as behind them. The two Warrows begin to inch toward the two glowing red eyes with their bows cocked. The growl of the beast continues at a steady grumble.

"Aim for the eyes," insists Philo.

The beast then sprints toward the four, then its low growl becomes a piercing roar. Both Warrows, bows filled with two arrows each, let go their projectiles. All four arrows find their mark and penetrate the head of the beast. It yelps as it falls to the ground dead, just two meters from where the four were standing.

Amolo is keeping a watch behind them. So far, there has been no movement from where they entered the cave.

"We are far enough into the cave. Let us leave the Neanderthal body here and see what we have in front of us," says Isolde.

As the four approach the fresh kill, Philo uses a flint to light a small branch on the cave floor.

As the small flame begins to brighten the cave, the four gazes upon the corpse of a *sabertooth panther*. The four inspect the animal; all four Warrow arrows have penetrated its head.

"A panther," whispers Philo.

"Now that's good eatin'," Turak whispers back to Philo.

Then the four hear another growl; only this time it appears to be the high-pitched growl of a panther kitten. The two Warrows load their bows with another two arrows each; Isolde pits her hands over the Warrows' bows to stop them from shooting. She then walks about three meters toward the growl. She bends down and picks up the kitten.

"Aww, a baby panther. It appears to be, maybe, thirty days old," remarks Isolde.

"What do we do with it?" asks Philo in a bewildered tone.

"Do with it . . . nothing. We can't leave it here for it will get eaten, either by another predator or the Neanderthals. We will take it with us, and I will raise it as my own," insists a whispering Isolde.

Amolo jumps up and down in approval.

"Great, just what we need on this journey . . . a baby. A panther baby," remarks Turak. Isolde holds up the baby and says, "It's a little girl. I will call her *Red*."

"Red? But she's black," says Philo,

"No, she's red," insists Isolde, then Isolde chuckles.

"I get it. I get it," answers Philo.

"So you want to take the baby and eat the mother?" asks Turak.

"Sounds about right," answers Philo.

"Works for me," remarks Turak.

Isolde holds baby Red to her chest and strokes her down her little back.

"Leave the meat on the ribs. I love panther ribs cooked over a fire," insists Philo, whispering to Turak.

"Thighs or legs?" whispers Turak.

"Thighs, more meat there," answers Philo.

Amolo stands there, shaking his head up and down in agreement with Philo.

"Will you two stop! Don't listen to them, Red. They only think with their stomachs," whispers Isolde, as she covers Red's ears.

Turak, Philo, and Amolo stop for a moment and look at Isolde, then Turak continues butchering the saber-toothed panther.

As the twilight begins to rise Turak has just completed butchering the saber-toothed panther, for that has been a long and arduous task. Once completed, he and Philo pack the meat neatly in Philo's sack. The four will have enough meat to sustain them until they reach the citadel of Lions Gate. Now the five, including baby Red, carefully walk to exit the cave, with Isolde carrying the kitten in her arms.

"It's longer than I remembered," whispers Turak.

Philo looks at Turak, and says, "Are you sure there is an end?"

It is a three-kilometer walk from the middle of the cave to its exit. While the cave does have its ups and downs, it is straight with a few offshoots that lead into an unknown void which are avoided by the travelers. As they approach the exit of the cave, they notice a scarlet haze encompassing the forest floor, for a fog has settled across the landscape. It is a thick fog as thick as pea soup. Well, Turak's pea soup, anyway. The five move cautiously out of the cave, for their visibility is only about five meters. While still in Wildwood, they will encounter the openness of the Grassy Plains before the dwarf sun is at its zenith. Amolo looks toward Isolde, waving his arms in an up and down motion indicating he will fly back to Wildwind and deliver the message Isolde has written for King Leo.

Isolde bends down toward Amolo's face, she places both her hands on his hairy cheeks, "Be careful, fly low and swift, and when you have completed your task, return to us. We will head straight north toward Lions Gate. Please be careful . . . Okay, my friend?"

Amolo nods his head up and down in acknowledgment. Isolde then kisses him on his forehead, closes her large eyes, and as she does, she whispers out loud, "Guardians of the Spirit World, bless this warrior, assist him in his task, then have him return to us safely."

Amolo then takes to the air and flies as fast as he possibly can, staying low within the forest itself, avoiding the large pterodactyls who linger above the tree line and who then, with their large powerful eyes, swoop down on its unsuspecting prey. Amolo flies in between the giant redwoods weaving in and out to avoid a collision with them. The Wiki notices serpents slithering along the low branches, seeking out their next meal. Then further up the forest he sees *tyrannosauruses* feasting on a meal of a large *curly-haired brown bear.*

Wildwood is awake in the scarlet glow of the twilight and as savage as it possibly can be. After a short while, Amolo sees straight ahead of him the tree city of Wildwind. He ascends to reach its boundaries, then approaches the wooden castle of King Leo. He lands on the porch connected to the king's private quarters. The King's Guard run toward Amolo, not knowing his intentions, but Amolo takes out the note written by Isolde and shows it to the captain of the guard. The captain reads the note, then quickly turns to one of the other guards and says to him, "Get the king. Quickly!"

A soldier enters the king's quarters, then moments later the king emerges on his private porch. The king notices a Wiki standing in the middle of it. As he approaches Amolo, the Wiki bows, then hands the king the note written by Isolde. The king then reads the note. As he is reading it, his expression turns to one of concern. The king looks directly at the Wiki and asks him, "You have seen them with your own eyes?"

Amolo shakes his head up and down, acknowledging the king's question.

"You are traveling with Turak?"

Once again, Amolo nods his head in acknowledgment. The king then turns to the captain of his guard and says to him, "Get me something to write with."

The king then pens a note acknowledging what Isolde has sent him and hands it to the Wiki.

"Give this to Isolde."

He then puts his arm on the Wiki's shoulder and says to him, "Thank you, friend of the Warrows, and be safe in your travels."

Amolo bows to the king, puts the note inside his vest, and takes to the air to be reconciled with the expedition.

After reading the note from Isolde, King Leo orders a regiment of his best warriors into Wildwood and straight to the caves described in Isolde's note. The squad will be led by *Lieutenant Krug*, his field commander, to hunt down the prehistoric beasts during the twilight when the nocturnal beasts are asleep in the caves. His orders are to exterminate them, then burn their bodies where they lay. The king's concern is Neanderthals in Wildwood, as he wonders how they have traveled so far from the Dark Forest, and what else has been driven out of that dark land, and why.

CHAPTER III

Kill 'Em All

Lieutenant Krug leads his legion of twenty Warrows out of the tree city of Wildwind. The warriors are all heavily armed with bows and arrows, as well as their swords made of pure gold. Four Wiki scouts accompany them and have taken to the air ahead of them to scout out the Neanderthal camp to assure their whereabouts and to report to Lieutenant Krug upon the Warrows' arrival at the caves before they will begin the slaughter of the Neanderthals. Lieutenant Krug stands at the bottom of the hidden staircase. He listens to the sounds of the forest with the Warrow's keen sense of hearing. The forest floor is abundant with the sounds of many footsteps both large and small which indicates that many predators of numerous sizes are wandering in the vicinity.

The lieutenant's first duty is to keep his squad safe from all that roam in this untamed forest. He then decides to travel on the lower branches of the giant trees as a prudent decision. The warriors will leap from tree branch to tree branch, then from tree to tree to avoid the predators lurking on the forest floor. For as a large group as they are traveling through the realm, they might attract many predators as they move within the branches of the forest. They must also stay alert of other beasts that lie and wait in the treetops, for - Wildwood is named that for a reason. The Warrows, being only about a meter in height which is tiny compared to the variety of species which lurks in this forest, they could be snapped up by a large predator with ease.

The Warrows move rapidly among the branches, then from above they are spotted by a large *horned eagle* standing almost two meters in height with a wingspan measuring about four meters wide. The eagle's large eyes have spotted the group moving along the low branches from the forest canopy high atop of the redwood trees. The predator, driven by its hunger, begins to descend from the canopy moving downward, hopping from tree limb to tree limb. The Warrows are moving fast, so the eagle must make its move quickly if it wants to have a successful hunt. The tiny warriors keep looking from side to side, making sure their path is clear from any and all beasts. A flock of *shadow ravens* sit above the group as they move along the branches, and caw as the group passes below them. The ravens are not a threat to the Warrows as they dine on small mammals which dwell in the forest, such as elephant mice and pouched squirrels, even though the ravens are large birds standing almost .61 meters in height.

The horned eagle is descending rapidly, hopping from tree branch to tree branch. It then decides to swoop down at the Warrows. It takes to the air in a rapid descent. As it moves through the air, it fixes its gaze on a single Warrow—the one that is the closest to it. As the eagle approaches the Warrow, he places his large talons in front of its descending body. The predator then spreads its wings to slow itself down. As it approaches its prey, it spreads its talons wide open. Then as it grasps its prey, it latches onto the Warrow's shoulders. As it clamps down on its victim, its grip clench deep into his flesh preventing the tiny warrior any means of escaping its destiny. Its powerful grasp leaves a stream of blood flowing into the air, then falling, splattering onto the ground like raindrops falling from the sky. As fast as the eagle has grabbed its prey, it turns its body upward and flies at a high speed past the Warrow group, as they don't even have time to react. The captured Warrow screams as the eagle takes him higher and higher into the treetops. While its prey squirms and tosses in its lethal grip, it settles on a large protruding branch and begins to devour the Warrow, first by plucking out its large eyes as they are the tastiest part of the body. The Warrow screams in agony and within moments his life is extinguished; thus, he becomes part of the ecosystem in this untamed land, as the "strong will survive while the meek shall perish to the strong's domination over them."

Lieutenant Krug is astounded by the rapid kill of one of his warriors. The group can do nothing as their comrade is now one hundred and fifty meters above the group, dead, and the main course of the large bird of prey.

The squad gathers their thoughts for a moment as they stare up at their comrade, watching as pieces of his flesh fall past them, slipping from the jaws of the large bird of prey, and landing on the forest floor. But none of his flesh goes to waste, for the rodents that roam the forest floor make a quick grasp of the scraps discarded by the large eagle. Lieutenant Krug orders his warriors to keep it together, for they still have a mission to accomplish. The lieutenant then orders the squad to keep moving, for standing still, they are a target for other predators that may have them in their line of sight.

The squad then continues to move along the branches. Off in the distance, one of the warriors spots a large *serpent* laying coiled in a ball on one of the thick branches above the moving squad and points to it as the rest of the squad moves to avoid the large beast to prevent additional casualties from happening on their journey.

A while later the Warrows approach the cave system where the Neanderthals have taken refuge. One of the Wiki scouts is waiting for the squad out of earshot of the beasts. The squad of Warrows gather around the Wiki scout to get a report from them on the goings-on within the tribe of the Neanderthal's. The *scout commander* attempts to communicate the situation to Lieutenant Krug by pointing to their location and using familiar sounds and gestures that are understood by the Warrows.

It is in the late afternoon when the Warrows arrive by the caves, and the Neanderthals will soon awaken when twilight begins to set. Then they will move about their campsite, so the squad must strike when the opportunity presents itself and when it is to their advantage, such as at the present time when the prehistoric beasts are asleep and will never see it coming. The Wiki scouts have determined that the tribe is bed down in four caves; thus, the caves are all alongside each other and that they do not interconnect with each other.

Standing on the branches at the outskirts of the Neanderthal camp, the lieutenant notices that there are torches unused and piled into a group together, lying on the ground. The lieutenant has an idea.

"We will light those torches. Once they are lit, we will throw them into each cave, forcing the beasts to leave due to the smoke and fire. When they run out, we can pick them off with our bows and arrows. Then we won't have to fight them hand-to-hand."

"Like an ambush, lieutenant," remarks one of the warriors.

"Exactly," responds the lieutenant.

"The Neanderthals will be in disarray, still half asleep, thus not expecting a slaughter," concludes the lieutenant.

As the Warrows descend from the tree branches, they creep up to the Neanderthal campsite. The squad align themselves in front of the cave entrances with their bows and arrows fully cocked and ready to shoot. Two of the warriors silently creep up to where the Neanderthals have stacked their pile of torches. The two Warrows then take their flints out of their vests which are hidden behind their coat of armor. They then strike the flints until the sparks created by the flints light eight of the torches. Once all of the torches are lit, they slowly slink up to each cave entrance, then they begin to run. Each Warrow flings two torches deep in each of the caves, filling the four caves with eight lit torches in total. Once that task is completed, they run about six meters to be alongside their comrades and set themselves and await the Neanderthals attempt to exit from the caves. The caves begin to fill with smoke and flames so thick that none of the Warrows can see into the caves past their entrances.

Thick smoke and colossal flames begin to escape from the caves. Coughing can be heard by the Warrows which are emitting from inside the caves. The warriors then begin to hear the sounds of footsteps moving about, then screams of fright and bewilderment. One by one the Neanderthals begin to flee out into the surrounding entrances and, as they do, one by one the Warrows begin to shoot their arrows into the fleeing beasts, picking off each of them as they exit the caves. Each flying arrow finds its target, and the Neanderthals' bodies begin to pile up outside of the cave entrances. The tribe of Neanderthals have all attempted to flee the caves and they have all been slaughtered by the arrows of the waiting Warrows. Eighteen Neanderthals in total have been killed; ten males and eight females lie dead on the ground. The Warrows, satisfied with their task, walk among the bodies, poking at them, ensuring that their quarry is no longer breathing life into their bodies. Lieutenant Krug then speaks to his warriors, "Pile their bodies in a single mound, then burn them, for their stench has offended my sense of smell."

The lieutenant then turns to two of his warriors and says to them, "Check out the caves and see if anything is worth salvaging."

The two Warrow privates nod their heads in acknowledgment and begin to comb through the caves.

"Lieutenant, what are Neanderthals doing living in - Wildwood? They would have had to cross the Grassy Plains to get here, and how could they have not been seen by the soldiers of the Northern Realm?" asks a Warrow soldier.

"Now those are good questions, private. Well, they are nocturnal and would have traveled by way of the dimindark, which may have been why they went unseen," replies the lieutenant.

"Let's hope that no other tribes have followed them and are somewhere else in Wildwood, sir," replies the soldier.

"But why would they leave the Dark Forest? They must have been driven out by something . . . or someone?" concludes the lieutenant.

"Let's hope we don't find out," answers the soldier.

The Neanderthals' bodies are then dragged into the middle of their campsite and piled high in a single mound, then they are all set afire. Once the flames catch, the fire begins to burn, its flames climbing higher and higher, emitting the stench of burning flesh which fouls the surrounding air. The Warrows stand and stare at the burning Neanderthal bodies for a long moment to ensure the flames have engulfed all of them. The two soldiers who have inspected the caves return with nothing odd to report. The lieutenant then turns to his warriors. "Let's get out of here before we attract beasts we'd rather avoid."

Once their task has been completed by burning the bodies of the foul beasts, the squad take back into the lower tree limbs of the redwood trees and begin their journey back to the tree city of Wildwind. The Warrows now travel closely together with their Wiki scouts flying overhead of them, looking out into the forest ahead, ready to report anything unusual and unexpected which might be lurking in the forest ahead of the squad. The small warriors will always defend their homeland in the face of adversity as they have been doing for the last two million full seasons.

CHAPTER IV

The Journey Northward of the Five

Amolo weaves through the air as he flies in between the large trees, flapping his wings as fast as he can muster, for he wants to rejoin his comrades before the dimindark settles over the landscape. As the Wiki gazes back behind him, he can see that he is being stalked by a flock of pterosaurs hot on his trail. The *pterodactyls* who are pursuing the Wiki have a wingspan of about thirteen meters; thus, because of their large size, they cannot navigate the lower realm of Wildwood as can the Wiki. As the six pterodactyls try to keep up with Amolo, one, then another, pterodactyl collide with the branches protruding out in the forest as Amolo dives and ducks in between the huge redwood trees. The remaining pterodactyls are closing in on the Wiki, as two of the pterosaurs change their pattern and begin to fly above the arthropod as to box the Wiki in. Amolo, now realizing that he is close to the Neanderthal camp, flies downward toward the forest floor. The pterosaurs are now directly behind the Wiki and are close enough that Amolo can feel the hot breath of his pursuers directly on his back. The Wiki makes a sharp left turn, and the pterosaurs follow forthwith, keeping a sharp eye on their quarry. Amolo then heads directly toward the cave in the Neanderthals' camp which passes through under the hills and exits on the northern hillside.

Amolo flies directly into the cave at full speed; his small size allows him to fly inside of it even with his wings expanded. The pterodactyls follow him. They are now right on his tail. But as they try to follow Amolo into the cave, their wings are much too large to pass through its entrance and the flock crashes into the cave entrance. With a loud crash, they pile upon one another.

Amolo continues his flight at full speed and exits the cave as he did in the morning with his four companions. The pterodactyls lie entangled upon one another, injured and without their meal intact; their collision causing part of the cave entrance to collapse which adds to the pterosaurs' injuries. Amolo lands after passing through the cave and is gasping for air, as he has flown so fast for so long. The cave exit is near the northern boundary of Wildwood; thus, the Grassy Plains and the terminus of the Northern Realm lie about seventy kilometers to the north.

Amolo will need to fly high but below the canopy to catch a glimpse of his companions. Once the Wiki has caught his breath, he takes off into the air with a slow ascent, keeping his scope to the north so as to find the whereabouts of the four moving toward the citadel of Lions Gate. He stops from time to time, landing on the branches midway up on the redwood trees about one hundred meters above the forest floor and scopes out the surrounding forest for signs of his companions. It is now afternoon and the scarlet hue of twilight is overhead, making it the best possible time to spot the four. As time lingers on, he sees a hooded figure darting between the redwoods followed by two smaller companions. He has found them.

Amolo then descends from high atop the tree line and swoops down and lands in front of the four. He jumps up and down in his delight of finding his companions. Isolde, Turak, and Philo seem as excited to see Amolo as he is to see them. The three embrace Amolo as if like meeting an old friend one has not seen for many seasons, even Red growls at his direction. Amolo then hands Isolde the note that King Leo has given to him to present to her.

"Thank you, Amolo. I'm glad you made it back safe and sound. We missed you. Let's see what the king has to say," Isolde says.

As Isolde reads the king's note, she turns to the three. "He will attack the Neanderthals today. He is sending a squad out to intercept them," Isolde concludes.

"Good, then our journey has started on a positive note," answers Turak.

"I am glad you are safe, Amolo, and back with us," Philo says to him.

Amolo bows his head in thanks for the kind words all have just spoken. The five then continue on their trek north. Isolde then asks Turak, "Do you know of another place to rest for the evening for the sun is creeping toward the horizon?"

"I know of a gully near the border to the Grassy Plains which is protected and can be used almost like a safehouse because of the struggle it will take to enter it. Not many predators can crawl down into it, for its decline and ascent are steep and deep," answers Turak.

"Is it far from here?" asks Isolde.

"We can make it if we pick up the pace, for it is not far from the Grassy Plains," Turak surmises.

The five continue now on a brisk walk, as they sustain their conversation. "The *Great Gully of Longmire*, I forgot about its whereabouts. It was used as a place of ambush by King Galen's soldiers in the Great War to lure the Malakai into the gully. Once they lured them into it, the king's soldiers bombarded the beasts with arrows and, the gully around them. They killed many a Malakai in that battle. we should be quite safe there," reminisces Isolde.

"You were there? In the Great War, my lady?" asks Turak.

"Yes, I was there, Master Warrow. I lay witness to the carnage that consumed the land. I remember it like it was yesterday. Those were the darkest of times. The Demon of Fire, he was called, for in his wake of destruction he set ablaze everything and everyone in his path in his lust for world domination. The world burned in his fury. His name was never uttered again for fear he would hear its calling and return to finish what he started. Let us hope those days never come upon us again, for if the Necromancer, or as he was called the Demon of Fire, reappears, it would surely be the end of times," answers Isolde.

"I have never heard his name spoken before, my lady. No one has. What was he called?" asks Philo.

Isolde stops and, with great hesitation, the White Witch gazes at both Warrows, then utters his name in a whisper, "He called himself *Naamah*, the conquer of all things."

The two Warrows and the Wiki look at one another; thus, Isolde can see fear emitting from their expressions. She places her hands on the shoulders of both Warrows and says to them, "Do not be afraid, for I have vanquished him to a place so dark that there is no beacon to guide him into the light."

"Are you sure?" asks Turak.

"I am sure, Master Warrow, I am sure, "Isolde retorts.

The five then continue their brisk walk through the forest, as Isolde looks up to the sky, she says out loud, "Evil will always try to return, for evil uses seduction to win over the weak of mind and body, whether verbally or physically. Thus, after it has converted the weak through its methods, then and only then will it reveal its true self to the masses. And by then, it's too late."

The five continue their journey. As the twilight begins to fade, they reach the Gully of Longmire on the edge of Wildwood. As the four gaze beyond the gully through the wall of redwood trees, they can see the beginning of the Grassy Plains—the gateway to the Northern Realm.

"Do you know of a way down Turak?" asks Philo.

"There is a path which descends into the gully. It hugs the steep walls. It's very narrow and it is hidden and difficult to find," answers Turak.

Isolde closes her large eyes and appears to meditate for a moment, then says, "This way."

She the points to her right.

"Follow me," she insists.

The two Warrows look at one another in bewilderment but follow Isolde anyway. The group walks about fifty meters, then Isolde approaches a group of bushes. She uses her walking stick to separate the foliage and turns to the Warrows. "Here is the path down," she says.

"How did you know where it was, my lady?" asks Turak.

Isolde looks at him and says, "A female's intuition, Master Warrow." She smiles at the two, then looks at Turak. "After you, Master Warrow."

Turak then leads the group down the steep decline. Its path clings to the gully wall which is only a meter wide.

"Stay close to the wall, for one misstep and one will fall at least one hundred meters down to the bottom of the gully," insists Turak.

The descent is a slow and arduous walk as the twilight is fading fast. They must move quickly as the beasts that roam in the dimindark will soon be about, roaming for their next meal. As the four carefully descend below ground level, the twin moons begin to rise over the gully; though being only half full, their illumination does give some relief to the bleakness of the dimindark. The sounds of crickets are the only sounds which can be heard. As they continue their descent, they can see the outline of *goliath frogs*—thirty-eight centimeters long, hopping in front of their path.

Turak turns to Philo. "Frog legs, yum!"

"I'd rather have the panther ribs," answers Philo.

As the travelers reach the bottom of the gully, Turak turns to Isolde and says, "There is a thicket of trees toward the middle of the gully where we should be able to set up camp, for the density of the trees should protect us from being seen, even from above." Isolde agrees.

As the group walks toward the thicket, they are guided by the twin moons' illumination for they dare not to light the torches they carry in their sacks until they have enclosed themselves inside the thicket of trees. When the five finally reach the thicket, they stand at its boundary.

"Is there a way in?" asks Philo.

"There's always a way in, we just have to find it," remarks Isolde.

Then the White Witch straddles its boundary while peering into its enclosure.

"Ah, here seems to be a path. A narrow one, but a path. Be careful the brambles are long and sharp . . . This way," she insists.

Isolde holds Red close to her chest, as she leads the four into the middle of the thicket of trees. After a trek of about twenty-five meters as they struggle through a thicket of brambles, they come across a clearing The thicket is like a protective wall, protecting and concealing what lies within.

As they reach the middle of the thicket, the group hears the sounds of running water.

"A running brook in the middle of the gully?" remarks Philo.

"It must come from an underground river that reveals itself as it runs through the gully," remarks Turak.

"Fresh water, how lovely," says Isolde.

As the five settle in for the night, they make a small contained fire and grill the panther ribs they butchered, while Isolde heats mutton milk for little Red over the small flames that was given to her by the maidens of Wildwind upon their leave from the Warrow village. The kitten requires fresh nourishment as she appears to be growing in leaps and bounds on a daily basis.

"I feel quite safe here. It is as if we are surrounded by a great wall of thorns," remarks Isolde.

"The brambles are so thick not even the glow of the flames appears to be able to penetrate beyond the inner forest wall," answers Philo.

Turak looks at them both. "We could hide here for eternity and never be found by anyone from the outside world."

"The perfect sanctuary," remarks Isolde.

"We have to remember this place . . . Just in case," remarks Philo.

"We know what you mean," answers Turak.

With their meal completed, the five gather round the campfire and begin to settle into a night's sleep, for in the morning they will begin the treacherous journey to cross the Grassy Plains. It is a two-day journey by foot to the citadel of Lions Gate. Thus, so far, this will be the most dangerous part of their adventure, for the five will be out in the open and vulnerable to the many predators that roam the plains and stalk the sky above.

Chapter V

Unlikely Alliances

As the dawn of twilight breaks over the eastern horizon, the five prepare to venture out of the Gully of Longmire, which borders the most northern edge of Wildwood where Grassy Plains inaugurate. Isolde heats a saucer of mutton milk over the simmering coals, which are the remnants of last night's fire, for baby Red to have as her breakfast.

"We need to leave this place as soon as possible, for we need to travel in the twilight and avoid the treachery of the dimindark," insists Isolde.

"We have gathered everything together and are ready when you are, my lady," remarks Turak.

"Okay, Red is fed. Let's leave," Isolde insists.

As the five meanders through the thicket one more time, they trace their steps back the way they initially entered the thicket. Once they exit the thorn thicket, they come to the clearing. They then begin the venture back up the steep path which will lead them back up to ground level. The sounds of songbirds fill their ears with joyful music, while the stillness within the thick forest initiate suspicion of an ever-lingering fear of an unprovoked attack that can come out of nowhere at any moment from any number of predators which lurk in this thick redwood forest. Turak and Philo have their bows filled with arrows and move cautiously and calculating, peering their large eyes from side to side, then front to back. Amolo stays by Isolde's side. His small sword grasped hard in one of his forehands, ready to be put into action if the need arises. Isolde holds baby Red tightly against her chest, as the panther takes her morning nap in Isolde's arms while her magical walking stick is grasped firmly in both her hands. As the five move forward through the last remnants of Wildwood, the gloom of the thick forest begins to brighten as the "Grassy Plains comes into focus and opens up in front of them.

As the five reach its border, they step out of Wildwood into the openness of the plains. A gale of such force hits the travelers with its full impact as there is nothing to block the ferocious gusts and the steady force of the constant whirlwind that has nothing to impede its motion for the openness of the "Grassy Plains has no boundaries.

The plains is a barren treeless realm with many, many hills which protrude up to fifteen meters in height and are spread through this realm. They extend as far as the castle of World's End at the extreme western edge of the supercontinent. Though the plains are known in the Western Realm as the *Plains of Auria*, they are a continuation of one another. With its tall grasses more than a meter tall making this territory a perfect place for the *plains raptors*, which are thirty-eight centimeters in height and hunt in packs that can number up to one hundred individuals. Their instinct is to lie and wait in ambush for many an unsuspecting victim to cross their path.

Isolde stands at its doorway and looks to and fro, then up to the cloud-covered sky and back down to the meter-high grass extending in front of them as far as their large eyes can see. A chill pierce through her bones with a gale blowing a steady twenty-five knots. The scarlet hues of the dwarf sun now taking on a dull burgundy aura with the thick cloud cover dulling its illumination. Nothing but open spaces lie ahead of the five, as the White Witch contemplates the journey of crossing this deadly realm, especially on foot. Will they be cunning enough to survive out in the open the two-day journey to the citadel of Lions Gate or will the predators that roam the plains be the victor?

Turak turns to Isolde. "The grasses are as tall as us three, we cannot look ahead and see into the distance."

Isolde looks down at the three, standing at 2.13 meters tall. Isolde answers, "I will be your eyes to gaze out over the plains, so, Turak, you must heed my commands and warnings and react instantaneously to them, understood?"

All three of the companions shake their heads in unison.

"The journey will be slow and arduous, but we must make haste if we are to survive the vastness of this open land," remarks Isolde.

Turak and Philo begin to use their golden swords as machetes to clear their path, as the five trek out onto the open plains.

"May the spirits of our guardians bless our journey and grant us safe passage across the plains," Isolde says in a whisper, as she gazes up to the cloud-covered sky.

Time seems to stand still as the Warrows steadily slash at the at the tall grasses to clear a path for the four who continue to move forward. Large herds of *plains bison* feeding on the tall grasses pay no attention to the travelers; their heads are engulfed downward, tearing and ripping their main staple of food. Their consumption is nonstop which will aid the beasts in building an extra layer of fat to combat the cold winter that is less than half a season from its full impact which will blanket the northland during the long winter season and will continue until the warming erupts to bring forth of the Season of Awakening. The force of the gale can take one's breath away, and the five take rest alongside a towering hill on the opposite side of the whirlwind blowing steadily from the west.

High above the travelers, which seems at the upper edge of the troposphere, are figures of large birds of prey. Being so high in the sky, they are unidentifiable to the large naked eyes of the travelers. Isolde says to her companions, "Look up."

"What are they, my lady?" asks Philo.

"I don't know for sure, but we need to keep an eye on their movements. We do not want to be their choice for their afternoon meal," Isolde answers.

Turak, standing five meters up on the side of the hill, turns to Isolde, and in a startled voice, calls out to the White Witch, "Look, my lady! Over to the north . . . The movement of the grasses, it seems as if there are many creatures being hidden by the tall grass moving fast . . . and they are coming toward us!"

Isolde cups her large eyes, for the thick cloud cover contributing to the dullness of the burgundy hue is impeding her vision. She then gasps. "Raptors! Quickly, to the top of the hill . . . Hurry!" she shouts.

Amolo flies to the hilltop, and what he sees, the Wiki begins to make sounds of panic and jumps up and down while pointing at the incoming barrage of the tiny dinosaurs. The four continue to climb up the steep incline of the hill which is about fifteen meters in height. Above the plains at the hill's pinnacle, the four lay witness to the large herd of the plains raptors advancing toward the five. The tall grasses twist and turn with the assault of the tiny dinosaurs rapidly heading straight toward them. The Warrows load their bows with arrows and begin to take aim at their attackers. Then from behind the hill at the backs of the five, the travelers hear the clamor of hooves echoing through the gale, making their way around the hill.

"*Centaurs!*" yells Philo.

Isolde turns in bewilderment and stares at a pride of Centaurs, at least thirty in number. The half-man half-horse warriors begin to charge in the direction of the tiny predators, letting loose a barrage of arrows which hit their mark with every release of their bows. Five of the Centaurs climb the hill and place themselves in front of the travelers to shield them from the attack of the raptors. The precise aim of the Centaurs has killed many of the predators, thus the tiny beasts begin to withdraw and head back onto the openness of the plains, abandoning their quest to attack the travelers.

The Centaurs have defeated the raptors. They then turn and head straight to the travelers.

The Centaurs approach the five, as Isolde advances toward which appears to be the leader of the tribe.

"My Lady Isolde," says the Centaur leader.

"My Lord Galgaliel . . . What are you doing here . . . in the middle of nowhere?"

"We were on a hunt, then we spotted you and your companions scurrying up the hill. I figured you were in need of assistance," summarizes Galgaliel.

Isolde approaches Galgaliel and embraces him, as he is an old friend of the White Witch.

"A thousand thanks, my lord. You saved our lives," answers Isolde.

"My lady, you have saved my life more times than I would like to admit, but you are most welcome," Galgaliel answers.

"What have we here . . . Warrows and a Wiki. My lady, such companions . . . an unlikely alliance, even for you," says Galgaliel. He continues, "Tell me, what you are doing here in this treacherous land and traveling by foot? Not a good choice."

Isolde nods her head in agreement. "Let me introduce you to my companions. Turak and Philo of Wildwind, and Amolo, our scout"—and uncovering the blanket she is holding close to her chest—"and this is Red, my wee one."

Galgaliel lets out a loud laugh.

Turak then says, "Now, Centaurs . . . truly an unlikely alliance."

Then all who are present laugh out loud and smile at one another.

"My Lord Galgaliel, we are on a quest to enter the Dark Forest and are heading first toward Lions Gate to gather supplies," Isolde tells the Centaur.

"The Dark Forest, my lady? Why? Entering that realm is a death sentence, even for such a powerful sorceress like yourself," remarks Galgaliel in a surprised manner.

"My lord, I am a defender of this world. My mother has raised me and trained me to repel evil at its core. You know that!" Isolde states.

Galgaliel shakes his head in acknowledgment. "I understand your principles, my lady. What makes you need to enter that dark realm?" asks the Centaur.

Isolde leans toward the Centaur lord and whispers to him, "I feel an evil is stirring in that dark place. I have felt it in my being. I must know for sure if evil has returned, and if it has . . . then it must be defeated. Again."

Galgaliel stares at the four companions, then lets out a sigh and says to the White Witch, "Well, that is too large a task for a sorceress, two Warrows, and a Wiki to handle alone."

Isolde then says, "Aha, don't forget about little Red."

Galgaliel then says to Isolde, "Traveling by foot across the plains is as dangerous as entering the Dark Forest itself. For if you are lucky enough to survive, it will still take you at least two days to get to Lions Gate by foot. I cannot, out of good conscience, allow you to continue by foot. My companions and I will escort you to the citadel, and on the way, we will discuss your trek into the dark realm . . . Okay?"

"As you insist, my lord," answers Isolde, as she bows her head in gratitude.

"On our backs we can arrive at Lions Gate before the twilight fades into the dimindark." Galgaliel looks at the three companions. "Hop on the backs of my soldiers and, my lady, will you do me the honor of riding with me?" the Centaur lord asks in a meek voice.

Isolde then hops on the back of Galgaliel and, once all of her companions are on the backs of the Centaurs, the tribe sets forth to the citadel of Lions Gate.

The Centaurs run at an accelerated gallop. Furthermore, they are almost as swift as *Lambo ponies.* They are as powerful as the *draft horses* of the Tehran armies as they steady themselves while the crosswind they are encountering blows at a harrowing gale.

Thirty Centaurs in all gallops as one across the plains, heading north as the gloom of the burgundy hue emulating through the thick cloud cover as beams of twilight peek through its boundaries as the dwarf sun begins to draw toward the west. The farther north the Centaur army and their new companions travel, the bitterness of the cold summons that the Season of Harvest is past its pinnacle, thus the winter season abounds much earlier on the calendar the farther north one travels.

The Centaurs travel on the easterly side of the hills which dot the plains, trying to avoid the full force of the gale as much as they possibly can, for the breath they draw becomes harder to maintain. As the cold gale slows their forward momentum, it becomes harder to steadily breathe and maintain their motion as they strive to meet their goal of arriving at the citadel before the twilight fades into the dimindark. The tribe gallops past large herds of bison and the enormous *northern elk* with their horns protruding three meters in every direction, standing five meters tall, seven meters long, and weighing up to 1,824 kilograms. Their meat is prized by Tehrans and Centaurs alike, also by many of the predators that hunt across the realm and attack from the sky.

The group rides through midday, then Galgaliel decides to stop for the tribe to gather a second wind before continuing on the last leg of their journey.

Tucked in alongside a towering hill, the group of thirty Centaurs and five riders rest and chow down a midday meal of raptor meat taken earlier from their battle on the plains. Small fires have been lit with just enough flame to cook the fresh meat, with twenty-five raptors being cooked on almost as many grills.

Turak turns to Philo and says to him, "I have not had raptor meat in a hundred seasons and, boy, this is delicious."

"I forgot how good it tastes," answers Philo.

Red is also enjoying the meat along with playing with her food as she consumes it in single gulps, then begging Isolde for more. Galgaliel then says to Isolde, "Eat well for we have about a hundred and ten kilometers yet to travel until we reach the citadel. We should arrive there before the twilight sets if we leave soon, as the dimindark arrives later in the day the farther north one travels."

The Centaurs put out the fires, and again the group begins the second leg of their journey north.

Later in the day as the dwarf sun hovers on the edge of the western horizon, the group of Centaurs and their riders arrive at the base of *Mt. Gryphon*, where, located at its pinnacle, lies the castle of Lions Gate. Mt. Gryphon rises two thousand five hundred meters above the Grassy Plains. At its base is the walled city of Lions Gate which boasts as many as ten thousand inhabitants and whose entrance is guarded by the soldiers of the reigning King Galen.

As the group approaches the single entrance to the walled city, a loud call goes out by means of the large stone trumpets carved into the turrets that abound the top of the city walls. Its call can be heard many kilometers in every direction, alerting the nearby troops in and around the citadel and its inhabitants of an unexpected arrival in which the soldiers may need assistance in case a battle may ensue. Galgaliel leads the troop of thirty Centaurs up to the guarded entrance to find the group surrounded by as many as fifty soldiers of the King's Guard, as well as the turrets filled with archers pointing their wares at the Centaurs.

Isolde slides off Galgaliel's back and walks toward the sergeant of the guard.

"*Sergeant Aimsworth,* it is nice to see you!" remarks Isolde.

"My Lady Isolde!" says the sergeant. As he approaches the White Witch, he bends on one knee and kisses her hand. He then looks up at her and speaks, "You are a most welcomed guest of the kingdom."

With that greeting, the soldiers lower their weapons, and the archers lower their bows and arrows. The sergeant then stands and gazes upon the group of Centaurs. He then takes a long stare at the riders which sit upon the backs of the beasts. The sergeant then gives a bewildered look at Isolde and says to her, "My lady traveling with Centaurs, Warrows, and a . . . and a—"

"A Wiki," Isolde says, finishing his sentence.

"Yes, my lady," answers Sergeant Aimsworth. "Such an unlikely alliance for you to be in the company of, my lady," remarks the sergeant.

"As unlikely as it may seem, sergeant, we would like to request an audience with King Galen, for we have an urgent matter to discuss with him," asks Isolde.

The sergeant bows his head and answers her, "But, of course, my lady."

The sergeant then turns to the soldiers in his command and orders them to clear a path for the troop and for the King's Guard to escort the visitors to the entrance of the citadel. Isolde then climbs back on Galgaliel's mount, as the troop is then escorted by fifteen of the King's Guard.

Thus they begin the steep walk which will take them up through the streets of the city of Lions Gate, concluding at the top of Mt. Gryphon which upon it the citadel rests. As the mixed group of travelers pass through the city, the inhabitants come out into the street to gaze upon the group of unlikely companions, many of which have never seen a Centaur, a Warrow, or a Wiki in the flesh; they have only heard of their existence through legends of the many ancient tales that have been passed down to them through the ages by their fathers and their fathers' fathers. The travelers are not greeted with cheers but with a silent glare of the suspicious nature from an untrusting city of simple folks just trying to survive on the edge of the wilds of Pangea. Chatter from the Tehrans can be heard by the travelers as they pass by the thousands of the city's inhabitants who have cluttered the streets of the walled city to catch a glimpse of this unlikely alliance as they continue their trek through the walled city up the steep path to the citadel.

A lone rider of the King's Guard is now sent ahead of the group to announce their arrival to the king and his court. As the group marches through the town, they glance from side to side at the onlookers.

"They look at us with wonder . . . and with distain, my lady," remarks Turak on the expressions of the onlooking Tehrans.

"They are not a trusting sort of being, Master Warrow. They are driven by greed, jealousy, and lust. A Tehran will kill his brother to possess his brother's wife," answers Isolde.

"That's terrible," remarks Philo.

Galgaliel turns to Philo and says, "No, my dear Warrow, that's Tehran nature."

"Tehran nature?" repeats Philo, then in a bewildered stare, then glances at Isolde.

Then the forward movement of the troop comes to a halt as the White Witch begins to speak. Isolde then says to all, "Many millions of seasons ago, the race of Tehrans began to dominate the planet. My mother, Elisheba, Queen of the Alicorns, went to have an audience with the kings of the three clans that ruled over the land. She offered them the insight given and preached to the Alicorns by the Guardians of the Spirit World which had been passed down to them by the Ancient of Days. My mother explained to the three kings of the many spiritual realms and their purpose, plus the names of the spirits and their duties that watch over this planet. She then instilled their commandments about living with and alongside nature to become one with all that there is. But the three kings were not interested in spirituality or anything other than power. Their only interest was weapons of mass destruction, greed, and lust. So they laughed at my mother, calling her a pawn of the Spirit World and mocking her to one another. My mother became very angry at the Tehran race as a whole for their disrespect of their creator. She then returned home to *Lemuria* to contemplate the future of the planet, even though she was anointed the protector of all that exists by the Guardians of the Spirit World. After many seasons of anguishing over the Tehran race, she decided that I, who she considered is pure of heart and soul and who was conceived and born from two Guardians and is a product of the Spirit World, shall, in her stead, assume her duties as the Watcher and one who can intercede on her behalf, thus allowing me to possess the power and the magic of the Alicorns. That is why I must face evil and vanquish it whenever it appears to threaten the existence of any and all life on Pangea. That is why I must venture into the Dark Forest to see for myself if evil has shown its ugly face again."

Everyone in the entourage have listened attentively. Not a word was spoken between any of them, for all are in awe of the White Witch for who she is and what she represents to the world as a whole.

The dimindark is now setting in as the lighted torches set by the castle entrance are the only illumination emanating to show the way as the company walks up to the iron gates of the citadel. As the company arrives, then stands before the Iron Gates another loud horn sound to announce the visitors at its entrance. The Iron Gates then slowly begin to swing open. The King's Guard, in single file, lead the company of Centaurs and their riders into the courtyard of the castle itself. Upon entering the courtyard, the King's Guard align themselves on both sides of the travelers to allow the company to pass in between them as a sign of respect to the Centaurs and their riders, especially Isolde who have been revered by King Galen for her remarkable courage in vanquishing the source of evil two million seasons past, ending the Great War.

Prince Quill, King Galen's younger brother and general of his armies, stands in the courtyard to greet the travelers. He approaches Isolde, as she dismounts from the back of Galgaliel. The two Tehrans embrace each other as they are the oldest of friends who have not seen one another for at least a hundred thousand seasons.

"My Lady Isolde, it is so good to see you," Prince Quill remarks.

Isolde looks him straight into his large eyes and says to him, "My lord, it has been way too long since we have seen one another. You have grown and now are a general, very impressive."

"Being the king's brother does help," the prince answers.

Then the two laugh together at his remarks. Prince Quill then gazes at the company of Centaurs, then notices two Warrows and a Wiki. The prince recognizes the Centaur leader and walks up to him. "My Lord Galgaliel, thank you for escorting the Lady Isolde across the "Grassy Plains. You and your warriors do us a great honor with your display of courage and loyalty to the lady."

Galgaliel bows his head to the prince and answers him, "My lord, the Centaurs will always serve and protect the lady that has saved our world from tyranny . . . with our last breath."

Then the two warriors bow toward one another, showing mutual respect.

Prince Quill then gazes in Isolde's direction and says, "Warrows, a Wiki, Centaurs. My lady, what is going on?"

"I need to speak to your brother and yourself, of course," answers Isolde.

Prince Quill pauses for a moment, then says to Isolde, "Is this about the goings-on within the Dark Forest, isn't it?"

"Yes, my lord, that is exactly why I am here," she remarks.

The prince then shakes his head in acknowledgment. "Giselle has felt a presence of evil in there also. It was only a matter of time before she anticipated that you would come calling."

"Well then, she is not a dumb as she looks," Isolde answers. "Isolde," says the prince.

"I know, I know. I'll behave myself . . . Maybe," answers Isolde.

The two walk arm in arm as they enter the main entrance of the citadel. Galgaliel, Turak, Philo, and Amolo follow the prince and Isolde into the citadel, walking two steps behind them. The company of Centaurs are offered the evening meal by the sergeant of the King's Guard and are led into the dining area used by them.

Once inside the citadel, Prince Quill leads the visitors into the great meeting room which is in the rear of the castle on the second floor facing the Dark Forest, whose border lies just a few kilometers to the north. The illumination of the twin moons shed light on the landscape whose iridescence shine about half full on this cold evening. The silhouette of the Dark Forest is visible in the distance as the castle sits atop Mt. Gryphon, high above the Grassy Plains which stretches out below them in every direction.

"A thick wall of darkness and evil," Isolde describes as to what she is witnessing, looking north directly into the forbidden land as the rest of the company gazes into the unknown as they all stand side by side and stare in bewilderment and fear. Then the doors from the inner castle swing open, and four of the King's Guard enter the meeting room.

One of the guards announces, "All Hail! Presenting King Galen!"

As the king enters the room, all in his presence bow to him. The king then looks directly at Isolde and smiles as he approaches her. The two embrace each other with affection and respect.

"Look at you, you look wonderful . . . A little tired but wonderful," the king remarks.

"Thank you, your majesty, you haven't aged a day," answers Isolde.

"You always know the right to say, my lady," answers King Galen.

The king looks around the room and stares at the Centaur, Warrows, and the Wiki. He then turns to Isolde and says to her, "Okay, my lady, explain to me the company you are keeping."

Isolde smiles at the king and explains her story to him beginning at Wildwind, leaving out no details of the adventure up till today upon arriving at Lions Gate.

Just as Isolde finishes her tale, the inner door of the meeting room swings open again, and the sorceress, Giselle, enters the room. Upon seeing

Giselle, Isolde's expression changes to a look of distain and disgust. Giselle walks up to the long table, where the group is seated, and stands alongside King Galen. Giselle stares in Isolde's direction and acknowledges her, "My Lady Isolde, it is a pleasure to see you again" as she bows to her.

"I'm sure it is," Isolde answers her sarcastically.

Prince Quill looks at Isolde and raises his eyebrows as to say "Be nice."

"I have felt your presence getting stronger the closer you traveled to Lions Gate," Giselle remarks.

"Then tell me, Giselle, since you have felt my presence, what feelings have you felt about the goings-on inside the dark realm?" asks Isolde.

"Evil," answers Giselle. She goes on, "But an evil presence that is darker . . . more consumed . . . more violent than we could have ever conceived of, my lady."

Isolde stands up and begins to wander around the meeting room, her expression showing a dire concern from what she has just listened to, for her feelings have been as equal.

Giselle then says to Isolde, "You know what I speak of, for you have felt it also, have you not?"

Baby Red jumps out of Isolde's arms and begins to run around the meeting room, playing with herself and tumbling around on the floor. Isolde smiles to herself watching the baby panther frolicking about.

"This evil is not the same evil that we have faced before, that is certain, for I feel its wrath is gaining strength, growing stronger every passing day," Isolde finishes her statement, staring at the silhouette of the dark realm.

"We need to assess what we are dealing with. I need to see for myself," Isolde says to King Galen.

Giselle interjects, "Surely you cannot mean to venture into the Dark Forest. it has been two million seasons since any Tehran has entered into that dark place."

Isolde then turns to Giselle and barks at her in a tone of distain, "Two million seasons ago I faced the Necromancer in the Dark Forest, alone. Where were you? You were hiding behind these castle walls, refusing to venture beyond them! You, a sorceress of great power with not an ounce of courage inside you!"

"My duty is to protect the king and the Royal Family!" Giselle barks back.

King Galen stands up and speaks, *"Enough!* Both of you! We cannot fight evil and one another at the same time."

"You are right, your highness. I apologize for my outburst," answers Isolde in a somber tone.

Giselle then says to Isolde, "There are many ways to fight evil, my lady, with many methods that can be used."

"Yes, there are, but in the end, evil must be destroyed once and for all, for that is the only acceptable conclusion to its existence," Isolde answers her.

"Evil will always try to find a way to return to spread its carnage and to dominate the planet by enslaving all that exists on it," concludes Prince Quill.

"I will venture into the Dark Forest along with Turak, Philo, and Amolo," proclaims Isolde.

"And myself," answers Galgaliel.

Isolde turns to him, but Galgaliel goes on to say, "Isolde, I will not allow you to enter that dark realm without me. I owe you my life which you have saved before more than once over the many seasons. It's a debt I need to repay."

Isolde smiles at the Centaur and nods her head in gratitude.

"All that is missing is a Tehran. I will accompany you, also," says Prince Quill.

Isolde begins to say something to the prince, but the prince interjects, "Ah, remember I am a prince, thus you cannot deny me." Prince Quill says with a smile.

Isolde then says, "Who can argue with a prince and a Centaur lord? I am grateful to you both."

King Galen then stands and walks by the six companions and pats each of them on their shoulders. He then stands at the head of the table and says, "Six unlikely companions, may the Guardian of the Spirits bless all of you and keep you safe."

Prince Quill then says, "We leave at the dawn of twilight. Now we should all get some rest. The maidens will show you to your quarters. Please follow them."

The companions then head to their respective quarters as the Dark Forest begins to awaken.

CHAPTER VI

Into the Darkness

The travelers have now settled into their quarters for the evening and most have fallen into a restless slumber, as the anticipation of heading into the unknown toward the most hostile of environments weighs heavy on their minds as well as their souls for no beings of a civilized nature have ventured into the Dark Forest for two million seasons out of fear and for their own self-preservation. What lies ahead for the six can be compared to walking willingly into the Underworld, weaponless and naked.

As the dimindark lingers on, the temperature in and around the citadel begins to drop precipitously as if the icy chill of the winter season has placed its grip on the northland. Isolde is awakened by the raw chill seeping deep into the confines of her quarters. She sits up, lights a candle, then uncovers baby Red to check on her status. The baby panther appears to be in a deep sleep, so Isolde returns her covers as to not to disturb the kitten. Isolde notices flash of lights flickering outside her window opening. She stands up and wraps her naked body with her blanket, which is woven of bison hide, and strolls to look out the window opening to view what is stirring in the darkness. Her quarters face north. She walks up to the opening and gazes at the silhouette of the Dark Forest whose massive canopy protrudes just a few kilometers from the castle itself. Isolde watches as many streaks of light find their way into the dark land, plunging into the planet's crust and setting off many explosions from their impact, whose explosions then ignite huge fires that light up the night sky much brighter than the scarlet hue of the twilight at midday.

Isolde quickly dresses herself and walks swiftly through the castle to the winding staircase that leads up the highest tower to gaze upon the carnage now brewing in the dark land. As she reaches the top of the tower, she finds Giselle already there, staring at the glow of the raging fires taking over the dark land. Antler bats by the thousands have taken to the air; their silhouettes cover the sky above the Dark Forest, dimming the illumination of the twin moons with their sheer mass. It appears the light of the fires and the heat generated by the flames have driven the bats out of their lairs and into the night sky to seek other accommodations for the colony.

Giselle turns to Isolde and speaks, "It appears the sleeper has awakened, my lady." Her voice is trembling with fear.

Isolde closes her large eyes, then says out loud, "I hope we are not too late."

King Galen and Queen Alexandra are next to appear on the top of the tower. The queen gasps at the horrific site and grabs ahold of the king's arm in fear of what she is witnessing. Both sorceresses turn toward the king but remain silent. The four then watch as the glow illuminating from inside the Dark Forest grows brighter and brighter against the bleakness of the dimindark. The streaks of light in the sky continue their rampage of plummeting to the ground throughout the Dark Forest.

King Galen, realizing his worst fears are coming to fruition, turns to Isolde. "My lady, I fear we now know that evil has shown its face to the world."

"I agree, your highness. But what we are witnessing the other realms may not, for they are geographically too far to see what we are seeing. But before we alert them, we must in fact be certain of what we are dealing with. Do you agree, your majesty?" asks Isolde.

"My trust is in your judgement, my lady, for you are the wise, the all-seeing prophet who has protected the world since before the Great War," the king surmises.

Isolde bows to the king in respect, then says, "Then we will proceed as planned, thus we will leave at the dawn of twilight."

Giselle is taken back by the adoration the king has bestowed on the White Witch, thus she peers at Isolde in defiance.

The castle is in a frenzy with soldiers running to and fro, trying to make sense of what they are witnessing of the goings-on inside of the Dark Forest.

Captain William, the captain and field commander of King Galen's troops, has put the army on full alert. He then seeks out Prince Quill who is his general. "My lord, the fortresses of Ravens Rock and Juul are directly in the midst of all the carnage."

Prince Quill shakes his head in agreement. "Send out riders to both posts immediately. Then upon their return, have them report directly to the king," Prince Quill insists.

"Not to you, my lord?" William asks, a little taken back by the prince's answer.

"I will be leaving shortly with Isolde and her companions on a trek inside the Dark Forest to see for ourselves who is responsible for all of this," the prince tells the captain.

"I see. As you wish, my lord," William answers.

Prince Quill then puts both his hands on the captain's shoulders. "Captain William, I give you full command of the King's armies. You are to act in my absence as the Commanding General of the armies, including the King's Guards. I give you full power over all that is under the king's rule, answering only to the king himself. I am counting on you," insists the prince.

"I will not let you down, your highness." William then bows to the prince.

William then sends out two squads to the fortresses to see how both are faring, as they are very close to the carnage since both fortresses are situated on the extreme flanks of the Northern Realm bordering the Dark Forest.

The smoke from the fires covers the land like a mist of morning fog as its substance is thick with ash from the burning trees that encase the dark realm, making it hard for all to breathe, thus making visibility almost impossible to see one's hand in front of one's face. It covers the northland and protrudes to the upper troposphere, squelching the illumination of the twin moons as well. Prince Quill then walks through the courtyard of the citadel to reassure the soldiers and enters the castle from its main entrance. He begins to wander the hallways, seeking Isolde. The corridors of the castle are abuzz with soldiers being assigned new posts, with an increase in security for the Royal Family's protection amid the uncertainty coming out of the Dark Forest. Quill stumbles across the two Warrows and the Wiki who are also wandering the hallways, searching to find the White Witch.

"Have you seen Isolde?" Prince Quill asks the three.

All three shake their heads no.

"We were going to check her quarters, my lord," responds Turak.

"Good idea. Let's head that way," responds the prince.

The four then head up to the guest quarters and go straight to Isolde's room. As the prince swings open the door to her room, the four find Isolde kneeling in front of *Princess Ella*, who is the daughter of King Galen and Queen Alexandra. Ella is three full seasons in age and is standing with Red encased in her arms. Isolde, kneeling, speaks to the princess, "Take care of Red till I return, princess. Treat her like she is yours."

Ella is holding the kitten close to her chest. All can hear the panther purring with her eyes closed, as she is content in Ella's arms. Ella looks up at Isolde and says to her, "Thank you, Isolde. I will always keep her close to me. I love her."

Queen Alexandra then says to Isolde, "We will treat her as one of the family. Thank you for this, my lady."

"No, thank you, your highness. The Dark Forest is too dangerous for a kitten to venture in to, especially after last night," responds Isolde.

As the queen and the princess exit Isolde's room with baby Red, Isolde tears up and begins to cry as controlled as she possibly can, watching the kitten leave without her. Isolde then notices the four standing just inside her room. She turns to them and says out loud, "I hope I see her again, for she is part of my soul now."

The four just stand there, not saying a word to anyone. Sadness fills their hearts, for they realize that they too may never see their family and friends again as they venture into the perils of the dark realm in which this journey could possibly be their last.

Galgaliel then walks into Isolde's quarters and witnesses a somber scene. He says to all, "Did someone die? Did I miss something?"

Isolde looks at the Centaur and says, "No, I just said goodbye to Red. I gave her to the princess to watch over her in my absence."

Galgaliel realizes the sadness that Isolde is feeling which has radiated to all.

"Don't worry, my lady, we will return," Galgaliel insists.

"From your lips to the Guardian of the Spirit World's ears, my lord," Isolde answers.

Galgaliel then says to all in the room, "Twilight is breaking over the horizon, we need to go."

Without saying a word to one another, the six head out of Isolde's quarters and into the hallway. The castle is still buzzing with soldiers moving about the corridors. As the six exit through the castle, they make their way into the courtyard where Prince Quill's personal guard is standing in the middle of the courtyard with his grip on the reigns of his steed. The draft horse is saddled and encased with armor with the prince's sword sheathed on the left side of his saddle, his daggers lined up on the right side. For the Warrows, the prince has filled two quivers each which number about one hundred arrows per quiver, which should be able to fend off many enemies, and he has done the same for the Centaur.

Galgaliel turns to Prince Quill, "Your highness, allow my warriors to defend Lions Gate and become part of your army until our return, for we have a common goal and are allies in battle."

"That is most appreciated, Lord Galgaliel." The prince contemplates on it for a moment then says to Galgaliel, "They will be an independent squad within the army." He continues, "I will relay that information to General William."

With that, the prince calls the general over and instructs him on the new addition to the army, as Galgaliel does the same to his warriors. Galgaliel instructs *Halgar*, his *sergeant at arms*, to assume command of the Centaurs in his absence. The Centaur agrees enthusiastically, for he realizes the importance and the necessity of Galgaliel's mission.

Prince Quill mounts his steed, and says to his companions, "This is *Knuckle Buster*, the toughest steed north of - Wildwood. He will carry you three alongside me."

The two Warrows and the Wiki climb aboard the draft horse, with the two Warrows seated behind the prince in the saddle and the Wiki sits in front of him. Galgaliel bows to Isolde in which she climbs on his back and readies herself for the ride to the Dark Forest. The six cover their faces with coverings made of elk skin tanned to protect against the ash-filled air.

With all mounted, the six begin their venture out of the main gate of the citadel. They begin their journey by riding down the steep dirt path descending Mt. Gryphon which leads through the town of Lions Gate, then through its main entrance. The cloud of smoke and ash is so thick that the six cannot even catch a glimpse of the forbidden land from outside the walled city, but they know the way, for the Dark Forest encompasses the way north as it is the beginning to the end of the civilized world.

The six companions move at a snail's pace entering the Grassy Plains as the visibility in front of them is almost nonexistent due to the smoke of the fires and the ash of the burning hardwoods. They shield their eyes, for the hot ash burns on contact with their exposed flesh.

"Lets us hope the smell of the fire and the lack of visibility shield us from the predators that roam the plains," remarks Prince Quill.

"If we do get attacked, we will never see them coming," answers Galgaliel.

"For sure, Galgaliel, but at this pace, it will take us much longer to travel the ten kilometers to the dark land," answers Isolde.

"Let us keep pace and let us all be silent as to not attract any attention," concludes Prince Quill.

All shake their heads in agreement. The sounds of the crackling of the burning hardwoods shield the soft thuds the hooves made by the draft horse and the Centaur, as the companions slowly prod along, taking it slowly one step at a time. Their movement is in a zigzag motion as the ground they are stepping on is hot to the touch from the embers resting on its surface. The long strands of grass which much of it has been burned making it easier to walk without making much sound eliminating the crunching under their hooves.

Galgaliel is in the lead position, guiding the six to avoid the trailing draft horse being burnt and reacting in a startled manner. The gale, which is constant on the plains, has subdued itself due to the thickness of the surrounding poison air projecting doom and gloom as if they are walking into the second coming of evil. As the six continue moving forward, they become startled for on their right flank they lay witness to a mass extinction of *red-tailed deer*, which have been asphyxiated from the poison air of smoke and ash. Hundreds lie dead, as the six gaze upon them in horror, for their dead carcasses stretch as far their large eyes could see into the dense fog; many with their fawns lying dead by their mother's side. The companions stop but for just a moment to gaze at the carnage they have stumbled upon. They look toward one another, then

Prince Quill whispers to all, "We must keep moving. It is death for all if we stop."

In the distance, all can hear the ripping of flesh from predators feasting on the carcasses of dead deer, but whatever is preying on them goes unseen, for the thickness of the smoke is shielding their identity. The Warrows immediately draw their bow and arrows to ready themselves in case of a surprise attack from out of the surrounding fog and smoke.

"Steady, boys," whispers Galgaliel who is also on alert with his bow and arrow in hand, ready to shoot at any unforeseen foe! Even Isolde has her golden sword, Casabel, grasped in both hands just in case. "Keep moving," whispers Prince Quill.

Then out of the fog of smoke, the six hear the sounds of a stampede pounding the ground as if there was an earthquake building which is coming toward them from their left flank. The six begin to almost panic, for they cannot see what is approaching them. Knuckle Buster, the prince's steed carrying the prince and his companions, starts to breathe heavy, its nostrils flaring. He then begins to circle in place, making it hard for the prince to control his movements. The Warrows and the Wiki hold on to the horse's mane and the prince's body to keep themselves from being thrown off the steed's back onto the surrounding charred ground. Then out of the fog they witness what is causing the ground to stir—Tehrans on horseback, soldiers of King Galen's army riding swiftly toward the south. Thirty of them, at least, riding at a full gallop blindly into the wall of smoke and fog. Prince Quill calls out to them but they do not hear his call, for they cannot hear him over the sounds of the pounding hooves and cannot see the travelers due to their swift speed and the thickness of the fog and smoke. They pass alongside the six, just ten meters from where they stand but have no idea that they were even there.

The companions glare at one another, for a company of soldiers appear to have fled from something or someone and are in a hurry to retreat from where they were.

"This is not good," remarks Philo.

"Border patrol. Soldiers from Ravens Rock assigned to monitor the goings-on in the Dark Forest," remarks the prince.

"They sure were in a hurry to leave from where they were," says Galgaliel.

"What could have made them panic to ride so swiftly when one cannot see a meter in front of their faces?" remarks Isolde.

"This is not good," says Philo again.

"I heard you the first time, Master Warrow," answers Prince Quill.

Galgaliel looks at the prince and says to him, "Philo is right, this is not good."

"We need to proceed with caution," remarks Isolde.

After a short while out of the smoke and fog, the six arrive at the wall of trees which stretch as far as their large eyes can see. The trees appear to be deformed in shape and reach to heights of about eighty meters.

The four dismount Knuckle Buster. As the six are poised together at its outskirts, they gaze out on the towering forest looming in front of them. They stare at it in awe and angst, for it is the mid of day and twilight is barely able to penetrate the thickness of the towering canopy. Their vision cannot permeate more than ten meters into the dense thicket. The smoke is beginning to lift, and the visibility is starting to improve. The gale that is constant on the Grassy Plains, which was stagnant while the smoke and ash dominated the air, is beginning to pick up as the mist is beginning to get pushed out by the increasing gusts.

"We made it this far," remarks Turak.

"You figured that out all by yourself . . . Turak," answers Philo.

"Wiseass," Turak comes back with.

Amolo chuckles at the both of them, which breaks the tension of the moment.

"What do we do with Knuckle Buster?" asks Galgaliel.

Isolde walks up to the draft horse and places both her hands on both sides of his face. She closes her eyes and places her face against his. Knuckle Buster, in response, closes his eyes, as the two seem to be able to communicate by their thoughts. After a few moments, Isolde and Knuckle Buster both open their eyes, Isolde kisses him on his snout, turns to her companions, and says to them, "He will wait for us in the shadows. He will be fine."

The rest of the companions turn to one another in bewilderment. Prince Quill then says in a whisper to all, "Well, she is a sorceress."

Isolde turns to him, "I'm more like a witch, your highness."

Prince Quill then addresses his companions, "No one but no one has entered this realm since the Great War two million seasons ago. While we enter this dark realm with trepidation, we must keep in mind the final goal we seek. Let us move in stealth and watch each other's backs. Are we ready?"

All shake their heads in acknowledgment.

"Okay then, let's go," concludes the prince.

Then the prince walks over to his steed and pats Knuckle Buster on the side of his head. "We will be back soon, my boy. Stay safe."

"Don't worry, he will be fine," remarks Isolde.

"Then why do I have a feeling like it's the last time I'm going to see him?" remarks Prince Quill.

"My spells will protect him, your highness. Do not fear for him," Isolde concludes.

As the six take their first steps into the dark realm, the temperature surrounding them seems to plummet, while the air seems heavy with traces of smoke and ash making it harder to breathe.

No crickets, no rodents, no life in the trees, just the sound of silence surrounds the companions.

"Do not speak above a whisper," whispers the prince to all.

In the distance the companions witness plumes of smoke reaching upward coming directly from the fallen meteorites. The smell of burning wood and brush irritates their nostrils thus, so they quickly cover their faces once again to protect themselves from what now could be poison air.

Turak looks up at Galgaliel and whispers to him, "Do you think the beasts that roam here have been driven out by the fires and smoke, Lord Galgaliel?"

"It's hard to say, Master Warrow. Maybe . . . Except the Malakai and the Neanderthals. Oh, and the *giant mole rats*. They all live underground in burrows. They all could escape the fires by their own means in theory," surmises Galgaliel.

"Giant mole rats, what in Hades are they?" whispers Philo.

"Something you would rather not see," surmises Prince Quill.

"Don't forget about the *blood ants*," adds Isolde.

"Blood ants?" questions Turak.

"Well, Turak, the ants are about thirty centimeters long and are attracted by blood, either from wounds afflicted or blood seeping from carcasses. They emerge from the ground like a caldera of a volcano pushing upward to eject its magma. They will devour their food until all that is left is the skeleton of its victims," explains Isolde.

The Warrows then glance at one another, and Philo swallows hard and whispers out loud, "Shit, we are doomed!"

"Blood ants are known only to exist here . . . in the Dark Forest. But with all the goings-on in the world right now, one never knows where they may wander, Master Warrow," answers the prince.

"That is why we must move in silence," whispers Isolde.

Amolo then flies up on the back of Galgaliel, and the Centaur looks back at him and smiles, "Don't worry, Amolo. I won't let anything happen to you."

"We must head for the pass at the base of the mountain chain known as the *Valley of Lost Souls,*" Isolde whispers to Prince Quill. She continues, "It is the only clear path that goes through to the Dark Tower. It is narrow but straight and will lead directly to the castle itself. But beware, it is a perfect place to be ambushed, for it is lined with many caves and crevices. A perfect environment for Malakai and Neanderthals to dwell and thrive."

As the dullness of the twilight begins to fade, it becomes harder and harder to see clearly as the diminadark is setting in fast. The six come across a large redwood tree and decide to make camp inside a hollow base of it which is large enough to house all six comfortably, being about four meters round.

As the companions begin to settle in for the night, their evening meal consists of bison and elk jerky, for they dare not light a fire which will attract one of the many beasts that roam this dark place. Then out of the darkness the six hear footsteps roaming the forest floor, many footsteps. Prince Quill motions with his finger perpendicular to his lips for all to be extremely silent. The Warrows seem to hold their breath in fear. The prince then peers out of the hollow and in the darkness in which he sees the outlines of figures standing straight up; many silhouettes walking bipedal through the forest. He turns to his companions and whispers, "Neanderthals."

Quill then pulls himself back in to the tree hollow. All six companions have their weapons drawn and ready to use. Then they hear the grunts and harsh sounds of the language of the Neanderthals, which identify the species to the prince and Galgaliel, who have encountered them many times in the wilds of Pangea. Then out of the darkness, a head pops into the tree hollow. The six remain perfectly still, hoping that they are not seen. The beast sniffs the air inside the hollow. It smells a familiar odor which is that of the Centaur. He then starts to slowly move into the tree hollow with his handmade spear—the weapon of a Neanderthal, which is carved from a part of a tree branch of a redwood tree and is sharpened to a keen edge which is then pointed in front of its path. The beast then steps inside the tree hollow. Prince Quill, dagger in hand, stabs the Neanderthal with his blade. It penetrates straight through its neck, covering the companions with its blood which is squirting it in all directions, killing it instantaneously. It happened so quickly that the beast did not make a sound. The prince grabs onto his body to stop it from falling to the ground to avoid the other beasts being alerted and coming to its aid.

Galgaliel then drags its lifeless body to the extreme back of the hollow away from the entrance. The tribe of Neanderthals continue to move about in the darkness. as the six continue to hear their footsteps. But now the sound appears to be moving away from them, as it is becoming more and more faint with each passing moment. The prince again peers out the entrance to the hollow, as once again the sound of silence dominates the dimindark.

"We must move the dead Neanderthal out of here, for it will attract predators that hunt in the darkness. The scent of blood and death can carry for many kilometers in the still of the night," whispers Prince Quill.

"I will move it now, for I can move swiftly in the dimindark without being seen," answers Galgaliel.

Prince Quill shakes his head in agreement.

Turak then says to the centaur, "I will go with you as an additional set of eyes."

"Thank you, Master Warrow," acknowledges Galgaliel.

The companions lay the body of the Neanderthal over the back of Galgaliel. Turak then climbs on the Centaur's back to hold the body in place, as the two attempt to move the dead Neanderthal away from where the six are camped for the night. As Galgaliel leaves the hollow, his gait is at a fast walk as the companions need the two to accomplish this task quickly but quietly so as to not attract the attention of any passersby. Galgaliel heads west, as the companions will move toward the north at the dawn of twilight in the direction of the Dark Tower. This way, if the body is discovered by any predators during the night, it will not affect their journey and they can continue their quest uninterrupted.

Galgaliel continues at this pace for about two kilometers. He then turns to Turak and whispers to him, "This is far enough away from the camp. Let's dump the beast here."

Turak unties his hands which was done to keep its body from rolling off the Centaur as he moved through the forest. The beast slides off Galgaliel and onto the forest floor. Both Galgaliel and Turak attempt to cover the dead Neanderthal with fallen dead leaves, hopefully to cover the odor of the beast. Then Galgaliel gingerly uses his hooves to spread dirt over the body until it is covered.

Turak taps Galgaliel on his neck and points to a bright light which appears to be coming from the west of where they are located now.

"Do you see that light?" whispers Turak.

Galgaliel shakes his head up and down, acknowledging Turak's question.

"We need to check it out," whispers Turak into Galgaliel's ear.

The two inches ever so slowly toward the fire lighting up the night sky. They travel about a kilometer, then they come upon a ridge. They then crawl up to its edge and set their gaze into the valley below. Turak then spots a fire glowing, lighting up the night sky about a half of a kilometer down in the valley below them. The two gaze upon the large fire; its brilliance is illuminating the valley for about fifty meters in every direction, allowing the two to get a good look at its inhabitants.

Sitting around the fire is a tribe of Malakai which seem to be feasting upon a meal.

"There seems to be about eight Malakai," whispers Turak into Galgaliel's ear.

Galgaliel turns to Turak. "That's the usual number of a Malakai tribe, give or take," he says in a whisper.

"There must be a cave system close to here where they are holding up in the twilight. They are nocturnal so we should be safe to travel once the sun rises," concludes Turak.

"I don't know about that. The canopy is so thick in here it may not matter because twilight does not penetrate to the forest floor with all its might," whispers Galgaliel.

"We need to tell the others," whispers Turak.

Galgaliel then turns to slowly walk back in the direction of the camp; the only sound being generated is the soft touch of Galgaliel's hooves on the forest floor.

Back at the campsite, Prince Quill keeps a vigil by the entrance of the hollow as he gazes out into the surrounding forest.

"They have been gone a while, what is taking them so long?" whispers Philo who appears to be worried about the two.

Isolde turns to Philo. "The forest is extremely silent. I surmise that many, many of the dark beasts that dwell here have either been driven out by the fires or they have climbed up high into the mountaintops to avoid the carnage we are witnessing," Isolde concludes in a whisper.

The prince then whispers to all, "Either way, that is not good. So what you are saying, Isolde, is that many dark beasts may now be roaming the Northern Realm or we may be walking into an ambush as we will go through the Valley of Lost Souls."

Isolde hesitates to answer for a moment, then says, "Both are a possibility, your highness."

Then out of the darkness the prince hears the soft sounds of movement on the forest floor coming toward the four. He draws his sword to ready. He then sees the shadowy figure of a Centaur coming toward the camp. He turns to the four.

"Galgaliel and Turak," he whispers.

"Thank the spirits above," whispers Philo.

The two approach the tree hollow and are met by the prince with a huge smile on his face.

"You weren't worried now, were you, your highness?"

The prince smiles and whispers, "No, not me."

Philo then answers, "With all due respect, your highness, you're full of shit."

The prince turns to Philo and retorts, "Yes, I was, Master Warrow. Yes, I was."

Then all smile at the return of the two.

The two tell the others the tale of the Malakai and about where they are camped and how they partly buried the Neanderthal body. With everyone now on high alert, not much sleep was achieved by any.

As the morning approaches, the forest appears to have brightened somewhat. But no one is for certain because the thickness of the canopy is suppressing twilight from penetrating its full aura onto the forest floor in which it casts many shadows, making the appearance that the dimindark is always present in one form or another. Then Turak inquires, "Has the sun risen?" as the Warrow sticks his head out of the hollow.

"Yes," answers Isolde.

The prince stands outside the entrance to the hollow. He gazes to and fro, then says to all, "This is as bright as it's gonna get, unfortunately. Let us be on our way."

As the six begin the next day of their adventure, Isolde takes the lead as she is the only one of the six who has ventured this deep into the Dark Forest as she defeated the Necromancer within the walls of the Dark Tower. But that was two million seasons ago, as she, along with the three kingdoms, the Centaurs, and the Warrow army, fought against the Necromancer in the Great War. Isolde will have to get her bearings, as the six continue on their quest.

Isolde leads her companions northwest through the dense forest. At about midday, the group comes to a clearing. Approximately six kilometers to the north lies the mountain chain whose cluster encompasses the Great Meteor Crater. Then north of the Great Crater is the castle of the Dark Tower where evil has manifested itself and has spread its essence throughout the supercontinent for more than two million seasons.

Upon gazing out onto the clearing, the twilight's scarlet hue is at its pinnacle, and the company can see much more clearly ahead of them than as the tree canopy is absent here.

"Once we cross this clearing, we must find the entrance to the Valley of Lost Souls. It lies between two mountains. It is a narrow pass, and its entrance is hidden from sight. But between which mountains, I don't remember. Not yet, anyway," Isolde regrettably remarks.

"It will come back to you, my lady. Do not fret, for we have faith in your judgement," answers Galgaliel.

"Other than the Malakai tribe, we have not encountered any other form of wildlife roaming the realm," remarks Turak.

Philo glances at Turak. "I hope you didn't just jinx us, Turak," answers Philo.

"Sorry, I was just thinking out loud," remarks Turak.

"Let us cross the valley while we have the ability to see clearly in the twilight," says Isolde.

Then the six steps into the clearing and walk at an accelerated pace in order to cross the clearing with the dwarf sun at its peak.

"Keep your eyes peeled in all directions. Also at the sky in case of an attack from one direction or another," orders the prince.

"The sun feels nice and warm. It has gotten so cold up here in the north," proclaims Philo.

"The winter season arrives early the farther north you travel. You get used to it, Master Warrow," answers Prince Quill.

"Not me, I like the warm weather. Warrows are a tropical species," remarks Turak, as he chuckles out loud.

"I can sure go for a hot cup of tea. It's been days since I had one," remarks Philo.

"Since we all have had one," retorts Turak.

About midway through the clearing, Amolo points to a set of tracks off to their right side which appear to be heading in the same direction as the six.

"Will you look at these tracks? They're huge!" remarks Philo.

"They must be ninety centimeters long," says a startled Turak.

Philo turns to Turak. "What could have made these?" inquires Philo.

"I would say Malakai tracks," remarks Turak.

Prince Quill bends down to get a closer look, then he turns toward Galgaliel and says to him, "Are you thinking what I am?"

Galgaliel shakes his head in agreement.

"What?" asks Turak.

The prince looks at Turak. "These are not the tracks of a Malakai but something worse, much worse," answers the prince.

"How can there be sometime worse than a Malakai?" remarks Philo,

"A *mammoth cave bear*," answers Prince Quill.

"What? Are you sure?" remarks Turak.

The prince and Galgaliel glance at one another, then the prince faces his companions. "I am sure," he says.

"What is a mammoth cave bear, your highness?" asks Philo.

"Well, Philo, these bears are only known to exist in the mountains surrounding the Dark Tower. They were used as guardians by the Necromancer to ward off any and all attacks by the Tehran Army. They fought alongside the Malakai in the Great War but have not been seen since that time, almost two million seasons ago. They are 7.6 meters in length and weight over two thousand kilograms, with teeth as long as twenty-five centimeters long. They make a Malakai seem tame in comparison," remarks the prince.

"So, we are heading right for it?" remarks Philo.

"Apparently so," answers Galgaliel.

"These tracks are maybe a day old. With any luck, he is far away from here by now," remarks the prince, as he gazes upon the landscape in the direction in which the six are heading.

"What if we come across it?" asks Philo.

"Run as fast as you can away from it. Engaging it in battle would be a massacre," remarks Galgaliel.

"They are on the top of the food chain," answers the prince.

As the six continue to head toward the direction of the Valley of Lost Souls, they are cognizant of the presence of the tracks of the mammoth bear as they continue the walk parallel to them. The mountains are now towering in front of them as they approach their border. Their peaks reaching 3,700 meters into the sky. At about three-quarters up their steep rocky slopes, the storm clouds that are ever-present and have been for the last two million seasons swirl with the velocity of the force of a hurricane, protecting the evil that dwells within. As the six approach the end of the clearing, the massive wall of redwood trees twice as thick as the part of the forest they have just passed through again encompass the way forward. Once again, as the six gaze the path ahead, they realize that with the thickness of the forest the twilight barely has the ability to penetrate through the canopy of the redwoods and down to the forest floor.

The prince looks toward Isolde. "Does any of this look familiar?"

"We must head in that direction," Isolde says, pointing to a clearly marked game trail.

"Be very leery, this trail is well used," says Galgaliel.

"But by what?" asks Turak.

No one then dares to answer Turak's question. As the six trek forward as silently as they can, all at once they hear a rustling in the forest ahead of them.

"What was that?" whispers Philo.

"Sshhhhh," remarks the prince.

Then from behind a large boulder in front of the companions they see a large single eye shine. Its iridescence glowing red, staring down at them.

Then out of the shadows leaps a Malakai who is now blocking their path. He is enormous in size, standing about five meters in height. In his right hand he grips a nail-laden club almost two meters long. He is swirling the club over his head and appears to be running toward the six. Before the companions can react, the Malakai closes in on them. As the beast gets within three meters of the six, from out of the dimindark a mammoth cave bear cuts the Malakai off by attacking him from out of the bleakness of the thick forest from his left flank. The bear's massive jaws encompass the entire body of the Malakai. It then crunches down on him.

The sounds of crushing bones and the accumulation of blood shooting into the air as the Malakai screams in agony from the bite of the massive beast. Its anguish only lasts a moment as it is crushed to death by the bear's massive jaws. The Malakai's body lies limp and broken in the jaws of the mammoth cave bear who ignores the six companions as its prize is clasped tightly in its jaws, thus it will shortly be consumed.

"Quickly, follow me," insists Isolde, as the six sprints along the game trail to move away from the massive beast. The bear continues to move to seek out an isolated place to feast on its meal. The six have their weapons in hand in case another attack out of the darkness takes place. They run and run as fast as they can muster. Then the six come to the end of the game trail and what appears to be a dead end where two mountain bases converge.

"We are trapped," says Turak, as fear grips his body.

Isolde then walks to the front of her companions and notices thick array of vines at the base where the mountains converge. The White Witch approaches the wall of vines, and with her walking stick, she opens a passage hidden by the vines and disappears inside of them. All are aghast. Where has she disappeared to? They all start calling to her out loud in a hysterical frenzy.

A moment later, Isolde sticks her head through the vines and says to all, "Well, are you coming?"

The companions are startled and happy to see their sorceresses alive.

"Come on, quickly!" Isolde insists.

As the companions pass through the sheet of vines, they enter the hidden entrance of the valley pass known as the Valley of Lost Souls.

Gasping for air after running to escape the mammoth cave bear, the six attempt to regain their composure. Isolde attempts to regain her memory to lead the six on the way forward. Turak and Philo gaze at their surroundings and try to take it all in. The mountain slopes are sheer, almost straight up in its incline. The forest is as dense as where they had just escaped from. The pass itself is narrow, maybe ten meters wide at its widest point as far as they can see into the dimindark. The brambles in and around the forest floor have also attached themselves to the bark of the trees and are thick and sharp and will need to be avoided as to not allow oneself to be cut and bloodied, which in turn will open an invitation to attract the many predators that roam this part of the dark land.

Philo gazes up into the trees and gasps. "Turak, tell me those are not webs, are they?" he gasps.

"Arachnids. Huge ones," answers Prince Quill.

"Their webs have to be almost thirty meters around," remarks Philo.

"Yeah, but how huge are the arachnids?" asks Turak.

"Probably three meters round, at least, and look . . . Their webs seem to cover so many trees," answers Galgaliel.

"Thanks, Galgaliel, that makes me feel so much better," remarks Philo.

"What's stuck in their webs?" asks Turak.

"Looks like it could be Neanderthals that will be consumed at a later date," answers Prince Quill.

"Let us be careful as to not join them," remarks Isolde.

"Good idea," answers Turak.

Galgaliel turns to Isolde and points on to the sides of the mountains that seem to be aglow with fires.

"Caves. Many, which are inhabited by Malakai and/or Neanderthals. Their fires glow in the dimindark and reflect where they are settled in," remarks Isolde.

"We need to find shelter ourselves," remarks Prince Quill.

"Let us look for an empty cave to rest for the night," remarks Galgaliel.

The six walk about three hundred meters and find a cave that is not crawling with either Malakai or Neanderthals.

Isolde then says, "Wait!"

Isolde then enters the cave alone. She speaks in the ancient language of the Alicorns and the top of her staff begins to glow like a beacon, lighting up the cave as far as her large eyes can see. It is a deep cave descending about fifty meters into the side of the mountain, thus it does appear to be empty. She waves to the others to follow her into it.

"Phew, it smells in here," says Philo.

Galgaliel then says, "Yes, Philo, it is the smell of death."

As the six gaze at the floor of the cave, they realize that it is covered with the bones discarded and picked clean which were the meals of the beasts that have inhabited the cave before them. At the back end of the cave, Turak and Philo light a small fire and begin to cook the evening meal of bison and elk steaks given to them by the chefs of Lions Gate.

Then after a hardy meal, the travelers settle in for the evening, for the six need a night of well-deserved rest. Galgaliel takes the first watch at the cave entrance, as the six take turns sleeping in shifts and rotating the watches for their own safety as the evening lingers on.

Then deep into the dimindark, on Philo's watch, the Warrow hears the shuffling of many feet along the forest floor by crunching the debris under their feet. But in this valley, the malaise of the darkness is ever-present, thus it doesn't appear to dissipate even in the twilight, as this deep valley and steep inclines of its palisades inhibit the rays of twilight to penetrate its full illumination onto the forest floor. The Warrow moves inside the cave to its entrance without making a sound and waits in repose to gaze upon the intruders heading in the direction of himself and his companions.

"Neanderthals," he whispers to himself. The Warrow stares intently into the dimindark. there appears to be five Neanderthals in total. They appear to be on a hunt with their handmade spears in hand, pointing directly in front of them. Philo cannot move to warn the others without creating a stir with the primitive beasts, thus giving away his position, so he must watch and wait to see what their actions will incur before arousing his companions. The Neanderthals walk in silence in a parallel line side by side, moving ever cautiously with only their dark silhouettes emitting out of the shadows, giving away their location in the bleakness of the dimindark. Philo draws his bow into its firing position, two arrows fill its bowstring. At the first incline that the beasts are closing in on his position, he will begin his barrage to cut them down where they stand.

One Neanderthal on the far side of the parallel line seems to have gotten stuck on something, for he appears to be unable to move forward. He begins to tussle and move his arms in a frenzy, but the more he resists the more tangled he appears to become. Philo looks in bewilderment and says to himself, "What the fuck is he doing, dancing? This is bizarre."

The Neanderthal then becomes agitated, thus his struggle becomes more apparent. His companions begin to rush to his aid. They call out to him in their bizarre language of grunts and groans. This awakens Philo's companions who rush to the cave entrance. Philo signals for all to be quiet and whispers to them, "Let's wait and see what happens."

The struggling Neanderthal now appears to be caught in a web—an arachnid's web of massive size which was not visible in the melancholy of the dimindark. The Neanderthal is now entangled throughout its entire body. Its companions struggle to cut it loose but to no avail, for the web is thick; it must be twenty-five millimeters round and as strong as a Malakai's grip. In trying to free the entangled Neanderthal, one of its companions appear to also become entangled in its gluelike adhesive.

Then out of the canopy descending silently is a large arachnid which must be three meters round, moving at an incredibly accelerated descent down its web. It approaches the two entangled Neanderthals. Then with the speed of a lightning bolt, the arachnid thrusts its front legs straight out on front of it and grabs ahold of the first Neanderthal who became entangled. It sinks its fifteen-centimeter fangs into the body of its prey, instantaneously paralyzing its victim. The Neanderthal screams in agony, but its resistance is futile for its body hangs limp and unable to resist its captor in lieu of the venom injected into its neck by the huge fangs it possesses. The other Neanderthal, who is also fully entangled, tries with all its might to free itself from the thick web, but it only becomes more entangled and is now unable to move at all. The other beasts move back and away from the carnage happening in front of them, for they cannot compete with the power and veracity of this huge arachnid. The large insect then begins to cover its victim with its thick silk, encasing its victim who is still alive but powerless to resist its captor. Then the arachnid turns its twelve eyes positioned on its huge head to the other entangled Neanderthal. The beast is screaming in a hysterical rant but is unable to move as the stickiness of the web has imprisoned it and encumbered its movements. The arachnid again sinks its huge fangs into its next victim whose boisterous screams echo throughout the valley, reverberating in every direction and making the frigidity of the dimindark seem even more barren.

Though this time the arachnid decides to chow down on its prey. It begins to suck the fluids of the Neanderthal into its hollow fangs; a massive amount of blood runs down the victim's body and drips onto the forest floor. The Neanderthal's fluids seem to be drawn out of its body at an accelerated pace, for after only a few moments all that appears left of the beast is its skin and bones dangling from the web itself for everything it was is now in the belly of the beast. Its three companions have fled away from the slaughter and ran in the direction they originally were heading, whooping and hollering in their primitive language to one another.

The six linger in the shadows as they witness the large arachnid latch onto its other victim encased in its web and ascend with the Neanderthal up to the top of the of the canopy of the Redwoods. Not a sound is uttered by its victim, for it is unable to move or scream in its silken tomb, though it is aware of its eventual fate; it is helpless to react in its paralytic state.

Philo then sits on the ground, trying to make sense at what he has just witnessed.

Isolde then bends down next to the Warrow. She pats him on his shoulder and says, "Philo, it's okay. We are all safe."

The Warrow then looks into Isolde's eyes, his expression filled with fear. "I know, my lady. I will be okay."

"Is it morning or is the dimindark still among us?" inquires Turak.

"It's hard to tell, Master Warrow. The cliffs are too sheer. We will not know the time of day till the dwarf sun is directly above us, peeking through the storm clouds in between the mountain peaks," answers Galgaliel.

"This is why they call it the Dark Forest, for this realm consists of pure evil and that is what drives it and gives it its strength," remarks the prince.

Turak turns to his companions and says, "I'll make a pot of tea. We will need our strength going forward."

Turak takes out a frying pan and places it over the simmering coals which were still glowing from the fire last night. In his pack he takes out eggs given to him by the chefs of Lions Gate.

"What have you got there, Turak?" asks Quill.

"Raptor eggs, enough to go around," Turak answers.

"Good, I'm starving," remarks Philo.

While Amolo smiles from ear to ear, he appears to be hungry, also. The companions eat a hearty meal which fills them up for the moment. Once the morning meal is completed, the companions once again head out of the cave and head in the direction of the Valley of Lost Souls. They head north in the direction of the Dark Tower.

The six cautiously walk in a single file, with Isolde leading the companions on this part of their journey, for she is the only one of the six that has tread in this land before. Galgaliel takes up the final position of the six, for he is the largest among them and could be a target, considering his formidable size and shape which is twice that and more among his companions; thus, he could be seen before any of the others, provoking an attack from one of their many adversaries lurking in the shadows.

The webs of the arachnids seem to be more abundant the deeper the companions travel into the entrance of Valley of Lost Souls. While the gloom of the forest has become somewhat brighter as the day lingers on, the scarlet rays projecting out of the dwarf sun are severely impeded by the dark storm clouds swirling just below the mountain peaks, making the visibility less than ten meters in every direction, including above them.

The companions can hear the branches crackling above their heads, echoing through the canopy from the movements of the massive arachnids moving about the treetops but are unable to home in on their locations due to the bleakness of the canopy. Are they being stalked?

Amolo fixes his gaze on the darkness above the company; an attack from above would be swift and final. The six travels on a well-marked trail in the center of the valley. At this point the canyon's width is only about fifteen meters, so there is no place to hide or escape in case of an attack from any direction. They must stay on high alert, keeping their gaze all around them, as well as above as to not be caught off guard. The temperature has dropped to about 273 kelvins, as the cold stagnant air lingers in the valley. There is not a gust of wind, as the scope of the surrounding mass of mountains encompasses them with their spires reaching toward the sky, blocking out the moving air as was when the companions were roaming through the forest itself. This part of the journey seems like entering a whole new realm with all new perils which could be encountered.

"A realm within a realm," remarks Prince Quill in a startled whisper.

"It gets worst from here on," whispers Isolde, as all eyes look up as leaves slowly fall among them from above.

"Traveling with you, my lady, is no fun," whispers Philo.

Isolde looks at the Warrow and smiles in his direction.

"With all respect, that is, my lady," Philo adds to his comment.

"Keep moving," whispers the prince.

Then all at once a huge arachnid drops directly in front of the companions not three meters from where they are standing. It gazes at them for a moment with its twelve eyes. The group is startled and aghast. The Centaur and Isolde draw their swords, while the prince and the Warrows rush to fill their bows with arrows.

The orange and black arachnid then begins to charge forward directly at the six with its front legs extended in front of it. The arachnid then leaps into the air, and as it does, it is met with a barrage of arrows in which all penetrate its large head. It lands directly on the Wiki, killed in midair.

The companions quickly rush to Amolo's aid and remove the huge arachnid from on top the Wiki. They then realize the Wiki has plunged his sword into the arachnid's abdomen while it landed on him, adding to its death. Though Amolo is covered with the arachnid's blood and guts, he appears to be unhurt.

"Are you okay?" asks Turak in a concerned tone.

Amolo shakes his head yes, as he wipes the blood and guts of the arachnid off of him.

"Yuck," remarks Philo. "You stink," he adds.

"And I thought they just smelled bad on the outside," adds Turak.

The companions then hear a rustling above them moving about the thick branches of the redwoods with many leaves falling in clumps around them; many, many more leaves than what they just have experienced.

"Oh shit, what are we to do?" asks Turak.

"Over there," points Isolde.

"Everyone, into that cave. Hurry!" insists Prince Quill.

The cave is about ten meters from where the six are standing, so the company begins to flee toward the cave entrance. The six companions run as fast as their legs can move. The brush is thick and the brambles are sharp, making many incisions on the six, slowing their pace as they make their way to the cave. Then around them in every direction they hear the sound of large objects hitting the forest floor with a thud. Turak looks back and sees arachnids slinking down their silky webs and onto the forest floor. There appear to be many large arachnids in pursuit of the six.

"Don't look back, just keep running forward!" yells Galgaliel.

The large arachnids appear to be sleeking down to the ground from a line of silk extending out from their thoraxes, landing on all sides of the six. One arachnid drops directly in front of the Centaur and, with his sword, Galgaliel instinctively plunges the large blade into its skull, killing it instantaneously. It collapses on the forest floor directly in front of Galgaliel.

Amolo takes to the air and, like a bolt of lightning, flies directly into the cave entrance followed by the prince and Isolde. Galgaliel stops at the entrance, turns, and begins a barrage of arrows into the pursuing arachnids as the beasts close in on the fleeing Warrows, killing the beasts directly behind the Warrows.

Isolde then walks out of the cave, holds her staff up to the sky, and speaks in the language of the Alicorns. She then closes her large eyes and says out loud, "I vanquish you back from whence you came."

She then plunges her staff into the ground, using all her might. Isolde sends a shock wave which reverberates throughout the forest. That shock wave acts like a tsunami uprooting some of the smaller trees, sending them flying into the air, thus slamming into the arachnids like a brick wall with its sheer force which sends them shooting back across the forest floor and splattering against the surface of the mountain walls on the opposite side of the valley.

Then all goes silent.

The only sounds heard are the six trying to catch their breath after the chase they have just experienced. They then gather themselves around the entrance of the cave and look out on the surrounding landscape.

This part of the forest has been decimated by the power of the sorceresses whilst the arachnids in pursuit of the six companions have been annihilated, with many torn apart by the force of the gale as their body pieces lie scattered about the forest.

Prince Quill turns to Isolde, "Thank you, my lady."

Philo gazes at the White Witch and says, "That was amazing."

"Philo, that was the power of the Alicorns," Isolde answers.

She then turns to Prince Quill. "We cannot linger here, your highness, for the dark forces that inhabit this land will come to see what has transpired here. We need to leave. Now!"

"I agree, but we will need to stay off of the trail for it will be used by those who seek the answers to this query."

The prince turns his gaze to the decimation of the surrounding forest.

"Let us hug the mountain walls for the valley will shortly begin to turn east directly toward the Dark Tower itself," Isolde answers.

"We will follow your lead, my lady," remarks Galgaliel.

The six quickly leave the devastation behind them to continue on their quest, staying off the well-marked trail and remaining close to the eastern side of the valley near the mountain walls. There are many caves that the six encounter as they head in the direction of the Great Meteor Crater.

As they approach each cave entrance, they pause and tread cautiously as they pass by each one, not knowing if a particular cave is inhabited by some of the beasts that roam this evil land. Then as they continue to walk, the ground under their feet begins to shake.

"What is that?" asks Philo.

The six stands still, fixed for a moment, and listen as again the ground shakes.

"Marching . . . and it's getting louder. Something is coming toward us!" remarks Prince Quill. "We need to hide or we will be seen by whatever is approaching us," whispers the prince to the company.

Isolde points to a cave not twenty meters from where they are and says, "Look, just ahead of us is another cave right beyond that large redwood. Hurry!"

The six moves quickly and cautiously and head toward the cave. The footsteps are getting louder, and the ground is shaking more and more. As the six head into the cave, the warriors have their swords and bows drawn in anticipation of an encounter with an unwelcome beast. But luckily for them the six have entered an uninhabited cave. At least, for the moment. There are remnants of past inhabitant's meals spread throughout the cave. The footsteps making the ground shake are getting louder and closer with each passing moment. Galgaliel can now see figures moving within the tree line marching about on the trail. The six back up into the shadows so as not to be seen by the moving beasts.

"What do you see, Galgaliel?" whispers Turak.

"Malakai . . . and . . . Neanderthals . . . marching together? How can this be, for they are each other's enemy?" Galgaliel whispers to all.

"Evil has set its ways into motion. I was afraid of that," remarks Isolde. She continues, "The Malakai and the Neanderthals have formed an alliance. It is as it was before."

"What does that mean?" asks Philo.

"It means that indeed an evil is taking form in the Dark Tower. It is stirring, gathering its army together, and once its army is at full strength, it will strike out on the world, destroying everything in its path, leaving nothing but devastation in its wake. I hope we are not too late to stop it," Isolde answers him.

The marching beasts have now come into full view of the six. "What are they wearing?" asks Turak.

Prince Quill answers, "Battle armor."

"The armor appears to be recently forged. It looks shiny and new," remarks Galgaliel.

Prince Quill turns to Isolde. "Like they are preparing for war!"

Isolde shakes her head in agreement.

"Are we heading into a trap?" responds Turak.

Isolde looks at Turak, then onto the others, and says, "We shall find out soon enough."

Chapter VII

The Dark Tower

After another night spent inside one more vacant cave, Turak awakens, and with sleep still on his mind and in his large eyes, he glances toward Philo who is keeping guard by the cave entrance. Isolde has made a pot of tea which arouses Turak's senses. He can smell its aroma which is simmering on the coals from last night's small fire. Turak grabs two tin cups and fills them to the brim and brings one to Philo. Philo nods his head in thanks, then Turak stands next to his friend and glances out of the cave into the surrounding landscape.

"Snow. I hate snow," he mutters.

"It's turned really cold, my friend, and the snow is coming down in buckets," remarks Philo.

"Great, just what we needed, but I guess it's better than the steady drizzle we have been in since we entered this realm," retorts Turak.

Prince Quill advances toward the two Warrows. "It is so still. When the snow falls, you can hear footsteps a kilometer away," the prince says, as he stares out into the forest in front of the two Warrows.

Isolde then says to the company, "We need to get moving as soon as possible while the day is young and most of the beasts that roam this dark land are asleep during the twilight."

The six then pack up their belongings and begin the next part of their journey.

The companions exit the cave and continue to walk on the eastern side of the mountain chain, staying close to its the sheer walls and noting to stay off the well-traveled trail in fear of running into Malakai and Neanderthals using it to commute to and fro from the Dark Tower itself. Then after walking many kilometers, the six come to an impasse. They now must turn eastward and follow the path the basin has laid out, for the valley will lead them in the direction in which they need to proceed. There is only silence among the company, for their voices, even at a whisper, will carry far in the stillness of the gorge. The prodding of their footsteps is the only sound generated as they move forward.

The snow is getting deeper with each moment that passes it seems to be coming down much harder than when they first started the days trek. Amolo who is now riding on Galgaliel's back taps him on his shoulder, the Wiki then points to the trail the six are leaving in the deepening snow for fear of being followed and attacked from their blind side. Galgaliel then takes his two fingers, points to his large eyes, then points behind the company as to say to the Wiki to keep an eye behind the marching warriors. Amolo understand Galgaliel's gestures and turns his body backward on the Centaur's back to watch behind the moving group with his bow and arrows in hand loaded and ready.

It is now midday. The temperature has continued to drop, thus it has gotten much colder the deeper. The six ventures into the canyon and the closer they get to the Dark Tower. As they approach the last spire of mountains, the valley opens up again into the bleakness of the open plains which is now set before them. The topography has now changed, with many hills which weave about like the great plains of the Northern Realm while its hills rise higher and higher and peaking in its center. At the highest hill in the center of the plains, the six can see the shape of the castle; the Dark Tower itself. Its dusky silhouette is rising high above the plains ten kilometers in the distance. Even in the bleakness of twilight and with storm clouds blocking the scarlet rays of the dwarf sun, the castle seems to be aglow with many fires burning in and around the citadel itself.

The six gathers under a cluster of redwood trees which dwarf the pine trees growing in a grove underneath the giants. From this vantage point, the six can observe the goings-on in and around the castle without being seen from above and hidden from the activity around them. They stare at the fortress in awe and loathe it out of fear.

"It seems the sleeper has awakened," remarks Prince Quill.

No one dares add any other opinion on his remark, for it is now indisputable. Galgaliel turns to Isolde and whispers, "What's the next move, my lady?"

Then all eyes turn to the White Witch, awaiting her answer. Isolde takes a deep breath, then lets out a long exhale, seemingly lost for words. She looks at her companions with an expression of concern and says, "We need to get into the castle."

The companions look at her in disbelief.

"What, are you crazy? With all due respect," says Philo.

"Excuse me, my lady, but there are swarms of Malakai and Neanderthals roaming all around the castle grounds and we don't know how many of them there are, plus what other beasts are inside the castle walls itself. Do you expect us to walk through the Iron Gate and say 'Hi, honey, I'm home?'" remarks Turak in an elevated response.

"He does have a point," answers Galgaliel.

Isolde then turns her gaze onto the plains for a moment. She then points to the only cluster of trees in the middle of the plains situated halfway to the castle itself and says, "There, that is where we can gain entrance into the castle."

Galgaliel stares out at the cluster of pine trees, then looks at Isolde. "Isolde, that is just a cluster of trees in the middle of nowhere which just happens to be surrounded by our enemies. How does that help us get inside the castle?"

Once again, all eyes turn to the White Witch for answers. Isolde then sits on a large rock facing her companions and begins to tell them a story. "The last battle of the Great War was fought right here on the Plains in front of the Dark Tower. Malakai, Neanderthals, and Tehrans placed under the spell of the evil Naamah fought the army of the three kingdoms, along with the Centaur army and the two kingdoms of Warrows, fought together in this final battle. It was the war to end all wars. Thousands of casualties on both sides. Their war-torn carcasses covered the plains, turning the soil red with their spilled blood.

"During the battle, I was surrounded by many Malakai. I realized I was fighting alone, so I retreated into that cluster of trees. The Malakai would not follow me into it, which I thought was a bit strange, then I realized why. The tree branches were covered with antler bats. Bats the size of a Warrow, huge and insatiable in appetite. They hunker and wait patiently for any creature to enter the tree cluster to feed on easy prey and the ground below them was covered with the bones of their victims. I set my staff aglow, creating a light brighter than the scarlet hues of the dwarf sun, thus the bats would not attack me with the brightness it was illuminating, so they flew off into the dimindark to flee from the light. There must have been thousands of them, for they covered the sky above and blocked the view of the dark swirling clouds hovering over the realm. Once I caught my breath, I then began to explore the cluster of trees and found an iron door cut into the side of a small hill. Through the magic of the Alicorns, I was able to unlock the door. I struggled to open it, for I figured it has not been opened in hundreds or even thousands of seasons. Once it was opened, I stepped inside. There was a hallway. With my staff aglow, I decided to follow where it went. I thought it would be safer than being on the open battlefield. The chamber was straight, long, and dark, supported by brick on all four sides, so it was made intentionally, I think, as an escape route as it seemed to go in the direction of the citadel. The long hallway is damp and dark. As I kept moving forward, I found out it was inhabited by enormous black scorpions four meters long. Again, my staff was illuminating a glow bright enough to blind any creature who unwillingly caught a glimpse of its rays. This kept the scorpions at bay, thus I was able to move forward. After many kilometers the hallway came to an end and opened up into the catacombs directly under the castle itself. More scorpions were moving about, only this time they had many chambers to hide in, but the fierce glow of my staff was my saving grace. Then after many dead ends and endless hallways, I was able to find my way up into the castle courtyard. It is there I confronted the evil Naamah. The castle was abandoned, with his entire army fighting on the plains. It was only he and I, one on one, his dark magic against my white magic. I called out to my mother to give me strength.

"Then the next thing I know my mother was standing next to me. I then climbed on her back, and the two of us quickly moved toward Naamah. My mother then spoke in the ancient language of the Alicorns, asking the Sun God, the Mighty *Apollonia*, for assistance in fighting the ultimate evil.

"As Naamah began his attack on us, Apollonia's spirit, giving us access to her magic, turned the end of my staff into the power of the sun. It projected a beam of light so bright and intense it set the Necromancer ablaze with flames so hot they instantly charred his body, destroying him. Then the castle walkway he was standing on began to crumble into the ground which opened wide like a crevice of an earthquake extending down into the molten core of the planet. The Necromancer was engulfed into the opening, sending him deep into the Underworld and vanquishing him from Pangea. Then once he was vanquished underground, the large crevice closed on top of him, sealing him off from the surface. As he was slayed, the spell the Necromancer had cast on his army was broken. Then every one of the beasts under his spell collapsed where they were standing; thus, they were freed from the spell cast upon them. The war was then over."

The companions observe a moment of silence to ponder the story they were just told.

"So now we know the true story of the end of the Great War." Galgaliel remarks.

"I'm glad you're on our side," says Prince Quill.

Then Isolde stands up and begins to pace. "It seems like I am back . . . back where I was two million seasons ago, facing the same situation with a familiar foe," Isolde concludes.

After a moment or so, Turak speaks to Isolde, "How can it be the same foe? Didn't you set Naamah afire and vanquish him to the Underworld? He was destroyed, wasn't he?"

"That is a question I have been asking myself ever since all the activity in the sky has begun," Isolde ponders out loud.

"Could it be a different necromancer, demon, or some other evil creature?" asks Prince Quill.

Isolde then locks eyes with the prince. "I don't know. Anything is possible, but what I do know is we need to find out what sort of evil is growing within the walls of the Dark Tower, for its power is intensifying. I can feel it growing. We will need to unleash the power of the three kingdoms upon it to destroy whatever or whoever this evil is," Isolde answers.

"I feel it would be better if we cross the plains in the dimindark," states Prince Quill.

"At night . . . remember the antler bats?" spurts Philo.

"We can blend into the landscape and use the cover of darkness to move across the plains without being seen," answers the prince.

"But the Malakai and Neanderthals have the ability to see in the dimindark. They are nocturnal," remarks Galgaliel.

"Yes, but they would not expect to see us in the dimindark or any other life-forms for that matter, plus the bats. The size and the mass of the bats will hopefully be gone when we enter the tree cluster, for in the dimindark is when they forage for food. It would be a bold move if we can pull it off," remarks Isolde. She then continues, "But six of us is too large a group to navigate the plains. We would be seen, for sure, then our quest would come to a bad ending and the world would suffer the consequences. I need to go forward, but I cannot ask any of you to continue further on this quest. It is much too dangerous."

The companions realize that Isolde is making logical sense, but what are they to do? They cannot let her go alone to the Dark Tower. They swore an oath to complete this mission with her. Turak turns to Philo; both nod their heads at one another. Then Turak addresses the company, "Philo and I will accompany you, my lady. We are the smallest of the group. We can move unseen, and we are the best archers. No offence." Turak gazes toward the prince.

"None taken," answers Quill.

Amolo begins to get very vocal, for he doesn't want to be left behind; he wants to accompany Isolde and the Warrows.

Isolde turns to the Wiki, "My dear Amolo, you are very brave, but you are the swiftest of all of us and you are needed here. In case we run into trouble, you can go for help and gather reinforcements."

Amolo gives a disappointed look to the group but understands Isolde's logic and agrees with her request.

Isolde then turns to her companions. "It's all settled then. We will wait for the cover of darkness to move onto the plains."

The six retreats into a nearby unoccupied cave to wait for the dimindark to settle in over the landscape. This cave is deep, at least twenty meters deep. At the back of the cave, Turak lights a small fire, then the companions settle around the flames for warmth, for the snow is still coming down hard and the temperature is continuing to drop. The snow on the ground is now almost fifty centimeters deep which will be difficult for the Warrows to navigate as the snow will be beyond their waist. Prince Quill, Galgaliel, and Amolo agree to wait in this cave until the three returns.

As the dimindark begins to settle over the landscape, the three companions begin to venture out of the cave. Isolde leads the three, for her footsteps will lessen the difficulties for the Warrows to move in the deepening snow as they trail behind her. The three jog as quickly as they can in the deep snow down the ridge leading to the plains, darting in between the pine trees which provide cover for them. As they reach the bottom of the ridge the landscape opens up, and Isolde will have to crouch as she moves for the tall grasses of the plains are only a meter tall and many are bent with the weight of the snow, some of which covers the Warrows as they move about but are only up to Isolde's thighs. The fires scattered on the plains by the evil's minion's light up the landscape as the three dart about, trying to stay out of the light and remain hidden in the darkness heading for the cluster of trees. Their pace has slowed, for Isolde is now having difficulty navigating in a crouched position in the deepening snow, plus the cold is taking its toll on all three. The bleakness of the dimindark has now deepened into total darkness reflected by the obscurity of the swirling storm clouds lingering above the plains which does not allow the night sky to penetrate and reflect unto the ground below them.

Neanderthals cross their path not ten meters from where there are hiding. The three now communicate through the language of sign pointing and using their hands and fingers as symbols instead of their voices so as to not alert their foes, who seem to be all around them, as they quietly move about the snow-ridden plain. The three then pause for a moment behind a cluster of sugar bushes to catch their breath. Then the companions watch as the Malakai and Neanderthals, who were camped by the tree cluster, begin to scurry about and moving away from the cluster of trees. They seem startled and afraid as they run about in all directions in the opposite direction of the oasis as if they are anticipating an attack. Then out of the center of the tree cluster a black mass flies up into the sky. Antler bats by the thousands make their nightly pilgrimage out of the tree cluster and into the wilds of Pangea to fill their insatiable appetites with their need for fresh meat. Their mass covers the night sky which appears to be a kilometer in length and half of that in width.

Philo leans toward the White Witch and whispers to her, "Timing is everything, my lady."

Isolde nods her head to Philo in agreement. The three are now halfway to the cluster of trees. Isolde realizes that they need to make their move quickly toward it while the Malakai and Neanderthals are distracted by the movements of the antler bats. Isolde signals to the Warrows to run and follow her. As the beasts move away from the cluster of pine trees, the three companions head directly for it as fast as their legs will take them. They clamor through the deepening snow, leaving a snowy trail behind them as they quickly move within the cover of darkness. Then after a short time the three enter the cluster of trees and continue to move deeper into this small forest. They hide behind the wide tree trunks of pine and oaks, watching their backs to make sure they have not been followed. They have successfully crossed the plain, thus they are now in the safety of the mass of trees hidden from the beasts roaming free.

Isolde then turns to Philo, trying to catch her breath. "You are right, Philo. Timing *is* everything."

"Good call, my lady," whispers a panting Turak.

"So far so good," remarks Isolde. "We need to keep moving, for we have left a trail in the snow that will lead our enemies directly to us," Isolde whispers.

"That's if they even notice," remarks Turak.

"Yes, Master Warrow, you may be right, but we just can't take that chance," Isolde concludes.

The Warrows draw their bows and fill them with arrows, while Isolde has her golden sword in hand, for they must be on high alert for an attack can come at any time from any direction.

"This small forest is bigger than it looked," Philo whispers to his companions.

"Be careful where you step," Isolde says to the Warrows.

The ground is covered with many bones of the antler bats' spoils—bison, elk, rodents, and many, many bones of Neanderthals and Malakai.

"No wonder the beasts were running for their lives. Look at how many bones of theirs there are . . . and they're all picked clean," Philo remarks in a whisper.

"Antler bats leave nothing behind—no flesh, no organs, only skeletons to identify their victims," Isolde explains.

She goes on, "Unlike blood ants, the bats will eat its victims to the bone in minutes."

"Blood Ants?" Philo asks.

"Yes, blood ants. Red ants who are thirty centimeters long and tear their victim's flesh. They like to take their time consuming their victims, so it can take days for them to completely eat their prey. It's an agonizing, torturous death. You have never heard of blood ants?" Isolde asks.

"No, my lady," Turak answers.

"Did you notice the mounds throughout the plains as we were heading here?" Isolde asks the two Warrows.

Both shake their heads yes.

"Those mounds are the blood ants calderas. They erupt from them like a volcano spewing lava, thus they are attracted by large amounts of blood spilled and absorbed into the ground as they live underground and are drawn by the smell of blood. That is why there is no trace of the warriors of the Great War killed here on the plains. The blood ants feasted on their flesh for a full season," Isolde tells the Warrows.

Philo and Turak swallow hard and shake their head in disgust of such a foul creature.

"Pretty gross, if you ask me," retorts Philo.

"Keep moving," insists Isolde.

The three walk at a moderate pace, prodding through the tree cluster. Then from behind them, they hear footsteps moving toward their direction. The footsteps are moving fast, and their thuds are getting louder with each passing moment.

"The beasts must have spotted our tracks! Prepare to fight!" Isolde remarks in a firm voice. The three companions duck behind the large trunks of the pine trees. They hear the muffled sound of the footsteps in the snow heading in their direction.

"Wait until they are almost upon us," whispers Isolde to the Warrows.

Four Neanderthals, who have spotted the three, trail into the cluster of trees. They are closing in on Isolde and the Warrows. As the four Neanderthals come within five meters of the three, the two Warrows spring out from behind the pine trees from which they were hiding behind and unleash a barrage of arrows at the beasts. Two Neanderthals have taken arrows directly in their heads, killing them both instantaneously. Turak then loads his bow again with two arrows and kills a third one, but the fourth is still coming at them. Isolde then steps out from behind the pine tree she was hiding behind and swings her golden sword at the beast, decapitating the Neanderthal with one swing of her arm, sending his head flying off his shoulders, and landing about three meters from where his dead body lays. The three then stand their ground, anticipating another attack. But, alas, no other foe has come forward. It looks like the four Neanderthals came at them alone with no others trailing behind them. The three gazes toward one another.

Isolde then says to the Warrows, "Leave them where they lie, the antler bats will do the cleanup. Let's go."

The companions then turn and continue their search for the Iron Door, as the Warrows follow Isolde deeper into the cluster of trees. Isolde points in the direction she believes where the Iron Door is located. Hidden behind the branches of a pine tree, she locates it.

The three stands before the hidden entrance and fix their gaze on it for a moment. The door is ornate, with the symbol of the Underworld which is the everlasting flames soaring up into the heavens encompassing a serpent figure of evil carved in gold onto its surface. Then all three begin to pull on its handle together. It barely moves, for it has been two million seasons since it has been opened and by the same Tehran who had opened it before. The three keep pulling on the Iron Door and slowly they make progress, for the door is made from solid iron fifteen centimeters thick. It is overgrown with vines and with buildup of mud over its base which has endured many seasons of neglect. Finally, when they are ajar the door to about sixty centimeters, the three decide to slip through the opening.

One by one the three step inside the doorway. Isolde speaks in the language of the Alicorns, thus igniting the end of her staff which begins to glow in a bright light similar to the scarlet hue of the dwarf sun. With each moment that passes, the brilliance of Isolde's staff intensifies until it is brighter than the sun's illumination, lighting up the long hallway that lies ahead of them.

In the distance the three hear the sound of *tick, tick, tick*.

"What is that noise?" asks Philo in a terrified voice.

Isolde looks at the two Warrows and answers Philo's question, "Scorpions. Giant ones . . . Four meters long, at least."

"I hate scorpions," answers Turak.

"The catacombs are crawling with them," answers Isolde.

"Still think this was a good idea, Turak?" Philo asks his companion.

"If we die, I blame you," Turak says, pointing to Philo.

Isolde looks from one Warrow to the other. "Stay close by my side, for the scorpions will be blinded by the light and unable to get a fix on us," Isolde demands.

Again, the three hear the sound of the vermin . . . *tick, tick, tick, tick*.

But this time it is continuous. There seems to be many, many more of the large scorpions than originally thought, moving in a frenzy throughout the catacombs. The intruders bring with them the smell of fresh meat, and the thought of being a hearty meal for these large insectoids is enough to make one's skin crawl in absolute fear. The hallway is extremely long with no exits for an extended period, so once the three commit themselves to this journey, there is no turning back, for they are walking into a calculated trap by the most aggressive and terrifying beasts on the planet.

The movement of the three is slow and cautious, for the timing of an attack thrusted by the scorpions will come at lightning speed and without warning. As they move forward and inch closer to the middle of the catacombs, the foul smell intensifies, invoking the three to cover their faces to avoid the nauseous feeling they are experiencing from the stench created which abounds in the stillness of the air.

"What is that smell?" asks Philo.

"Two million seasons of death," answers Isolde.

"That's a comforting thought," remarks Turak.

The three continue to move forward. Then in the distance they can see shadows moving back and forth as they approach the outshoots of other hallways intersecting the one they are traveling on. These figures seem to move at an accelerated pace, lurking at the edge of the darkness just outside the light.

"Once we pass the outer hallways intersecting with this one, we will need eyes behind us, as well, for an attack can them come from either side," Isolde notes.

Turak reaches into his backpack and pulls out a used torch, but it still has enough oil coating it to light. Maybe it can assist in warding off the beasts. As the three pass the first opening, Isolde lances her staff straight in front of her, making the large arachnids waiting for them to pass by the opening back away in a frenzy, for the beasts have no tolerance to light of any kind considering they have been existing in complete darkness since the beginning of time. Isolde stands at the opening, waving her staff back and forth, ensuring the large scorpions will not come toward the three. Turak, with his torch lit, turns, facing behind the three and continues to walk backward, sword in hand, pointing in front of him.

As the three approach the Great Chamber of the catacombs, they can see a huge glow of light which appears to be generating from inside of it. Isolde seems puzzled.

"What is that light, my lady?" asks Philo.

"I'm not sure," answers Isolde.

As the three steps into the Great Chamber, it is aglow. Its walls are aligned with torches lit every five meters or so, emitting an immense luminosity throughout the chamber. It is as if they were standing outside in the twilight. The chamber must be thirty meters long and just as high. As the three move deeper into the chamber, they can hear an intense *tick, tick, tick, tick* coming from behind them from the hallway in which they just exited. It is now filled with the large scorpions which have hurled toward them and have clustered around the entrance of the chamber, filling up the hallway but have stopped just short of the Great Chamber and linger in the darkness just out of the light. The three can hear the frenzy of the scorpions moving in the hallway. Their movements are echoing the sound of their steps throughout the catacombs which is chilling and breathtaking to the three companions.

Turak looks toward Philo and says, "Damn, we have to go back that way."

As the three move toward the center of the chamber, they notice a line of torches fixed in the ground standing three meters high, forming a circle around five large obelisks protruding out of the brick floor. The obelisks are about five meters high and about forty-five centimeters square. As they approach these obelisks, they notice five figures chained, one to each obelisk. The three glances at one another with a confused look on their faces. They approach the figures with extreme caution; their weapons drawn in anticipation of a grim encounter. Isolde leads the two Warrows, sword in hand, toward the circle of flames. Then the three stand at its boundary and stare at the five bound figures.

"Who are they?" asks Turak.

Isolde turns to the Warrow but does not respond to him, for she knows not the answer to his question. Isolde notices that the five figures are all dressed in white and are all adorned with long blond hair with fair features. "Tehrans of a higher order," Isolde presumes. They all are wearing golden armor, signifying they are warriors of some kind, but attached to what army? She also notices that the five are bound only at the wrists and appear able to hardly move about at all. By the length and weight of their heavy chains, they appear to be constructed of chromium.

The five look weak and battered and gaze at Isolde and the Warrows with large eyes that have seemed to have lost the will to live.

Isolde then approaches the five.

"*Stop!* Do not cross the circle of fire, for it is bewitched with a killing curse. One cannot enter, and we cannot exit," says a chained figure.

Isolde gazes from one to the other, then says to the chained figure who just spoke to them, "Who are you? How did you get here?"

The last figure on the left raises his head and says to Isolde in a defeated tone, "I am Oriel."

Isolde gasps, then places her hand over her mouth. "Oh, my word!" Isolde then drops to one knee and bows to the five.

Turak and Philo are confused, for they know not of whom Isolde is addressing.

Isolde then stands, opens her arms with her palms upward, and turns to the Warrows and says, "The Watchers, the protectors of all beings, the Angels of Life."

{The Watchers were conceived by the Ancient of Days at the creation of time and space. The deity created five in total, each with a designated purpose to watch over life, water, land, sky, and spirit. They were created out of a thrust of the Ancient of Days' breath which then breathed life into them as the Immortal Angels—half Tehran, half Spirit—to observe and protect over all that exists until the End of Time.}

"My Lord Oriel, I am Isolde, daughter of Elisheba. I have come forth from the Islands of Lemuria as a Siren to all that are righteous and to walk among the land to safeguard the platitude of the laws entrusted to the Alicorns set forth by the Ancient of Days."

"My Lady Isolde, I know of who you are and have watched you throughout the many millennia you have wandered throughout the land. For you are the righteous and the just among the Tehran order, for you were conceived by divine design, for we are the same, for we dedicate our souls to the same cause to the ones who are born of flesh and blood."

Oriel points to the White Witch. "For we, who are of spirit, abide by the laws entrusted to us by the Ancient of Days," Oriel answers her.

"My Lord, who has imprisoned you and why," Isolde asks.

Oriel gazes at Isolde, then hangs his head in shame. He then begins to tell the tale of their capture.

"After Naamah was destroyed and you sent his charred body to dwell forever in the bowels of the Underworld, a stirring began to occur in the Spirit Realm. Evil became enraged. The anger of Evil and his minions grew steadily over the many seasons, for his desire for total domination of this world was stopped in its tracks by you and your mother. He then swore to destroy all that is good, especially the race of Alicorns, for they were instrumental in the destruction of Naamah which was Evil's offspring. His meteor storm was conceived to invoke his minions, such as the Malakai and the Neanderthals, plus other dark creatures to gather in the Dark Forest to prepare for his second. He then sent his most trusted disciple to carry out his will. His first target was us, the Watchers, for without our vision the Spirit World is blinded from seeing the evil spreading throughout the land, for we are their eyes and ears to the firmament of all things. With the Watchers out of the way, Evil can proceed."

"My Lord, who is Evil's disciple?" Isolde asks with dread in her voice.

"Why, Abaddon, of course," Oriel answers.

"The Destroyer," Isolde remarks, as her flesh pales in fear.

"Naamah was Evil's offspring?"

"He was. That is why Evil's wrath is unprecedented, thus driven by extreme hatred for all things good, especially you and the Alicorns," answers Oriel.

"He will begin with a drought to deprive the crops to fulfill the completion of their task," answers *Raphael*, the *Watcher of the Sky*.

"Then with no rain, the rivers will dry and life in them will cease to exist," says *Hamal*, the *Watcher of the Waters*.

"Then the land will turn barren, the trees will die, and all life that depends on them will follow suit," says *Ariel*, the *Watcher Who Oversees the Land*.

"Then all life will either bend to Evil's will or be destroyed by his hand," says *Raziel*, the *Watcher of All Living Things That Walk and Slither on the Planet.*"

"If the world bends to evil's will, their lives will be damned, along with their souls to dwell in the bowels of the Underworld for all eternity," concludes Oriel.

"Evil is setting its will into motion, gathering its army, then it will release its wrath on the world. We haven't much time, Lord Oriel," concludes Isolde.

"Time, my lady, is dwindling down rapidly, for when evil has gathered its full strength, that is when it will strike. It is coming whether we are ready or not," surmises Oriel.

"What am I to do?" Isolde asks the Watchers.

"Do? Do what you have done before. Align with the army of the three kingdoms and the two Warrow tribes to fight Evil's minions, then you and only you will have to face the Evil Lord Abaddon in an epic battle for the survival of this world. Either light will prevail or the world will fall into shadow, for it is your destiny, Isolde," concludes Oriel.

"How do I free you and your companions?" Isolde asks Oriel.

"Only the magic of the Alicorns has the power to break these bonds and relinquish this curse. Elisheba will know. Trust your mother, for she is wise and powerful. More powerful than you can ever imagine," Oriel states to Isolde.

Oriel then struggles to stand to face the three, the heavy chains that bound the five are a heavy burden on their weak frames, for their imprisonment in these dungeons has been for many a millennia initiated by Evil itself, camouflaged in goodness to hide its evil intension by shape shifting itself into a magnificent *eagle of paradise* which would have been sent by the Spirit Guardians to guide the Watchers to the Still Waters of *eternal life* which would cleanse their souls and their minds of impurity, only to find themselves trapped in between the Spirit World and the Underworld; thus, becoming the prisoners of Evil itself and thus placing the unbreakable curse upon them.

Oriel struggles, then finally gets to his feet, and as he does, he spreads his wings, which spread six meters wide, and speaks to the three, "Now, go! War is coming. Prepare the world to fight or plan for the world to be destroyed."

As the three turn to walk back to the hallway infested with the large scorpions, Oriel calls out to Isolde one more time, "Isolde, remember, you are from Lemuria and was raised of Elisheba. The magic of the Alicorns lies within you. In time, it will reveal itself to you, for it is in your soul . . . Allow the sleeper to awaken."

Isolde nods her head to Oriel in acknowledgment but wonders to herself what he meant by "The magic of the Alicorns lies within you. In time it will reveal itself to you?" *I don't understand what that means, I guess in time I will find out.*

The three position themselves before the long dark hallway which will lead them back to the Iron Door. The movements of the scorpions lingering in the darkness seem frenzied. It is as if they are anticipating attacking the intruders once they enter the long dark hallway.

Isolde then closes her large eyes and again she thinks to herself, *The magic of the Alicorn's lies within you.*

As she did when the three originally entered the hallway from the Dark Forest, she speaks in the language of the Alicorns, and again she sets the end of her staff aglow with the brightness of the dwarf sun. The movement of the scorpions moving about the long dark hallway begin to scatter out of the light. She turns to her companions. "Run! Stay alongside me and *run!*"

The three begin to run as hard and as fast as their legs will allow. The Warrows have a hard time keeping up with the Tehran witch as she is almost two meters taller than them with a stride four times theirs. The Warrows then begin to fall behind, as Isolde keeps setting the pace. The movements of the scorpions become feverish, as the three move closer to the exit of the long hallway, staying just out of the light inching closer to the lagging Warrows. Finally, Isolde is the first to reach the Iron Door. She quickly turns and points her staff toward her companions and sees the hallway immediately behind the Warrows filled top to bottom with the four-meter arachnids in their pursuit of them. As the beasts close in on the Warrows, Isolde then yells out loud, "No!"

Then the glow from her staff intensifies ten times, its beam and heat generated by the staff incinerates the scorpions in their tracks. The hallway is now clear of the beasts.

Turak turns to Isolde and says, "My lady, how did you do that?"

Isolde looks at Turak and says to him, "I have no idea."

Philo then says to Isolde, "Unleash the power of the Alicorns. Oriel was right!"

Isolde looks at the two and murmurs out loud, "I have much yet to learn."

The three open the Iron Door. Then as they leave the dark corridor, they close the door behind them so as to not let anything living inside escape to the outside world.

"We made it! We made it!" Philo whispers to his companions.

Turak looks at him. "Now we have to make it back to the safety of the cave. That will be no easy task."

"I need some corn whisky . . . badly," remarks Philo. He then continues, "Thanks, Turak, like I needed to be reminded of that!"

"Okay then, let's go as quietly as we can through this patch of forest. Let's just take one step at a time, okay?" remarks Isolde.

Then the three begin their venture back through to the safety of the cave where their companions are waiting for them.

CHAPTER VIII

The Journey Back

Galgaliel, Prince Quill, and their Wiki companion, Amolo, have been patiently waiting for the return of Isolde and the two Warrows for two long days. In that time, the forest has become infested from the increased amount of Malakai and Neanderthals making their way back and forth and to and from the Dark Tower and its surrounding areas. The activity in the valley below has increased ten times in the same time frame.

Galgaliel stands in the shadows of the cave entrance and stares out at the surrounding snow-covered landscape. He turns to Prince Quill. "It's been two days. Where are they?" he says with deep concern.

"There has been so much movement from the filthy beasts the last couple of days with their comings and goings, I don't know how Isolde and the Warrows can move about unseen, let alone make it back here," says the prince.

"We have to do something. The waiting is driving me nuts," insists Galgaliel.

The snow has continued to fall steadily; it's accumulation now stands taller than a Warrow, and a Wiki. Galgaliel continues to observe an increase in the fires surrounding the castle grounds, as more and more Malakai and Neanderthals march past their cave hideaway heading toward the Dark Tower. It is as if they are being summoned to do so by a higher calling to bring all the forces of evil that dwell on the supercontinent together on a single plane. The Neanderthals have become the taskmasters over the

Malakai using the grunts and groans of their primitive language to lead the large one-eyed beasts through the deep snow by using their bullwhips as weapons to crack them above their heads to keep them at bay to lead them on the designated path of travel. The Malakai resent the smaller beasts controlling them; they make their displeasure known by growling at the Neanderthals and turning toward them with hostility as they are led through the forest.

As the day lingers on the wind begins to pick up, turning the calm snowfall into a blizzard where the visibility is less than a meter in front of oneself. Then the activity of the beasts moving about the forest ceases with the weather turning worst. Soon there is no movement at all, for all have taken shelter from the oncoming snowstorm. Two Neanderthals losing their way spot the cave where the three have held up and move toward it, seeking shelter from the storm. Galgaliel, keeping watch over the cave, spots two figures in the blowing snow heading straight toward their cave. He steps back as to not be seen by the oncoming figures. He then realizes that the two figures are Neanderthals. The Centaur turns to his two companions and whispers, "We have company!"

Galgaliel slowly backs away from the cave entrance and moves toward the back of the cave and waits with his companions in the shadows. Then in a few moments two Neanderthals walk through the cave entrance. They then shake the snow off of their hair-covered bodies.

Galgaliel moves to set his bow with arrows, then the Neanderthals hear the shuffling in the back of the cave and turn in the direction of the noise. They are quickly met with a barrage of arrows thrusted in their direction from out of the shadows from the three companions which find their way directly into the skulls of the two Neanderthals, killing them both instantly, splattering pieces of their brains, and plunging their blood all over the entrance of the cave walls and floor. The two Neanderthals then fall on the cave floor with a soft thud.

"Whew, that was close," whispers Prince Quill.

Then the prince and Galgaliel drag the two dead Neanderthals to the back of the cave, hiding their bodies in the shadows in case more intruders follow their path seeking shelter.

"Phew, they smell," says Galgaliel.

Amolo holds his nose so as to not smell the odor the beasts are emitting. Galgaliel then again walks up to the cave entrance to continue his watch. The Centaur then notices out of the grove of pine trees a large figure coming toward the cave. He again turns to his companions and says to them, "Damn, we have another figure coming at us."

Again, Galgaliel moves toward the back of the cave alongside his companions, and the three load their bow with arrows, anticipating another unwelcomed intruder. Then moments later, stepping inside the cave is Isolde, followed by the two Warrows.

Galgaliel stares in disbelief. Amolo flies to his two Warrow friends and hugs them both at the same time. Prince Quill and Galgaliel then embrace the three. Then the prince says to the three, "We were a little worried about you, weren't we, Galgaliel?"

"Just a little, but I knew you would be alright," Galgaliel answers.

Then the prince and Amolo glance at the Centaur, then Galgaliel says, "Okay, okay, I was a little worried."

"A little?" answers the prince.

"Okay, a lot, but they are back and safe." answers Galgaliel.

"Phew, what's that smell?" asks Philo.

"That would be the two unwanted guests that came to visit us," answers the prince.

"Unwanted guests?" remarks Isolde.

"Yes, Neanderthals. They are just over there," answers Galgaliel.

"Neanderthals, just the way I like them, dead with arrows through their heads," remarks Turak.

"My lady, tell us about your journey. What did you find out?" asks Prince Quill.

Isolde then tells the three of their adventure from beginning to end which takes some time to tell as she does not leave out any detail of their encounters.

When all is said and done, Prince Quill paces for a time, then says to all, "We must leave at the dawn of twilight and make haste back to Lions Gate and inform the king."

"We will need a plan on how to fight this new foe," Isolde remarks.

"We will need a gathering of the three kingdoms to set forth a battle plan, my lady, only then can evil be defeated," answers the prince.

"For sure," Isolde answers him.

The blizzard continues through the dimindark and into the dawn of twilight, as the dwarf sun begins to brighten the morning sky. The six companions venture out of the cave and begin their journey back to the citadel of Lions Gate. This time around, Galgaliel leads the six, for his size and stature can move easier through the deepening snow, making a path for his companions to follow, while the Warrows and the Wiki hitch a ride on the Centaur's back.

The prince and Isolde follow in his tracks, making their trek easier to move in the deep snow. The wind is still howling, blowing the falling snow sideways directly into their faces. The temperature has fallen to what feels like 263 kelvins, but the six have to keep moving for to stand still is to freeze to death in this now frozen land. With the miserable weather, the landscape is void of any of the beasts that roam the black land, giving the six companions a better opportunity to make up time and make haste to venture out of the Dark Forest.

The six have continued throughout the twilight and have traveled about halfway through the Valley of Lost Souls, but they need to find an empty cave to hold up before the dimindark begins to set in. That will be a feat considering the weather has driven all the beasts into hiding. Once again, they have stayed off the market trails and have traveled close to the mountain slopes, hoping to move undetected throughout the forest. The dimindark begins to emanate as the ambience of the dwarf sun is setting. The six spot a cave about twenty meters in front of their path. Finding shelter now is their top priority, for the temperature seems to have continued to drop as it now feels like about 255 kelvins; thus, they will need to get out of this harsh weather for they will not survive in this cold out in the open. As the six approach a cave entrance, they move toward it cautiously, with Philo peeking his large eyes into the cave to ascertain if it is unoccupied. The Warrow can only glimpse about three meters into the deep cave even with his large eyes that enhance his vision in the despondency of the dimindark. Philo stares into the cave for moments on end for to choose the wrong action will put all of the companions lives at risk.

Philo then turns to Isolde. "I smell something coming from the cave, my lady, but I can't make out what it is," states Philo sounding scared.

Isolde moves around the Warrow, then stands in the center of the cave entrance. She then speaks in the language of the Alicorn's, then points the end of her staff into the cave. The end of her staff glows a bright beam of light and the entire cave illuminates like the dwarf sun gleaming at its pinnacle. Then out of the back of the cave a large figure, blinded by the light, panics, then begins to charge toward the light. Isolde jumps out of its way. Then a large *red mountain bear* three meters long and about nine hundred kilograms rushes past the White Witch and sprints out of the cave into the forest, running as fast as his legs can take it.

Isolde, laying on the ground, looks up at Philo and says to him, "Good call, Master Warrow."

"Are you okay?" asks Turak.

"I'm fine . . . A little shaken but fine, Turak. Thanks for asking."

Isolde quickly gets to her feet so she is the first to enter the cave, still with her the end of her staff aglow. She can see all the way into the back of the cave which is now empty of all life. She turns to her companions and says to them, "It's now safe to enter. It's empty."

The cave is about fifteen meters deep with many bones scattered about its floor. It seems that this cave is used daily for shelter by the many beasts that roam the Dark Forest.

Prince Quill turns to Turak and say to him, "Turak, get a fire going for its bitterly cold, then melt some snow to brew some tea. We need to warm up."

Turak nods his head to the prince in acknowledgment. Amolo motions to the prince that he will take the first watch. As the night lingers on there is no movement in the forest, for the bitter cold has kept the beasts that roam this land at bay and hunkered wherever they have found shelter from the storm.

For two days the six companions travel in the shadows through the Valley of Lost Souls back into the gloom of the dark realm, moving ever cautiously so as not to be seen by the wild beasts and the minions of evil traveling throughout this realm. On the afternoon of the third day the six come to the edge of the forest and gaze out upon the Grassy Plains in which their journey began. Cold and hungry and in need of a well-deserved rest, the citadel of Lions Gate is now just a sprint away. The six breathe a sigh of relief, but they are not out of the woods yet, so to speak.

Isolde kneels in the deep snow, closes her large eyes, and once again speaks in the magical language of the Alicorns with her voice just above a whisper. Then moments later, Knuckle Buster appears out of thin air, for she has now taken away the *spell of invisibility*. The horse seems pleased to see the six, especially his master, Prince Quill.

"Now I feel better," remarks Philo.

A sense of relief has come over the six, as the prince, along with Philo and Turak, mount the horse, while Amolo rides on the back of Galgaliel, along with Isolde.

Prince Quill turns to his companions and says, "Follow me and let's get the fuck out of here."

"I need a bath," says Philo.

"You sure do, phew!" answers Turak.

The companions chuckle at Turak's remark, then the six begin the journey across the plains in the direction of Lions Gate, which shall take them to the castle just in time for the dimindark to begin to set in over the Northern Realm.

Chapter IX

Evil's Far Reach

The Neptune Sea off the western coast of the supercontinent is abundant with marine life and many other creatures that inhabit this water realm. Some as large as the *Mosasaurus* inhabit these waters in the warm Summer Season, topping out at twenty meters long and weighing as much as fourteen thousand kilograms. These fierce predators consume vast amounts of fish and sea mammals, including the *green sea whales*. They have also been known to prey on many a fisherman the likes of Tehrans and dwarfs. This vast ocean is dotted with many small to medium islands scattered throughout its vast seaways; most are uninhabited, but a few do have settlements on them whose populations consist mostly of exiled Tehrans and dwarfs who have been banished by their respective kingdoms for capital crimes against the crown, never to return. For if they ever reappear, they will be tortured, then executed upon their arrival. Sailing the waters of Pangea is more dangerous than journeying through its continental wilderness, for one cannot hide from the marine predators or in its depths or in the expanse of the open oceans.

The Western Realm is ruled by *King Baltazar* who rules with a firm hand in the capital city of World's End, which is located on the cliffs overlooking the Neptune Sea. The king is advised and always accompanied by his sorceress who has been in his service for more than a million seasons, the Grand Witch *Ursula*, who is the king's personal sorceress and his concoctress of potions.

Legend has it she was born of nonmagical parents, thus she was schooled in the ways of the magic by Oriel himself, as he was drawn to her beauty and her innate abilities. Fearless and without conscience, she is a loyal comrade of the Watcher. In her mind she owes her soul and her being to him, for through his teachings she has developed her abilities as a conjurer of the magical arts. She was born on the small island off the southern coast known as the *Isle of Isabella*. It is a magical island whose aura can be seen for many kilometers. It is surrounded by treacherous waters known as the breeding grounds for the *sword shark* and the plesiosaur; both are abounding sea creatures of enormous size and appetite, making the island inaccessible by sea.

The king has in his service his royal armada created to protect his kingdom by sea in case of an attack from the many nomadic tribes who roam the vast openness of the watery realm and are known as the *Marauders of the Sea*. These pirates number in the thousands and they can maintain several ships under one's control with crews as many as thirty per vessel, thus they sail on all of the free oceans of the world creating havoc wherever they go. They are the anarchists; as a result, they have become the enemies of all the civilized tribes that dwell along the coasts.

As Ursula stands on the balcony of her private quarters in the castle of World's End, she gazes out on the open vastness of the Neptune Sea whose waters have been building in wave size and turbulence over the last three full seasons. World's End is a fishing city, for many of its inhabitants earn their wares on the open ocean to feed its citizens of the many varieties of fish and other sea creatures abundant in these waters. Well abundant until recently, for there has been a large influx of predator fish and marine reptiles who have taken up residence along its rocky coastline, consuming many species of fish and devastating their populations which are the preferred staple of life for the Tehrans of this city to consume. Recently, many a fishing vessel has not returned to port whilst their crews have gone missing at sea.

King Baltazar joins Ursula on her balcony, for he is troubled with the recent losses of many of the fishing vessels of the city folk, along with the loss of ships from his armada. Ursula turns to the king as he enters her quarters. He then approaches her as she stands alongside her at the stone railing on her balcony, both then stare out at the open sea.

"What is thy bidding, my king?" Ursula asks Baltazar.

The king stares out on the sea for a moment, then turns to the sorceress and says, "The sea has become very violent. Never before have I seen the waters so angry."

"I suspect there is more than meets the eye, your majesty," Ursula answers.

"Tell me, my lady, what you are feeling?" the king asks.

"I have felt an evil building in the north whose black hand is ever far-reaching. As a result, the waters have reacted to its increasing control over the wildlings that roam the land and the seas," Ursula answers with disdain in her voice.

"Are you sure?" the king asks.

"I have no other explanation for the recent activities occurring around us, your majesty."

"Could it be another Necromancer?" the king asks.

"I am not sure what this evil is, but it is different than Naamah. I fear the worst, for I have not been able to contact Oriel for answers to my questions. He always answers my thoughts. I fear for his being as it has been too long that season after season he has remained silent and elusive from me. It is a blackness that hovers over us sent directly from Evil itself, thus I feel Oriel has become entangled within it," Ursula somberly answers.

"Well, that explains a lot," remarks King Baltazar, as again he gazes out over the ocean.

"If Oriel is in trouble, he may have found where evil is hiding. I will hunt down the reason for his disappearance and kill anyone that gets in my way and tries to stop me," Ursula says in a firm voice.

The king then turns to Ursula. "Violence is not the answer, my lady."

Ursula then turns to the king. "It is the solution to the problem, your majesty."

"Ursula, you are my most trusted advisor. I need your clear thinking in matters of the crown," the king says in a firm tone.

"My thoughts are clear and my actions are swift and concise, your majesty," she answers.

King Baltazar is silent for a long moment, then says to Ursula, "I hope so, for all of our sakes."

Ursula then says, "Lions Gate is at the forefront of the Dark Forest. King Galen would have a better explanation of what is happening there."

King Baltazar then answers, "Perhaps."

"We can send an *ivory eagle* to Lions Gate with a message for the king, your majesty," Ursula retorts.

"That seems the logical thing to do. Good idea," answers the king.

King Baltazar, along with Ursula, compose a letter in the king's study addressed to King Galen, explaining the unusual goings-on in the Western Realm and the premonitions Ursula has been having about the darkness spreading over the land originating in the Dark Forest.

King Baltazar includes in his letter's summary, "Are the premonitions that Ursula has been experiencing correct? And if she is correct in her assumptions, will you need assistance in suppressing the evil presence from spreading throughout the supercontinent?"

Ursula, sitting alongside the king, then asks him, "Do you think we should also send an eagle to the Southern Realm? Maybe Queen Lazuli has experienced much of what we have."

King Baltazar turns to Ursula and says to her, "I don't want to deal with that bitch queen, if I don't have to. She's a fucking nightmare on a normal basis, let alone in a time of crisis. If her actions make the difference in our favor, she'll want everyone to eat her pussy out of gratitude."

Laughing hysterically, Ursula continues, "I understand, your majesty, but she does have a flock of pterodactyls under her control which would be most effective in case we need to go to war."

"We will just have to remember that if and when we need her assistance," the king surmises.

In the early afternoon, King Baltazar's ivory eagle is sent out of World's End with the king's message strapped to the eagle's left leg; thus, it is then sent to begin its journey to fly to the citadel of Lions Gate. The sheer size of the eagle, at almost two meters in height encompassing a wingspan of five meters wide, allows it to have the ability to reach Lions Gate before the dimindark engulfs the reaches of the Northern Realm. Though there are many predators which encompass the skies of Pangea, due to the size and ferociousness of the eagle, most predators are likely to avoid the messenger in flight.

Meanwhile in the Northern Realm, Isolde and her companions have returned to the safety of Lions Gate. Having ridden across the Grassy Plains, they have thus returned whilst the dwarf sun is fading toward the horizon. As the six companions ride through the Iron Gate of the citadel, a call goes out from the king's guards to announce to the king the return of the prince and his companions.

"Welcome back, my lord," says Sergeant *Kash Moulton* to the prince.

"It's good to be back, sergeant," answers the prince.

"Was your journey successful, my lord?" the sergeant asks.

"Well, it's all a matter of what you consider successful, sergeant. We are still alive so that I consider that a plus," retorts the prince.

"And we have all of our limbs still intact," adds Philo.

"I have sent a guard to inform the king of your arrival. He will want to meet with you right away, my lord," says the sergeant.

"Very good, sergeant," answers the prince.

As the six head into the main entrance of the castle, little Red runs toward Isolde like a child who has missed its mother who has been away from home for a long spell. Isolde bends down, and the cub jumps into Isolde's waiting arms as she embraces her with lots of kisses to follow.

"I have missed you, my little girl. I hope you were a good kitten while I was away," Isolde says to her.

"She was perfect," answers Princess Ella.

"Thank you, my lady, for watching over her," answers Isolde.

As the six head toward the entrance of the citadel, the captain of the King's Guard comes to meet them.

"My lord, the king and Giselle are waiting for you in the meeting room," he says.

"Very well, captain," answers the prince.

"I will escort you and your companions to him," the captain insists.

Isolde and Galgaliel gaze toward each other, then Galgaliel says to her, "That was fast. I wonder what's up."

"We shall find out soon enough," Isolde answers.

As the six are escorted to the king's meeting room, they enter the room. On the windowsill is an ivory eagle perched on its ledge. The six stand and stare at the predator bird for a moment, then gaze toward one another.

"A messenger?" Isolde says in a startled voice.

Then before the six can take a seat at the large rectangular table, the king and Giselle are already seated in anticipation to hear what has been discovered on their expedition into the bowls of the dark realm.

"This should be interesting," Galgaliel mutters under his breath to Isolde.

"I'm glad you all have returned safely," remarks the king.

"Thank you, brother. A messenger eagle . . . from whom?" "From King Baltazar," the king retorts.

"King Baltazar?" Isolde says in a startled voice.

"His sorceress, Ursula, whom you are all familiar with has had many premonitions on a darkness that dwells in the Dark Forest. He goes on to say that the seas have been turbulent, abounding with large predators feeding on the creatures of the sea which is his kingdom's staple of food," King Galen says, reading from the message sent from the king of the Western Realm.

"So evil is stretching its reach, gathering its forces from the creatures who dwell in the seas, as well as the those who roam over the land. Ursula is correct. What I am about to tell you, your majesty, of what we encountered on our journey confirms Ursula's premonitions," Isolde answers.

Isolde tells King Galen and Giselle of their journey from beginning to end and the encounters they have had along the way, especially of Oriel and the Watchers imprisoned in the dungeons of the Dark Tower and the emergence of Abaddon, who sits on the left side of Evil itself and is about to invade the whole of Pangea.

King Galen, upon hearing Isolde's tale of woe, covers his face with his hand and looks down, then closes his large eyes in despair for he is stunned by the news he has just heard.

Giselle gazes toward the White Witch but is lost for words.

"Your majesty . . . your majesty," Isolde repeats.

King Galen then looks up at Isolde but does not say a word to anyone.

"Your majesty, you will need to answer King Baltazar's message and inform him of our encounter. Send his eagle back to him with your message attached," Isolde insists.

The king nods his head in agreement. Then Prince Quill says to his brother, "We need to send an ivory eagle to Queen Lazuli, also. She must be told of what is about to happen. We will need her army and her pterodactyls to join us to fight off Abaddon's march on the world."

Again, King Galen nods his head in agreement.

Isolde interrupts, "The Warrows and the other kingdoms must also be informed." Isolde then stands and faces the group. "The kingdoms have kept the truce for two ages, millions of seasons of peace without war with virtually no contact with one another. Can we come together to fight a common enemy?"

She then turns to King Galen and reprises, "We will have to, if all the races of the world want to survive in freedom, or kneel to bondage and watch the world fall into shadow."

King Galen turns to his brother. "Quill, compose a letter to the other kingdoms. Send King Baltazar's eagle back to him with our message. Then send *Norbit*, our swiftest eagle, to Queen Lazuli and inform her of the situation. Then send two more eagles to the two Warrow villages, for they are part of this world, thus we will need their assistance in this upcoming war if we are to be victorious."

"It shall be done, my brother," answers the prince.

King Galen then quickly leaves the meeting room escorted by his personal guard. The six are left alone in the room and, for a long moment, not a word is spoken.

Isolde looks toward Giselle in a concerned gaze. "Is the king alright? He looks confused," Isolde insists.

Giselle then answers Isolde, "He has the look of dismay, for he will need time to process all that he has heard."

"We do not have time to wait and *process* the situation. We need to act. Now! For Evil is coming for us all and there is nothing anyone can do to stop it from marching on the world," Isolde says in a firm tone toward Giselle.

Prince Quill turns to his companions and says to them, "The rest of you have a hearty meal. I need to have a talk with my brother."

The prince gets up, and he is quickly followed by Giselle, Galgaliel, and Isolde. He stops and looks toward the three.

Isolde then says to him, "We all need to have a word with your brother."

The prince nods his head in agreement, and the four go forth to seek out the king.

King Galen is on the top of the castle's highest tower. He stands on the walkway between the two spires with his two children, *Prince Elton*, almost fourteen full seasons of age, whilst he is holding his tiny daughter, Princess Ella. The three are looking out on the increasing swirl of storm clouds engulfed over the mountain peaks of the Dark Forest.

"The storm seems to be increasing, my father," says Elton.

"It does appear to get a little worst with each day that passes, my son," answers the king.

"The air is so bitterly cold. I am ready for the Season of Awakening," Elton concludes.

The king glances at his son, smiles then says, "Me too."

Then appearing in the sky above the citadel are four ivory eagles; one appears to be heading west in the direction of the Western Realm, while the other three appear to be flying south, presumably to the Palace of the Rising Sun, home of Queen Lazuli, and the two Warrow villages nestled in the untamed forest of Wildwood.

"Look, Father, four messenger eagles," Prince Elton says in an excitable tone.

The three then stare at four flying large birds for a moment without saying a word to one other until they are out of the sight of their large eyes. Then King Galen looks at his son and says to him, "Yes, my son, they are on a journey with messages to the kings and queen of the other realms, and to the Warrow villages of Wildwind and Southold. I have sent them all to deliver sad news."

Before Prince Elton can ask why, Prince Quill, Isolde, Giselle, and Galgaliel step onto the top of the tower and walk to where the king and his children are standing.

"Brother, we need to have a word with you," requests Prince Quill.

King Galen then says to his son, "Elton, here, take your sister. Now go and find your mother."

"As you wish, Father," answers Elton.

The king then turns and faces the four.

"Your majesty, we need to come up with some kind of plan," requests Isolde.

"I know," answers the king.

Then the thick clouds covering the sky begin to stir and swirl about. All standing on top of the tower turn their gaze to the turbulence within the clouds stirring above them.

Giselle turns to Isolde and screams, "We are under attack!"

Then bursting out from the cloud cover, a massive flock of *savage hornbills* emerge through their ice crystals.

{Savage hornbills are enormous birds of prey weighing in as much as 226 kilograms with a wingspan of seven meters with beaks as long as fifty centimeters and as sharp as a sword's edge. Their primary food is antler bats and small mammals who dwell in the treetops and in the thick underbrush of the Dark Forest, but they also have been known to roam the seas near the coast throughout the supercontinent as they also feed on the sea life that dwells at or near the ocean surface and on the creatures that come ashore to rest and mate on its rocky coast and sandy beaches.}

"Take cover!" commands the king.

Then the King's Guards turn and face the large birds as they begin their descent on the castle and its surrounding areas. The king and his companions run toward the exit that leads to the stairway that descends back into the castle, with Prince Elton running ahead of the four with his sister in his arms. The warriors load their bows with arrows and continue to fire arrow after arrow toward the large birds of prey. The sky is filled with the large predators. A hundred, maybe more, are in full descent toward the Tehrans in and around the castle, in its courtyards, and on its walls. The sky fills with the arrows aimed at the attacking birds, and many have found their mark by the true aim of the archers in the king's service.

The hornbills swoop down at lightning speed, picking off Tehran after Tehran, while clamping down on their bodies with their enormous sharp beaks, then taking their victims high into the sky while in their grasps, consuming them limb by limb as they scan the ground from high above the landscape to scope out their next victims.

Then one of the hornbills catches a glimpse of the young prince who is running frantically with the princess in his arms. The large predator hones in on the two, as Prince Elton approaches the exit door. One hornbill sleeks through the arrows being hurled at it by the king's archers. It swoops down in the direction of the fleeing young prince. His large beak then grabs the princess out of the Prince Elton's arms. As he clamps down on her tiny body, a barrage of arrows penetrates the beast in numerous parts of its body, while three of the arrows become embedded in its enormous head, killing it instantaneously. The beast then drops to the tower floor with a huge thud. But the response has been in vain; the damage has been done.

Princess Ella has become a victim of this huge predator as her crushed body lays lifeless, embedded in its powerful beak.

The king and his companions scream in unison at the horror of this massacre of the tiny princess which they have all just witnessed with their own eyes but were futile to stop.

The four rushes to the princess' aid. As they come upon her, they find her body broken, bloodied, and lifeless. Isolde and King Galen both remove the tiny lifeless body from the huge beak of her dead attacker. Death has come on swift wings for the princess by the villain of the unseen death who has stricken her from above. Prince Elton and the king scream in their grief for the loss of a daughter and a sister.

The King's Guard surround the princess thus. They continue to fend off the attackers with their arrows, as the hornbills continue their barrage on the helpless.

"Your majesty, you must get inside the tower!" insists one of the King's Guard.

But the king is overcome with grief and sadness at the loss of his child so he ignores the pleads of his guardians. Finally, Galgaliel grabs ahold of the king's arm and lifts him and his daughter at bay to safety inside the tower.

Once inside, the four surround the king and his son who are both kneeling alongside the princess's lifeless body; the king clasping her body tightly up against his, as the two royals scream in despair. The four companions just stand in place and gaze at one another, not knowing how to console the two royals.

After a long while, Prince Quill turns to his brother and says to him, "Galen, we need to bring Ella back into the castle, and we must tell Alexandra how all of this unfolded."

Four more of the King's Guard run into the tower to check on the king and stop and stare at the horror of the sight of the dead princess.

Prince Quill turns to them. "Take the king, the prince, and the princess to his quarters and go look for the queen and bring her to them."

The sergeant of the guard nods his head in acknowledgment. Galgaliel and Isolde accompany the king.

Prince Quill grabs Giselle aside and says to her in a whisper, "You will need to prepare Ella's body for burial. The Rising Ceremony will be done at a later date when evil is extinguished. She will be laid to rest in the *Tomb of Eternal Light*."

Giselle shakes her head in agreement, then leaves to make the preparations for the princess to have eternal rest among the great kings and queens of the past who have served this realm since the beginning of this families reign as far back as the First Age.

While all the mayhem involving the princess has been taking place, the savage hornbills cover the sky with their presence, thus they have been ravaging the inhabitants of Lions Gate and have killed and consumed many by swooping down and picking off one Tehran after the other in their huge beaks. The courtyard of the citadel and the surrounding areas have become a dumping ground for the body parts discarded by the large predators as they ravage their victims in flight. The blood of their victims is sprayed down upon the fleeing townsfolk like a deluge on a rainy day, covering them in streams of torrent red and bits of body parts. The screams of the victims being torn apart can be heard as far as the border of the Dark Forest some ten kilometers to the north. The protectors of the citadel show they will not back down in the fight against these invaders, as they continue to launch their arrows at the incoming charge of these large predators; their stationary positions make them an easy target and a simple meal for the predators to consume. The attack from above appears to go on and on for some time until the large birds have satisfied their hunger. Then slowly many begin to drift off back to the north in the direction of the Dark Forest from whence they came.

Then finally after all of the predators have retreated away from the citadel, a calm covers the castle. The icy breeze that was blowing from the north then diminishes, thus a stillness now encompasses the air. The smell of death surrounds the survivors and lingers in its placidity; the only sounds that are reverberating in and around the castle are the distant cries of the wounded and the sobbing of the victims' families and friends slaughtered by the attackers from above.

Captain William, standing in the center of the courtyard and covered with blood and bits of body parts, looks in disbelief as he scopes out his surroundings.

"How could this have happened?" he mutters to himself as he gazes at the snow-covered ground coated in red and laden in guts as far as his large eyes can observe which have been spewed from the bodies torn apart in midair. The captain is just standing there in disbelief when a private of the King's Guard approaches him in haste. The private has a deep gash in his left arm and is bleeding profusely. Captain William turns to the private and says to him, "Private, you need to take care of that wound right away."

"Yes, sir, but you are needed in the king's quarters," the private states.

"The king's quarters . . . why?" asks the captain.

"Princess Ella has been killed," says the private, as he stares at the ground in front of him.

"Killed? How?" asks the captain in an excited tone.

"She and Prince Elton were attacked by the hornbills. The prince has some deep cuts on him but he is okay, but the princess was killed in the attack," the private tells William.

With that, the captain turns and begins to run to the aid of the Royal Family.

As the captain runs through the castle and climbs the long and winding staircase that leads to the king's private quarters, the large doorway leading into the royal's wing of the castle are cloistered with the king's soldiers and hand maidens of the queen, most of whom appear to be dazed and confused at the loss of the tiny princess. As the soldiers clear a way for the captain to gain entrance to the royal's quarters, he stands in the entrance of their bedroom and watches as the Royal Family mourns the loss of their tiny daughter.

The Royal Family is surrounded by the traveling companions, as well as Giselle who is attempting to comfort the king and the queen in their time of grief. Captain William approaches Prince Quill, and the two go off in a corner of the room to discuss the events of the day. Then after a while, Giselle speaks in private to the Royal Family.

"Your majesties, I need to prepare the princess' body for burial. I know this is hard on both of you, but it needs to be done."

The king looks at Giselle and says to her, "I understand, my lady."

The king then looks to his wife. "Alexandra, it's time to let her go. Giselle will take her now and get her ready to rest in eternal peace. Okay, my love?"

The queen nods her head and runs out of the room, sobbing for her daughter. She is followed by her handmaidens for they will not leave her side. The king then turns to his brother in a confused state of mind. He places both his hands on his brother's shoulders and speaks to him.

"Quill, I give you all the powers I possess, for I cannot lead at this moment in time. They are yours to command, the kingdom and all contained within it, until I am fit to lead again."

Prince Quill bows to his brother and says to him, "I will be the custodian of the realm in your absence, my brother, but only until you decide to rule once more."

With that, the king excuses himself and leaves the room to be with his family.

As the king exits the room, the companions and the royal army commanders gather on the veranda outside the royal's quarters.

Isolde turns to all on the veranda and says, "This was no random act by the hornbills. This was premeditated. Evil is beginning its war on the world by his minions venturing out of the Dark Forest to begin their attack on the innocents of Pangea."

Prince Quill looks at Isolde. "I have drafted letters to Queen Lazuli, King Baltazar. and the two Warrow kings. I have sent the ivory eagles to their kingdoms. As soon as we get a response, we can make our plans to take on the evil residing in the north."

"By then it may be too late," responds Giselle.

"She is right. Time is of the essence, your highness," Isolde says, as she turns to the prince.

Galgaliel then says to all, "To go back through the Dark Forest is too dangerous. Abaddon will be expecting us to do that."

"But if we attack by sea, he will be blindsided," Prince Quill surmises.

"By sea?" Giselle boasts out.

"The *Sea of Storms* is frozen over in the winter season. We will be able to walk on the ice. With its close proximity to the Dark Tower, we can conduct a surprise attack on the castle," Isolde concludes.

"Attack the Dark Tower . . . that's suicide," Captain William says.

"Is there another way, captain?" The prince asks.

"We can fight on two fronts. A march through the Dark Forest can be a diversion," remarks Turak.

"Very good, Master Warrow, you are learning," surmises Prince Quill.

The prince goes on to say, "After the princess is buried, we will gather ourselves and begin our march northward. As for now, let us all just grieve together."

Two days after the death of the princess, she is laid to rest in the Tomb of Eternal Light, lying alongside the kings and queens of old—one hundred and twenty generations of the king's family rest in eternal sleep in the huge tomb which overlooks the Sea of Storms on the hillsides of Lions Gate. As the procession of mourners leave the tomb, they pass the company of guards posted outside its entrance. They have been standing guard at this post every moment of every day to protect the remains of the dead for over two millennia. They have stood guard out of respect of their lineage and royal titles, and to repel anyone who would disrespect and desecrate their bodies. The procedures King Galen follows for eternal rest was written by King Lionel before the First Age as the first king of the Northern Realm and an ancient ancestor of King Galen.

{Burial of the dead allows the Tehran soul to sleep within the corpse, thus it will not be released to enter the Spirit World as it would be by the ritual of the Rising Ceremony. This will protect the soul of the deceased if Evil is waiting for the soul to be released, for then it can abduct the soul and use it to commit evil deeds against the living. The Ancient of Days can release it himself and personally have it escorted to the Spirit World by the Guardians of the Spirit World, if he so chooses to assure safe passage so the soul can live in eternal peace.}

CHAPTER X

The Penance of Queen Lazuli

The ivory eagles have completed their mission and have found their way to their destinations. Upon reading the letters drafted by Prince Quill, the five kingdoms call on their commanders to strategize individually their next move. In the Southern Realm in the Castle of the Rising Sun, Queen Lazuli summons the general of her stealth warriors, her all-female death squad—the Daughters of Shayla led by their general, Harlee Antonia, with her second in command, Captain *Ivy Denali*. Accompanying the queen is her sorceress for the last million seasons, *Aveline the Conjurer*, who is the spiritual advisor and war counsel to the queen. Aveline is the queen's most trusted companion. The Daughters of Shayla consist of twelve warriors who operate in the shadows as assassins for the queen. They carry out the commands she instills on them, thus they are her most trusted warriors. This secret squad acts independently from the rest of the queen's army and answers only to the queen herself, thus they are known throughout the supercontinent as *the killers who strike in the shadows*.

The queen calls an emergency meeting of her commanders.

As the gathering of the warriors commence in the queen's meeting room. Lazuli addresses Harlee Antonia, "It appears there is a stirring in the north. An evil that once terrorized the land ages ago appears to be once again building its army of beasts to spread its horror on the known world."

She then hands over to Harlee the letter drafted by Prince Quill for her to read.

As Harlee begins to scroll through the letter, she talks out loud, "Your majesty, this is not good. The Watchers are imprisoned in the dungeons of the Dark Tower. Now I understand all of the mayhem that has been happening throughout the realm."

"It seems Abaddon the Destroyer is behind all of this. He makes Naamah seem like a timid child, but he is just a puppet of Evil itself. A messenger boy sent to do Evil's bidding," concludes Lazuli.

Harlee looks toward the queen. "Legends say he is very powerful." Harlee then directs her next statement to Aveline. "Didn't you see this coming? You are a sorceress with great powers, are you not?"

"I am, but I have been blinded by the capture of Oriel and the rest of the Watchers," Aveline answers.

"Oriel not sharing his visions with you, doesn't that seem a little odd, sorceress?" Harlee then turns to the queen. "Your majesty, we have never encountered an enemy of his stature before. His powers have to be ten times that of Naamah. With Evil controlling him thus giving him more power, if he controls the Malakai and the nomadic tribes of Neanderthals, plus the beasts that roam the many forests throughout the supercontinent, he will be most difficult to defeat in battle, even if we ally with the other kingdoms. It will be a war to end all wars," Harlee insists.

With that, Queen Lazuli stands and walks to the end of the balcony which adjoins her quarters and gazes out over the Southern Ocean. Harlee continues to glare at Aveline in despisement. The seas are glistening in the sun's scarlet hue as it rises up to greet the dawn as a new day is beginning. As the queen continues to peer out on the Southern Ocean, she gazes down at the waves gently breaking on the rocky shoreline at the base of the citadel, sending its spray across the rocks that protect the coastline. With her back to the two assassins, Lazuli speaks out loud, "I need to see for myself the mayhem that is occurring throughout our realm and on the seas."

She then turns to Harlee and Ivy. She continues, "I will call on *Samael*, my beloved pterosaur. On his swift wings, he will guide me throughout our realm and beyond and across the sea so I can make a determination on how to confront our enemy."

"As you wish, your majesty," both females answer together.

Lazuli then says to the two warriors, "Now go, prepare your squad for war. For it is coming and it will soon be upon us."

Both Harlee and Ivy nod their heads in acknowledgment.

Lazuli then turns to her sorceress. "Aveline, you will watch over the kingdom in my absence, for you will be my successor if I cannot rule or in my demise as Delphina is not in a position to lead. Do you accept my invitation?"

"I will do whatever you ask of me, your majesty."

As the two assassins exit the queen's quarters, Lazuli calls for her handmaidens to get her riding attire ready which includes her red hooded cape which extends down just above her ankles. Lazuli, standing alone facing the sea, pushes aside the straps that sit on her shoulders that hold up her short black leather dress, allowing it to fall to the brick floor of her balcony. The queen stands there in all her nakedness; her thin curvy body glistening in the scarlet hue of the morning twilight. She then lifts both arms to the heavens and raises her head to the sky. She then closes her large eyes and, in a whisper, calls out to her pterosaur, Samael.

"Samael, king of the raptors, your queen is in need of your presence. Come to me . . . Come to me now."

The queen continues to stand for a long moment, with her arms extended into the air in silence. She continues to concentrate on calling her pterosaur to her.

{Samael is the largest and most feared pterosaur in all of Pangea. He has been the queen's companion for as long as any Tehran can remember. It is not known how she has come to align herself with this beast; its loyalty to his queen is uncompromised. He is the alpha male of his own flock of at least twenty other pterosaurs who will follow his lead to their deaths.}

As the queen stands naked on her balcony, a stirring among her subjects begins to unravel. Cries of fear echo throughout the castle and its surrounding areas. Many Tehrans scream out loud in fear of the monstrous beasts bearing down on the citadel.

"Pterosaur! Pterosaur!" many scream, as Samael is spotted closing in on the citadel, descending through the cloud cover. Queen Lazuli smiles to herself, knowing that her most faithful subject is about to arrive at her beckoning. The pterosaur descends to just above the highest tower of the citadel and flies out onto the open ocean for about half a kilometer. It then turns and circles back toward the castle, slowing its pace and slowly landing on the balcony right in front of the naked queen herself. He then lets out a scream so loud it echoes through the kingdom and shakes the castle to the core with its deafening screech. The handmaidens who have returned with the queen's attire cower in the corners of the balcony, as Samael continues to screech louder and louder. Then Lazuli steps forward. She approaches the pterosaur, and with both her hands, she embraces Samael's long snout and kisses him on it.

"There, there, my most loyal subject. Welcome home, my boy. It has been far too long since we last embraced," Lazuli whispers to him.

Samael rubs his snout on the queen's face, and Lazuli smiles in satisfaction of her pterosaur returning to her side. The queen then turns to her handmaidens and says in a firm tone, "My attire."

Then the three handmaidens approach the queen with extreme caution for fear of the large raptor attacking them as they come close to her. The handmaidens begin to dress the queen for the flight atop Samael's back. The queen dresses in battle-like attire, which is tanned leather, hard and almost impossible for any blade to penetrate as it is woven together with spider silk from the large arachnids who dwell in the Dark Forest that adhere the pieces of the battle armor together. Last but not least, she wraps herself in her red hooded cape. Then with a brush of her hand, her maidens retreat back inside the castle walls as fast as they can scurry as far away from the large pterosaur as they can.

Samael lowers his long neck for the queen to climb upon his back, and once she does, he raises his long neck and head, and flaps his colossal wings which sends an enormous gust of air stirring through the balcony. He screams a scream so loud as is typical of the behavior of the raptor upon taking to the air. He then leans forward, then takes to the air.

As the pterosaur climbs higher and higher, the warm tropical air flows through the queen's long black locks which fall below her waist and is now blowing in the wind as Samael continues to climb above the clouds. The queen directs the pterosaur to fly out over the Southern Ocean. As they do, Lazuli witnesses the stirrings going on by the creatures that dwell in and below the calm tropical waters. She witnesses *plesiosauruses* swimming in large schools just off the coast, while many species of fish scatter furiously to stay away from the large aquatic reptiles' jaws. She and Samael fly farther from the coast. They watch as whales break the surface of the water, their blowholes spouting water high in the air. Then after some time, about two hundred kilometers off the western coast, Lazuli spots a rogue megalodon. The enormous shark measuring about twenty-one meters long and can weight up to sixty-five thousand kilograms is just below the ocean's surface. Seeing this is a such a rare sight, for those who witness this largest sea predator in the open ocean rarely live to tell the tale. Lazuli then spots in the distance the many scattered islands that dot the oceans throughout both hemispheres; some are inhabited by nomadic tribes who have chosen to live in isolation and have done so for many a millennium. Some isolated islands are hideaways for the marauders who terrorize the coastal waters of the supercontinent from time to time. Most islands remain uninhabited due to the remoteness in which they lie, for the oceans are filled with treacherous predators and the odds of reaching these lands safely is remote at best.

She then directs Samael to continue to fly west, and at about 400 kilometers off the western coast of Pangea, they come across a small group of islands called the *Umbrella Islands* which have been named so due to their brolly shape. She directs Samael to land on the largest island in the small chain named *Tortola*. This ancient island is the benediction of Queen Lazuli's ancestors as the legend passed down to the queen from generation after generation from millennia to millennia, which is written in the ancient scribes, for the queen's lineage was written here on the ancient tablets of her ancestors which documented their existence originating from this island chain. These tablets were scribed before the First Age of Pangea billions of seasons ago and traveled with the tribe when they proceeded to treacherously sail to the mainland of Pangea. There they have been preserved in the royal library in the Palace of the Rising Sun.

Upon approaching the Island of Tortola, Lazuli directs Samael to land before the Great Cave of her ancestors. Their tribe originated in this cave at the beginning of time. It is from this location they ventured across the Southern Ocean and settled on the mainland of Pangea on the tip of the *Westin Peninsula*. She has not visited these islands since before the Great War which ended the First Age. She came at that time to pray to her ancestors for guidance. She has returned here once again in these dire times to ask their spirits for guidance, as well as their blessings one last time since war will soon be thrust upon the world in this Modern Age.

Queen Lazuli leads Samael into the large cave entrance which spans thirty meters high and forty meters across. Inside the cave there are ancient structures built a billion seasons ago which are embedded in its stone walls where the tribe of her ancestors originated and raised their young, who then lived together in harmony with one another in the ancient times. Lazuli gazes at the ancient structures in awe for they speak to her as the souls of the departed linger in the ancient ruins. She was raised as a sorceress by her mother, *Queen Ina*, also known as the *Keeper of the Ancient Artifacts* and one of the main *Scribes* of the *Ancient Tablets* which tell of the world's beginnings, its triumphs, as well as its struggles. A powerful sorceress was Queen Ina who schooled her daughter in the ancient ways of magic and the correct execution of the ancient spells. Therefore, Lazuli is familiar with the ancient ways which have been handed down from generation to generation to generation.

She grabs a wooden branch lying on the cave floor. She then speaks in the ancient language of her ancestors and ignites the end of the branch into a torch. She then leads Samael into its dark reaches into the bowels of the cave some two kilometers from its entrance. Once they reach the end of the cave, Samael settles in in the far corner of the cave out of the light of the lit torch. Lazuli then climbs the steps leading up to the altar in which her distant ancestors prayed to the Ancient of Days for guidance, forgiveness, strength in battle, and the direction in which to lead their tribe of fellow Tehrans. It is here, according to the writings of the ancient scribes, that they were commanded by the deity to venture across the ocean and to settle on the mainland of Pangea *for the survival of the tribe.*

Upon the altar, Lazuli lights the torches stemming out of the altar's floor which were left in place by her ancestors; this in which lights the surrounding area where her ancestors prayed. Once all of the torches are lit, Queen Lazuli then kneels upon the altar in front of the marble statue of the Ancient of Days who is positioned pointing down at his worshipers. The deity is surrounded by statues of the Watchers who are the Guardians who oversee the planet of all the livings thing that adorn the world in all its forms and who are his most trusted servants and advisors. She then bows her head in reverence and begins to pray to the *Deity of Creation*. She closes her large eyes, and as she does, she can feel in her soul the spirits of her ancestors surrounding her being, engulfing her consciousness with wisdom and of the goings-on in the modern world in which she lives. They also fill her thoughts with the instincts of survival and tactics to confront the Evil that has encompassed the modern day. Lazuli is a leader without conscience or empathy toward her enemies or any other that gets in her way of power, riches, and lust. The queen prays for what seems like days, but in reality, is only a short period of time.

Then in her semiconscious state, she hears a stirring from behind her; footsteps moving in her direction which continue their approach on her. Kneeling, she slowly turns her body toward the noise coming toward her and sees three male Tehrans now standing about three meters from where she is kneeling. She says not a word but stares at them in a glaring eye. The queen then stands and faces the three. She thinks to herself, *Nomads, vagabonds who live on their wits to survive so far away from the modern world in the middle of the ocean.* Before speaking, Lazuli thinks to herself, *Could they be my ancient ancestors who stayed behind when the tribe left and ventured to mainland of Pangea?*

One of the nomads speaks, "Well, what do we have here?"

Another of the nomads answers the first, "I think we have a piece of ass for us all to share!"

Then all three laugh out loud amongst each other.

Lazuli then thinks to herself again, *No ancestor of mine would be so disrespectful of a female.*

She then answers them, "So you think I am here to be shared amongst you and to give you pleasure, do you?"

"I think we will have our way with you in any way we want," the first Tehran answers.

"Oh, you think so?" she retorts.

"Where did you come from, bitch?" asks the third Tehran.

Lazuli then gazes from one Tehran to the other. She then says to them, "I come from across the sea!"

"The sea? I did not see any boat!" the first Tehran barks in her direction.

"I did not come by boat, I flew," she answers.

"Oh, so now you are a fucking bird, huh?" says the second Tehran.

"No, I am a *queen!*" she retorts.

Then out of the shadows Samael walks quietly up to his queen. He approaches her from behind as to not be seen by the three Tehrans. Then out of the darkness and into the light of the torches pierces his long snout; his essence is gleaming in the light of the torches. The pterosaur then places his long snout on the queen's shoulder. His saliva oozes down to the brick steps of the altar. His large yellow eyes are now staring straight at the three Tehrans. The three marauders seeing Samael are now frozen with fear!

Lazuli then says to them, "How dare you treat a queen in that manner. Now you shall pay for your deplorable behavior!"

Samael lifts his large head straight up into the air and lets go a screech so loud it shakes the walls of the cave, and some of the loose boulders holding in place the dwellings attached to the cave walls begin to falter to the ground. Lazuli then laughs and says to the three in a mocking tone as she points her left arm straight at the three Tehran's, and says to them in an elevated tone, "You are nothing! I am a raging river . . . You are but a babbling brook. You will now feel the wrath of *my* raging current!"

Samael then thrusts his body forward and leaps over the queen toward the three Tehrans, crushing two of them with his large feet as his scaly body lands hard on top of the two. He then begins to engulf the third Tehran with his enormous jaws consisting of hundreds of sharp fangs in which Samael consumes the first one in a single bite. As the pterosaur bites down on his victim, the Tehran's organs, blood, and pieces of body parts splatter all along the base of the altar, settling on the brick floor in bloody clumps. Holding on to the other two Tehrans in his sharp claws, he squeezes their crushed bodies and blood begins to purge from every orifice of their being. He then eats them one at a time, piece by piece, tearing into their flesh and splattering their blood and guts which again covers the altar steps while crushing their bones in his powerful jaws.

The brick floor is amassed in red with pools of blood and body parts scattered about this holy place. Lazuli watches the carnage that Samael has instilled on the queen's enemies and smiles to herself, for this is her revenge—to watch her foes being devoured, which is her just reward for their horrid words and actions toward her. She looks toward Samael, then pets him on his shoulders.

"There you go, my boy. Eat our enemies. Enjoy your meal of flesh and blood, for revenge is a dish best served fresh."

She then laughs in a loud mocking tone which echoes throughout the huge cave.

Once Samael has finished consuming the three Tehrans, he and Lazuli begin their walk back toward the cave entrance. The two slowly walk through the cave past the many structures built billions of seasons ago. Lazuli gazes in awe at the way her ancient ancestors once lived and thrived on this remote island.

"Such a simple life without the demands of a kingdom to rule over or having the responsibility of making the decisions that impact thousands of lives," she continues to contemplate to herself.

"Maybe one day I can return to this place and stay for a while. Wouldn't that be nice?"

She feels elated in the home of her ancient ancestors as she is surrounded by the presence of her forefathers and foremothers as their spirits swirl about her. It is as if they are embracing her in their arms as one would embrace an infant child close to their essence for love, comfort, and protection. A feeling of gratification fills the queen's soul to the core with hope and direction, plus an excitation that she has not felt since the days of old, long, long ago with the fond memories instilled in her when she lived in this hallowed cave as a small Tehran child.

Lazuli decides to stay the night in the cave. As she wanders throughout its diameter, she comes across the dwelling she was raised in as a small child, and without apprehension or hesitation, she excitably goes inside which is like finding a long-lost friend whom she has not seen for ages. The hovel is small consisting of four rooms, with many of her parents' wares still in the same place where they were left so long ago. Though dust and grime cover the structure and its interior, these long-lost memories that were hidden in the back of her mind now come to the forefront of her thoughts. As she settles in for the night, a warm feeling comes over her and fills her soul with comfort. She will have the soundest sleep she can remember since leaving this place.

Then as the morning approaches, Lazuli awakens fully revived; feeling as she once did in her youth before the trials and tribulations of the crown which now sits upon her head and weighs down her thoughts in despair and responsibility. She now longs for the days of old when life was simple, carefree, and easy, surrounded by family and friends. As the cave begins to refract the scarlet glow of the dwarf sun rising over the Southern Ocean, Lazuli realizes that she must return to her place. As she would like to live in exile, that is not her reality. She must carry on with her destiny and continue to rule over her realm with an iron fist.

As the two exit the cave, Lazuli looks back and bows in respect to those who once walked upon this land and called it home and are now part of the Spirit World, looking over her and guiding the very essence of her soul. She then turns toward Samael. The pterosaur lowers his body close to the ground in anticipation of his queen ascending upon his back. Lazuli then covers herself with her red cape, then flips the hood attached to it upon her head covering her long black silky hair. She then climbs upon

Samael's back. Once upon him, she glances one last time at the empty cave and smiles to herself, knowing that her past is alive in her present.

Queen Lazuli leans toward Samael's head and whispers in his ear, followed by a kiss on the top of his large, elongated head. Then with a lunge forward, Samael slowly takes to the air; his long leathery wings creating a huge gust of wind and a dusky cloud in the wake of his soaring figure. Higher and higher Samael climbs into the clear skies of the troposphere. Once he reaches the geostrophic current, the pterosaur is then able to glide on the warm tropical thermals afforded to him in this region of the globe. Lazuli directs him to circle the small group of islands which appear tiny from this altitude. Lazuli can see what appears to be many small colonies on a few of the larger islands spewing life in this remote archipelago. She contemplates to herself on how life has spread out among the globe and wonders what lies beyond into the far reaches of the unknown world and what possible hazards and life-forms have yet to be discovered. Lazuli then motions to Samael to head east, back in the direction of the Pangean mainland. Her thoughts and feelings are now with the souls she has encountered in the cave of her ancient ancestors and the hopes that they will direct her in the upcoming war that seems to be inevitable; that they will lead her to victory and ensure the survival of her species and her kingdom.

CHAPTER XI

The Best Laid Plans

Queen Lazuli has circled the Southern Realm riding atop of Samael prior to her return to her palace, thus she has witnessed the disturbances Aveline has felt over the past seasons, such as large herds of predator beasts swarming throughout and above the forests and the Grassy Plains, which is uncharacteristic of many of their behaviors since many are solitary species. Something has brought them together to hunt and roam the realm in packs. Most disturbing to the queen is the presence of *Wolfen packs* in the realm which she has witnessed from the air atop Samael.

The Wolfen, the large *ebony wolves* who stand two meters at the shoulder and almost three meters in length with their large glowing orange eyes, dwell exclusively in the north country of Pangea. Though this specie does roam in large packs, they have never before been documented south of the *Plains of Auria* and are now roaming near the border town of *Ronin* near the boundary of the Southern Wildwood.

"They are being controlled by an outside force, for certain," Lazuli contemplates to herself.

"Abaddon's reach appears to be stronger and far wider than anticipated. His powers appear to be much greater than his predecessor of evil incarnate, Naamah, the Demon of Fire."

Upon landing with Samael back on her private porch, the queen is met by her three handmaidens who cower in the corners, trying to avoid eye contact with her pterosaur out of fear for their lives. As Lazuli dismounts

Samael, she once again embraces his long snout and kisses him on it. She then whispers in his ear to share her affection with him once again, "I will call for you again, my beloved. Soon . . . for you and your flock will be needed in battle. Stay close, my most trusted friend."

She then stands to his side. Samael then begins to flap his enormous wings, moving the air around him like the force of a hurricane. Then leaning forward, he starts to ascend into the sky. Lazuli watches his silhouette as it begins to slowly diminish as Samael ascends higher and higher into the wild blue yonder.

As Samael's voyage exceeds her line of sight, Lazuli turns to her handmaidens with an angry glare. They immediately run to her side and assist her in undressing out of her flying attire. She stands there naked, facing the three handmaidens. Then one of her handmaidens hands her one of her leather dresses. She slips it over her head onto her naked body; the outfit barely covers her slim figure and leaves nothing to the imagination. Once dressed, the queen turns to one of her handmaidens. She orders one of them to immediately summon Aveline and *General Levi Wult*, the commander of her army, to her quarters. She then turns to one of the other two handmaidens and asks her, "Where is my daughter?"

The handmaiden keeps her large eyes on the ground in front of her and answers the queen, "She is in her courtyard outside of her quarters, your majesty."

"Send her to me, now!"

The handmaiden bows to the queen and answers, "Yes, your majesty." She backs up the length of the porch to the queen's quarters. She then turns and hurries to the princess' quarters to relay the queen's order to Delphina.

Lazuli turns to the last handmaiden and says to her, "Bring me Harlee Antonia and Ivy Denali immediately!"

The queen then sits at the long rectangular table situated in the middle of her private porch, awaiting the arrival of her daughter, her sorceress, her assassins, and her general. Lazuli stares out onto the Southern Ocean; the view of the sea stretches endlessly to the horizon. The motion of the waves instills a calm being whilst the scarlet hue of the twilight reflecting off the surface of the sea appear to place her in a hypnotic state of mind. She closes her large eyes, then listens to the waves as they break then crash onto the rocky shoreline, sending its watery spray high up into the air in which Lazuli can feel the mist of the spray across her face and arms, sending a cool sensation throughout her body. The aroma of the salt air fills her nostrils. She takes a deep breath. The fresh air fills her lungs which instills in her a tranquility she has been searching to find within herself for many a millennium.

Within a short time, Aveline and General Levi appear on her porch and the tranquility she was radiating seem to disappear as Lazuli catches a glimpse of the two. Reality begins to set in. She now finds herself back into the present with the responsibilities that come with her royal title. Lazuli stares at the two for a moment, then says to them, "Sit, both of you."

Aveline and Levi take their seats at the table.

"Your majesty, I was worried about you, for you have been gone for days," Aveline says with concern in her voice.

Lazuli glares at the sorceress. "I'm fine, but what I have seen makes me worry about what is going to happen in our world."

"What have you seen, your majesty?" asks the general.

Lazuli stares at the two. "Wolfen . . . in the Southern Realm, for one!"

"Wolfen? Here?" asks the general in a startled voice.

"Are you sure, your majesty?"

Lazuli becomes enraged at the general questioning her words. Lazuli walks toward the table, then stands across the table from General Levi. She then leans on the table and looks directly into the general's large eyes. "Are you questioning my words, general? For if you are, I will have you laden with arrows by your own troops until all that is left of you is a bloody fucking mess."

General Levi lowers his head. "I'm sorry, your majesty. I didn't mean to question you, but . . . but the thought of Wolfen in our realm. It just came out . . . I'm sorry."

Lazuli again stares at the general. "You are the commander of *my* armies. I expect more from you, general. Think before you speak, or I'll cut your tongue out and feed it to the rats roaming the catacombs. Understand, general?"

"Yes, yes, your majesty, I understand. Again, let me say I am so sorry," Levi reiterates to Lazuli.

As the queen looks up, Harlee Antonia and Ivy are standing at the entrance to the porch.

"Ladies, come and join us," says Lazuli.

General Harlee and Captain Ivy take their seats at the table alongside the others. Moments later, Princess Delphina enters the porch and hurries to the table to join the others.

"Nice of you to join us, my daughter," remarks Queen Lazuli.

"Sorry, Mother, to keep you waiting," Delphina answers.

Lazuli glares at her daughter, displaying her unhappiness with Delphina's tardiness to her command. Lazuli does not answer her daughter or even acknowledge her apology.

Lazuli turns and faces the ocean to calm herself and to collect her thoughts, for General Levi and Delphina have upset the queen. Before she initiates anything rash and impulsive, Lazuli realizes she needs to think in a logical manner and express herself clearly and concisely to all assembled.

Once Lazuli's composure has been regained, she faces her trusted advisors and begins to speak to them. "The time has come to prepare for war. Once again, we must face an adversary sent to destroy the world by Evil itself. Though it has been more than two million seasons since the Great War, Evil Has been planning its revenge all along and it is just now starting to put its plan in motion. We will need to coordinate with the other kingdoms for we cannot do it alone as that would be suicide."

A long silence comes over the gathering. Then Harlee Antonia speaks, "Your majesty, may I speak?"

"Of course," Lazuli answers.

"Your majesty, Abaddon is the one who sits on the left side of Evil itself. His powers are granted to him by the deity. With such power, he would expect the world to cower at his presence, thus he would not expect an attack on the Dark Tower for that would be a brazen and unexpected act and one which would catch him by surprise, don't you think?"

General Levi shakes his head in disbelief, then says to Harlee, "Attack him . . . in the Dark Tower?"

"Yes, general, either that or he will decimate the entire world. Look, the Dark Tower is his stronghold. He fears nothing while inside its walls for he feels secure in his fortress, secure enough that he has no fear especially for his own life and the lives of his minions in his own fortress," Harlee concludes.

"A surprise attack?" answers Queen Lazuli.

"Yes, your majesty, but we will need a diversion to achieve this," Harlee answers.

General Levi has a look of disbelief in his eyes and questions Harlee Antonia, "And just how do you perceive to attack Abaddon in his own fortress, general?"

Harlee then stands and begins to walk around the porch, then she turns to all assembled. "We will need the armies of the three kingdoms to march on the Grassy Plains before the Dark Tower. Once his minions begin to do battle with the troops assembled there, my squad and I will secretly enter the Dark Tower, free the Watchers, and kill the evil Abaddon."

General Levi begins to laugh out loud. Shaking his head, he says, "That's preposterous! You can never pull it off."

Harlee glares at Levi and answers him, "Do you have a better idea, general? If so, now is the time to tell us!"

All eyes turn to General Levi and no one utters a word; all stare in his direction, awaiting an answer. Levi looks down at the table and does not say a word.

Lazuli then stares in his direction and says to the general, "This is twice you have disappointed me today, general. Do not disappoint me again, ever, for you will pay a heavy price. Do you understand?"

Levi looks up at the queen. "I understand."

Lazuli turns to one of her personal guards posted by the porch exit; eight guards in total always protect the queen. She commands one of them to "Go get the Royal Scribes and bring them to me."

She then faces another of her personal guards and says to him, "Assemble four ivory eagles here on my porch. They will be needed shortly."

Lazuli then turns to all assembled. "I will have the eagles deliver this plan to the other kingdoms and request a gathering of all the kingdoms as soon as possible."

Within a short period of time, the Royal Scribes have written the words Queen Lazuli has dictated to them. The queen's personal guards have lined up her ivory eagles on the porch's stone railing—four of the swiftest of the queen's messengers. Once completed and affixed with the queen's royal seal, the royal guards attach the messages to the eagles' left legs inside their attached pouches which designate them as carrier messengers. Then each individual eagle is instructed as to which kingdom they are to immediately venture to. Queen Lazuli then releases the messengers to do their duty. The four ivory eagles spring from the stone railings, then climb high into the sky; each individual eagle flying on the path designated by the queen.

Before the day's end and prior to the dimindark settling in over the supercontinent, the ivory eagle messengers arrive at their destinations.

Chapter XII

The Forgotten Warriors

Above the storm clouds that encompass the peaks of the Black Mountains some 4,200 meters above the forest floor in the interior of Dark Forest live a solitary species that has been able to thrive for millions of seasons in an environment of permafrost and year-round below freezing temperatures. This allusive and forgotten species is known throughout the supercontinent as the Centaurs. These beings, half horse half Tehran, are pure warriors who have thrived in the most hostile environment known on all of Pangea. Their population is undocumented, as is their laws and traditions. As a matter of fact, the only known truths known about them comes from a few small bands of warriors who have abandoned their isolated life above the storm clouds and now wander emancipated throughout the supercontinent. As a species, the Centaurs have witnessed firsthand the carnage created by the Demon of Fire and have fought against his evil, while they also share the same homeland with many foul and evil creatures who roam at or below their habitable range on the mountain slopes, as well as the forest floor.

The Centaurs are led by the oldest and wisest of their species, *Lord Khamael*. Before the First Age when the world was young, even before the continents converged, it was foretold that the Ancient of Days appeared to Khamael in a dream and instilled in him the foundations of *Centaur Law*. It is with this enlightenment which transformed his soul. He was tasked by the deity to lead his race by this doctrine which were now embedded in his essence to guide the Centaurs in times of peace, as well as war. Thus, he has done so ever since. Khamael is very, very old, thus he is very, very wise as well. He is loved and respected by all within his tribe for his virtues, his wisdom, and his courage.

On the treacherous slopes of the Black Mountains entrenched with snow accompanied by a freezing wind blowing from the north at a velocity of a gale is *Ormarath,* captain of the Centaur scouts. His squad of ten have been keeping a watchful eye on the movements in and around the Dark Tower ever since the meteors have started falling and landing abundantly throughout the realm.

"Captain, Malakai and Neanderthals continue to mass in and around the Dark Tower," reports *Lika,* a seasoned scout in the Centaur ranks.

"How many do you estimate, Lika?" asks Ormarath.

"It's hard to say, captain. There are many fires burning in and around the castle with much movement going on day and night. I would estimate maybe ten thousand," Lika retorts.

"Ten thousand?" Ormarath says in a startled tone, then shakes his head in disbelief.

The other scouts who have accompanied Lika shake their heads in agreement with him.

"Most are camped on the Grassy Plains surrounding the castle," Lika adds.

"Malakai and Neanderthals, working together . . . Those of which were enemies are now allies," Ormarath, distraught, mumbles to himself out loud.

"Captain, sir . . . The only reason that they would amass and act as one army with that amount of force is that they are controlled by an *evil force,* preparing them to go to war, but why? And for whom?" Lika states in a puzzled tone.

"This appears to be a reiteration of what happened more than two million seasons ago which preceded the start of the Great War of the Second Age. The foul creatures amassed then before the Demon of Fire first showed his ugly face to the world. It appears that indeed history is repeating itself, Lika," Ormarath concludes.

The captain begins to pace and appears to be in deep thought. Then after a short time of pacing, he stops, then turns and addresses his company, "I need to take a closer look at what is happening in and around the Dark Tower. I will descend down the mountain and take a look around for myself."

Lika looks at the captain and says to him, "Ormarath, I will accompany you. Hey, like old times when we were colts. The two of us together again on another adventure."

Ormarath looks at Lika and says to him, "Yes, like old times. The only one missing now is Galgaliel. The three of us were inseparable then."

"I often wonder about your brother. I hope he is alive and well, for he has been gone for ages, roaming the wilds of Pangea," Lika answers.

"He is the smartest and the bravest of us. I feel he is fine. He is just chasing his dreams of freedom and adventure," Ormarath replies.

Then Ormarath turns to his squad and gives them instructions to wait for them at this location until the dawn of the new day, for if they do not return by the dawn of twilight, they are to return to the Centaur Village of *Frostford* and report to Lord Khamael what they have witnessed so far on their mission.

Immediately, Lika and Ormarath turn and begin their descent down the steep ledges and rocky outcrops of the mountainside. The two tread carefully, for their footing could easily give way below their hooves as the mountain side has eroded in a massive way over the millions of seasons due to the constant gale and nonstop torrential rain. As the two continue to descend further down the steep incline, they come upon the boundary of the thick storm clouds which cover the peaks of the entire mountain chain about five hundred meters below their peaks where there is no visibility. The swirling of the gale force winds which blow in every direction makes it almost impossible for the two to see more than a meter in front of themselves. This storm has been continuous as far back as anyone can remember, and it doesn't appear that it will ever let up. It has covered these peaks since before the Great War of the Second Age when Evil was thought to have taken control of the mountain chain to project its presence to all who inhabit the supercontinent and to do its bidding by causing terror through the vile deeds it continuously supports and was the mastermind behind them throughout the known world.

As the two carefully step into the mass of dark grey, twilight turns from scarlet hue which was above the cloud cover to a dark burgundy drab fog as thick as pea soup. The force of the gale makes it impossible to hear anything but the howling wind blowing through this monsoon. An enemy could be right in front of oneself, and one would never know it is there until it is too late. Both Centaurs have their swords drawn and pointing outward in front of them as to tread very carefully as to not attract the enemy they are stalking. The two warriors walk side by side with their heads spinning like a top looking to and fro, then fore and aft, watching all sides of their forward motion.

Lika then sees a shadowy outline right in front of the two Centaurs. He puts his arm across the chest of Ormarath to stop his forward motion. He then points with his sword hand out in front of the two of them. Then out of the thick fog walking toward the two Centaurs are three Neanderthals. As fate would have it, none of the foul beasts are paying attention as they walk through the storm as they are covering their large eyes to block the wind from impairing their vision and staring at the ground in front of their feet. One of the foul beasts looks up, but before he can make a sound, his head is separated from his shoulders by a thrust of Lika's sword. The head of the beast flies three meters into the air, as his body falls lifeless to the ground.

Ormarath then swings his sword mightily and decapitates the other two Neanderthals with a single swing of his sword, sending a flow of blood shooting high into the air as their severed arteries gush from the opening where their heads used to be attached to their bodies. The two Centaurs are now covered with the splattered blood of their enemies, as the Neanderthals' lifeless bodies lay on the ground in front of the two Centaurs. The two Centaurs then gaze to one another.

"Are you okay?" asks Lika.

"I'm fine, but they're not!" Ormarath answers.

Lika looks down on himself, then to his companion and says, "I hate being covered by Neanderthal blood. Yuck!"

As Lika tries to wipe the blood from his face and body, Ormarath looks at his companion with a grin and says to him, "Better their blood on us than our own."

"True, Ormarath, we need to keep our eyes peeled," Lika answers. He then continues, "What do we do with their bodies?"

Ormarath looks bewildered at Lika. "Do? Nothing. Leave them here to rot. Besides, they will not be found in this mayhem."

"Sounds good to me," Lika answers.

"I can't see anything in front of us. We need to quickly descend below this cloud cover before we run into any more unwanted encounters," Ormarath states.

The two slowly continue their descent down the mountain again, treading carefully so as to not slip and slide down the steep mountain slope which will alert their enemies then bring the army of evil on them. As the two Centaurs reach the lower boundary of the cloud cover, they now have the ability to gaze onto the Dark Tower itself, surrounded by the vastness of the Grassy Plains as they peer down into the valley about eight thousand meters below them.

Then what the two Centaurs witness with their own eyes sends a chill down their spines. Ormarath gasps, then turns to Lika. "My word, will you look at that! Fires, hundreds of them covering the entire circumference of the plains itself."

The two Centaurs stand facing the Grassy Plains at such a horrific sight, shaking their heads in disbelief for moments on end. Then after a long pause, Lika makes an educated assessment. "You and your scouts were right, Malakai and Neanderthal's together shoulder to shoulder as one army, and their numbers seem also correct."

"How can this be?" Ormarath asks out loud.

The two Centaurs watch hidden between two huge boulders which have settled in a rut on the edge of the mountain slope. Then they can hear through the blowing wind footsteps above their position. Both turn and look up. Two Neanderthal scouts are wandering through the mountain slopes, looking for signs of anything unusual to report back to their tribesmen. Their conversation is indecipherable to the Centaurs as it consists mainly of grunts of groans. Omarath reaches behind him and pulls two arrows out of his quill, then gazes in Lika's direction. Lika nods to Ormarath, and then he pulls two arrows out of his quill. As the two beasts walk directly above the Centaurs, Lika and Ormarath let loose of their arrows. All four arrows find their mark with the thrust and accuracy of the archer's skill which splits both of the Neanderthals heads wide open, killing them both instantaneously. Both Neanderthals topple over and fall off the ledge they were walking on, landing in between the two Centaurs. They have fallen about five meters and landed with a thud and a crunch of their bones against the granite rock below the Centaurs' feet.

Lika looks at his companion. "Phew, they really stink. Do they ever bathe?" Lika asks Ormarath.

"They are wildlings. Cleanliness is not a priority to them." Ormarath gazes again at the Grassy Plains below them. "We need to get a closer look. Follow me," Ormarath says to Lika.

The rain and sleet continue to pound the two as they move down the mountain slope in the direction of the Dark Tower while the temperature continues to drop near freezing to about 273.15 Kelvins. The dwarf sun has set in the west and is now below the horizon. The dimindark has begun to settle in over the realm, dropping the temperature even further, thus the rain and sleet has now turned to a thick snow, making it impossible to see more than three meters ahead of themselves.

The quickly accumulating snow should cover their hoof tracks as they move along the mountain slope. The glow of the many fires on the plain lights up its entirety, casting a dark shadow on the Dark Tower itself. As the two Centaurs descend closer to the valley, the number of the foul beasts begin to increase rapidly, while the fires glow will make the Centaurs more susceptible to being seen and attacked by their enemies.

"Try to stay in the shadows," Ormarath whispers to his companion.

The blustery wind being driven by the downdrafts created by the topographic barrier of the mountain walls which is blowing to the south may be able to carry the scent of the Centaurs into the valley below as the Neanderthals rely heavily on scent to hunt and could alert the beasts of the presence of the intruders.

It now appears the odds are against the Centaurs.

"Great, now it's snowing, like a wall of white," complains Lika.

"I know, they'll be able to see us coming two kilometers away," Ormarath surmises in a somber tone.

"If that is our destiny, so be it!" adds Lika.

Ormarath nods his head in agreement. He then says to him, "Well then, let's finish what we started."

The two then continue to move cautiously down in the direction of the basin below. The Centaurs can hear the sound of dull footsteps all around them, trancing through the snow-covered ground, which is starting to quickly accumulate. The storm is quickly turning into a blizzard with the wind continuing to blow at the force of a gale. The two dart in between clusters of trees which are spread throughout the mountain slope. Then all at once there seems to be a stirring all around them by both Malakai and Neanderthals. The two then watch as the stirring turns into a frenzy which starts to unfold before their large eyes.

"They must have caught our scent," observes Ormarath.

The Centaurs see glimpses of shadows in every direction, so the two stand fast, hidden in a cluster of pine trees; their bows filled with arrows, awaiting an attack from one of the many beasts moving around them. Then two Neanderthals stop directly in front of the cluster of trees in which the two Centaurs are hiding. They sniff the air to pinpoint the exact location of their quarry. The Neanderthals gaze into the tree cluster in the direction of the hiding Centaurs. Then from behind the foul beasts, large glowing orange eyes can be seen by the Centaurs, many of them peering out of a cluster of trees directly next to where the Centaurs are hiding. The Neanderthals stand completely still as a low rumble of many growls pierce the air which can be heard through the blowing gale.

The confused Neanderthals just stare into the blackness now, facing the cluster of trees with the glowing eyes staring at them. Then jolting out from the cluster of trees charging the foul beasts are Wolfen, six of them in total. They quickly and ferociously pounce on the two Neanderthals, brutally closing their large jaws on the beasts' body parts. Arms and legs are torn off the beasts by the Wolfens' huge and powerful jaws. The sound of flesh ripping apart the Neanderthals appendages sending the gushing of blood which purges the air and shoots in every direction covering the Wolfen and the surrounding landscape with the Neanderthals bodily fluids and chunks of their body parts. The Centaurs remain perfectly still, hidden in the cluster of pine trees. They watch in horror as the Wolfen retreat back to the cluster of trees that they were hiding in; only this time their jaws are filled with the body parts and organs of the two Neanderthals—a hearty meal which will satisfy their hunger . . . for now. All that is left of the two Neanderthals are the bloody stumps of their torso and heads lying in a massive pool of their own blood which contrasts against the white snow-covered surroundings. Their attack was so swift and final that not a sound was made by the foul beasts. It was a quick and brutal death that they both have succumbed to.

Ormarath leans over to Lika and whispers to him, "We need to get outta here and fast or we're next." Lika nods his head in agreement.

The Centaurs quickly gallop out of their hiding place and head down the mountain slope. The two gallops for about one hundred eighty meters and come to another cluster of trees; this is a large tree cluster which appears to be about three hundred meters long and about one hundred meters wide which creeps along the mountain slope. This is an ample hideaway for the time being.

Lika turns to Ormarath while trying to catch his breath. "Wolfen in the Dark Forest, Ormarath. What is going on?"

Ormarath stares into the great void surrounding them and says, "The world is upside down now, Lika. Right is now wrong. Immoral is now moral. Evil is now righteous. A darkness is starting to further its reach out into the known world, for it feels like just before the start of the Great War." Ormarath then looks at Lika and stares straight into his large eyes. "I feel the end of days will soon be upon us all."

The two Centaurs then continue on their quest to reach the base of the Dark Tower. So far, the two warriors have felt a sensation as if unknown forces have been keeping a watchful eye over them, so they keep advancing closer to the valley floor without being noticed by the many foul beasts moving about all around them, surrounding them at times. Their agility allows them to move quickly, avoiding themselves from being seen. Realizing that none of their quarry is expecting outsiders to be this deep into their territory, that reassurance keeps them moving forward.

As the Centaurs reach the final cluster of trees just before the plains begin, they find themselves positioned directly in front of the castle itself. The castle is now a mere fifty meters from where they stand. Ormarath and Lika gaze upward and stare at the sheer size and mass of the castle. Its stone walls protrude upward at least thirty meters from the valley floor. On top of the stone walls on all sides are patrol paths wide enough for thirty Neanderthals to stand shoulder to shoulder, which is wider than the streets inside the walled city of Lions Gate. The paths are lined with Malakai which seem to be moving about. They appear to be being used as sentries for their immense size and height as they can see farther into the surrounding landscape with their huge cycloptic eye, rather than the Neanderthals which are short in stature and rely on scent rather than vision, especially with the hundreds of fires aiding them in their duty by lighting up the surrounding plains, keeping the Centaurs' scent at bay. The beasts are armed with their nail-laden clubs which are swung over their large shoulders and can be brought into action with their mighty strength in mere seconds to wreak havoc on their enemies, who are much, much smaller in size and scope.

"What do we do now, Ormarath?" Lika whispers, as a squad of Neanderthals marches in front of the two Centaurs who remain unseen by lingering in the shadows of the cluster of trees.

Ormarath then whispers to his companion, "Look at the base of the castle cut in the hill it sits on. It looks like caves, every twenty meters or so."

Lika stares from one cave to the other and whispers, "They look more like holes dug into the hillside for they are perfectly round, don't you think?"

Ormarath again stares at the holes and whispers, "Who could have dug holes into the hill side ten meters round and why?"

Then out of the darkness, two Neanderthals come wandering close to the hillside. They pass one of the holes about sixty meters from the hidden Centaurs. Then out of the blackness of one of the holes, four black figures lunge out on the two unsuspecting beasts. They then pounce on the two Neanderthals, who never knew what hit them. Four large black scorpions four meters in length have the two Neanderthals firmly in their grasp. The large insects have grabbed ahold of the beasts with a tremendous force of their meter-long fingers, and in their frenzy, they slice off the Neanderthals' heads and their legs below the knees. Then the four are fighting amongst each other for their piece of food, then tear their bodies into pieces so each of the insects have sections of the Neanderthals' body to feast on.

Even in the murky glow of the dimindark, the two Centaurs can see the silhouettes of the large insects tearing the Neanderthals apart, sending their blood shooting five meters into the air, at least, while pieces of the bodies are now clasped tightly into all four of the insects' mandibles. Once the carnage has subsided and satisfied with their scraps, the scorpions bite down on the severed pieces of the foul beasts' bodies as they retreat backward into their hole and into the gloom of their sanctuary.

The two Centaurs gasp for air in fear from what they have just witnessed. Lika turns to Ormarath and whispers in a frightened tone, "Scorpions, out in the open air. Lord of the Spirits . . . how can this be?"

"They have left the lair of what must be tunnels that lead directly out of the catacombs below the castle, for never before have they ever been seen out in the open air before this moment," Ormarath states.

"You are right, my friend. The end of days is truly upon us!" Lika retorts.

Then out of the darkness, high above the castle in the highest tower, a radiant glow begins to emanate from the window openings some ninety meters above the plains. The glow begins to appear to slowly increase in intensity until its magnitude appears incandescent; as if one is staring directly into the rays of a white dwarf star. The Centaurs and all within the castle's proximity have to look away and cover their large eyes to save from forever losing their sight. Then lightning begins to be ejected from all sides of the towers window openings, striking the ground in all directions around the castle and setting the ground where they have struck into a fiery blaze. Many lightning bolts strike within several tree clusters, sending many trees ablaze and dispatching their flames throughout the nearby forest, burning everything in its wake like an out of control wildfire

Then all at once the white glow, which was being emitted from the top of the tower, goes dark. A dark figure is now standing in its place. The figure itself is emitting a glow; a dark red glow almost like a silhouette on fire surrounding its body. Even from where the Centaurs are hiding, they can hear the crackle sending forth from its iridescence. Standing beside the figure on both its sides are Neanderthals. The beasts appear to be dwarfed by the black figure which appears to stand three meters taller than the Neanderthals and larger than the size of a normal male Tehran. At its flank is a Malakai dressed in full battle armor, its nail-laden club in hand. It appears to stand, ready to do battle. The Dark Entity appears to be almost Tehran in nature, but upon its head lies a glowing crown sitting tall which seems to be about thirty centimeters in height. A crown can only mean one thing, that this Dark Figure has proclaimed to be a king of some sort. The figure stretches out both of its arms, then raises them up to the sky, and as it does, flames ignite from the palms of its hands and shoot up beyond the cloud cover which seems to reach up to the heavens. The wind, which was blowing at a gale, has now receded then all goes dead silent, except for the sound of the fires surrounding the landscape. Crackling, the smoke it is emitting covers the surrounding landscape in a thick fog.

Ormarath turns to Lika and says, "What are we witnessing?"

Lika doesn't answer but continues to stare at the figure in black standing tall, looking down upon the beasts now beginning to congregate close to the castle itself. Lika then turns to his companion and says to him, "If I wasn't seeing this with my own eyes, I wouldn't believe it."

A hush comes over the landscape and the Dark Figure now begins to speak to the masses. "My disciples . . . are you ready to serve your king?"

Its voice reverberates throughout the landscape. The Malakai and Neanderthals, ten thousand strong, stands in unison at the foot of the castle, yelling and clanging their swords in unison in anticipation of a victorious campaign that they are about to embark on.

The Dark Figure continues.

"Soon darkness will cover all of the known world and all that live and breathe Pangean air will be our slaves to do with as we please." Again, a roar comes over the gathering.

"Muster your courage and ready yourselves for *war*, for we will strike when the leaders of the Tehran clans least expect it, for I, Abaddon, the Keeper of Keys, the Ambassador of Fire, I am the prince of the Underworld. I, who sits on the left side of evil, will lead you to victory where I will judge the fates of all things living. Then when I sit on my rightful throne as ruler of this world, I will rule over all beings who live and breathe Pangean air."

Again, a roar from the beasts gathered amplifies through the plains; only this time, the decibel of their roar is almost deafening.

Ormarath and Lika turn toward one another, then Ormarath says, "Abaddon the Destroyer . . . Then the legend is true, he lives . . . And he is now upon us."

Lika then adds, "And with an army the likes of which we have never seen."

Then Abaddon continues to speak to the masses. "Tonight, we begin my judgement . . . Bring out the prisoners," he commands.

Then the black gates of the castle slowly open . . . And as they continue to open wider Malakai begin to exit the interior of the castle grounds. The cyclops beasts are all dressed in battle armor; thus, they appear to be forming a circle as the march forward. Then in the middle of their circle exiting the Black Gates are what appears to be condemned Tehran soldiers. Their hands and legs are in bound in shackles. They are whipped by the giant cyclops as they exit the Black Gates. They are forced to move slowly out onto the plains for their movements are limited. It also appears their will to live has also been broken. As they move forward, the Malakai, who number around one hundred or so close, ranks on the condemned which squeezes the Tehrans closer together. There appear to be about thirty Tehran prisoners, at least.

The Malakai encircling them use whips which crack across their backs and necks to keep them moving forward. Ormarath notices the armor the Tehran soldiers are wearing, he says to Lika, "Look, Lika, look at the armor the soldiers are wearing, do you recognize it?"

Lika cups his large eyes, then turns to Ormarath and says, "The armor is that of the Northern Realm. They are King Galen's soldiers."

Slowly all the prisoners have exited the castle and are standing in front of the Black Gates. Then the Malakai, in their barbaric nature, instruct the condemned Tehrans to stand fast and turn and face their king. Then Abaddon, staring down on them from the balcony high above the assembled atop the highest tower, speaks to all assembled in a harrowing tone.

"Prisoners of the Black Prince, I will now judge you all for your crimes against your king." Abaddon pauses for a long moment, his gaze turns from side to side. He then raises his hand and points to the prisoners standing below him.

"For your crimes of treason, I sentence all of you to death. You shall all die on the cross and your blood will be spilled to nourish the Underworld."

Lika turns to his companion. "He's going to crucify all of them. Oh no."

The Malakai then lead the soldiers out into the middle of the plains where over thirty *saltire* or X-shaped crosses cut and carved out of the enormous redwood trees which are the most abundant hardwood in the forest. The crosses have all been laid on the ground side by side forming a single row for the many executions about to commence.

The Neanderthals, which number around sixty, then begin to remove the shackles from the Tehran prisoners one prisoner at a time, a tedious and long process. As each Tehran soldier is freed from their bondage, the Malakai then forcefully place each of them on top of the crosses which are laid on the frozen ground in front of each of them. One by one the prisoners' boots and armor are removed and placed in a large pile just behind the row of crosses. The Malakai forcibly hold their arms and legs of the prisoners squarely on each beam of the cross. The resistance of the Tehrans is futile, as the Malakai use their enormous strength to accomplish this feat. Then four Neanderthals, one on each of the prisoner's limbs, begin to drive nails fifteen centimeters long into their hands and feet. Blood gushes from the open wounds and the screams of agony echo through the frozen air which can be heard reverberating high into the mountain slopes. The Malakai and Neanderthals move slowly from prisoner to prisoner, nailing them each to the crosses one at a time; it seems like the screams of torture never seem to end. The snow-covered ground below the downed crosses is now saturated with the blood of the crucified whose radiance seem to glow black in the light of the many torches being held by the Neanderthals which brighten the plains more radiant than the twilight at its zenith high in the sky. The torture continues deep into the dimindark, as the process is slow and arduous. Then as the last prisoner is nailed to his cross, the Malakai look up to Abaddon, still standing and staring at them from the balcony and awaiting further instructions.

Abaddon then addresses the Malakai, "Place them in position."

The Malakai then stand up the crosses and move them into the holes dug to keep the crosses erect. The Black Prince then says to them in a boisterous tone, "Slice them all in their abdomen and let their blood flow to the ground below them!"

The Malakai again carry out the orders of their king. The blood of the crucified flow out of their bodies, making what appears to be a colossal lake of red surrounding the crucified. Then once the flowing blood begins to saturate through the snow and begins to be absorbed into the ground.

Then the frozen ground begins to shake all around them, like an earthquake beginning to separate the planet's crust. The beasts begin to run toward the castle as the other beasts standing at its entrance begin to flow inside the Black Gates. Lika and Ormarath keep their balance by hanging on to the nearby tree limbs, still hiding in the shadows as they continue their vigil, overseeing the carnage happening in front of them. The ground then begins to lift up into mounds all around the erect crosses, then the mounds continue to grow taller lifting up into a caldera, similar to a volcano growing larger from its expansion of magma being drawn into it which is intensifying and appears it is about to erupt. The mounds push up to about three meters tall in a blink of an eye. Then all at once the mounds erupt . . . Blood ants thirty centimeters in length which are a deep burgundy color.

The insects emerge from the mounds in a feeding frenzy attracted by the aroma of the spilled blood. These insects live below ground and wander through the planet's crust, foraging burrows like volcanic tubes hundreds of kilometers long where their queen gives birth the hundreds of thousands of them each millennium. The ants flow out of the calderas like lava flowing out of a volcano and spilling out over the ground. The ants swarm toward the crucified half-dead prisoners and swarm the area all around the crosses. The ants cover the crucified helpless bodies with their own. The condemned soldiers scream as pieces of their bodies are torn off and consumed by the large insects; killing them slowly, eating their bodies piece by piece.

The Malakai and Neanderthals scamper toward the Black Gate to avoid being consumed by the large insects.

Ormarath and Lika realize that now is their opportunity to return to the mountaintops and escape the carnage all around them, so they begin their ascent up the mountain, and as they do, the two hesitate for a moment for the screams of the soldiers have intensified and are now blood-curdling in despair. The two turn to witness the carnage that the ants have created. The blood ants attack, swarming each crucified body and continuing their feeding frenzy until all that is left of their victims are their skeletons dangling on the crosses. The soldiers' flesh and organs have been ingested by these large insects and they have done so in just mere moments, for there are thousands of them running all over the plains continuing their search for more food to ingest.

A handful of Neanderthals have been caught trying to make their way back to the Black Gates, but they are slow and move clumsily in the tall grasses and deepening snow. The blood ants catch up to them easily as their movements are swift and precise. They continue their carnage on the Neanderthals that they have now run down. The ants swarm the beasts; hundreds of the insects tear their flesh and organs into pieces and immediately consume them. When they have finished their consumption of fallen Neanderthals, they leave just their intact skeletons lying on the snow-covered ground in a large pool of their own blood, for everything of flesh has been consumed.

"I cannot watch anymore. I am getting sick to my stomach," Ormarath states.

So the two gallop swiftly up the mountain slope as fast as their legs can take them, but the forest is now swarming with Malakai and Neanderthals hiding in the intensive woodland of the tree clusters, trying to avoid being killed and eaten by the large foraging insects. As the centaurs race by them, they take many of them out with the precision of their skills as their arrows have all hit their target. Their pace has not slowed in their attack of them as they too are fearful for their own lives.

As the Centaurs approach the storm cloud, the wind intensifies and the visibility becomes almost nonexistent. They now must slow their pace back to a walk. The wind is blowing at a steady gale of around sixty-five knots, blowing the sleet and snow directly in their faces and blinding their ability to see more than two meters in front of them. The temperature seems to have dropped to about 263 Kelvins, hindering their ability to make accurate decisions as they feel frozen to the bone.

"Keep moving," Ormarath whispers to Lika.

Both have their bows filled with arrows as they tread carefully up the incline. It takes the two a long time to pass through the pounding storm, but as they exit the cloud cover, they gallop fiercely back in the direction of their awaiting squad.

The two Centaurs run at a full gallop until they are totally exhausted and both cannot run any longer.

Ormarath then holds up his arm and says to Lika as he gasps for air, "Slow it down. I need to catch my breath."

Lika nods his head in agreement. For a long moment as they continue at a walk there is an awkward silence between them; a denial at what they have both just witnessed. Then after a few moments, Lika breaks the silence. "What did we just witness, Ormarath?"

Ormarath gazes down toward the frozen snow-covered ground and in a somber tone answers, "The beginning of the end." He then continues, "War will be upon us soon. A war which no one has ever conceived would ever happen."

"We have been through this before," Lika responds.

"Not like this. We need to get back to Frostford as quickly as we can. Lord Khamael must be told immediately. He will know what to do," Ormarath answers.

Just before the dawn of twilight, Ormarath and Lika come upon their waiting squad.

"We were beginning to get worried," states one of the scouts.

"You both look like shit," another scout interjects.

Ormarath gives the scout a dirty look, then another scout asks, "What did you see?"

A long silence then follows until Ormarath says in a somber tone, "The beginning of the end."

The squad look toward one another, then Lika demands, "We need to get to Frostford. Now!"

The squad's reaction is one of shock as the returning warriors seem unhinged and uneasy in their behavior, so they dare not ask about their encounters. They look toward one another for answers, but not one of them speaks. They just prepare for the journey back to their village by gathering their wares.

"We need to leave now!" Ormarath orders.

Within moments, the squad departs their campsite and begin the half-day journey back to the Centaur Village of Frostford.

CHAPTER XIII

The Tale and Its Consequences

The Centaur squad returns to their village of Frostford. Their village is located alongside the peak of *Mt. Hialeah*, one of the tallest peaks of the mountain chain within the Dark Forest. The village is built into the cave complexes that are abundant on the mountain slopes. This is where the Centaurs have called home for more than two million seasons isolated from the rest of Pangea.

As the squad pauses at the entrance of Lord Khamael's cave, Ormarath directs his statements to the sentries posted at its entrance. "I must see Lord Khamael immediately," Ormarath insists to the sentries standing their post. The sentries gaze at the war-torn warriors, and one of the guards says to Ormarath, "Wait here. I will announce your presence."

The sentry then turns and enters the cave.

Ormarath then turns to his squad, "Go get cleaned up and rest. Lika and I will speak to the lord."

The rest of the squad then scurries off toward their dwellings to be reunited with their loved ones whom they have not seen for many a day and night. As the squad heads toward their individual caves, they are met by their fillies along with their colts, who jump and run to their fathers creating quite a stir within the village. The warriors seem content to be home with their families once again, at least for the time being.

Within a few moments the sentry returns and speaks to the two warriors. "Lord Khamael will see you. Follow me, commander."

The two enter Lord Khamael's cave. It is a tremendous cave with many offshoots, but like any Centaur dwelling, it is absent of much comfort for the Centaurs spend most of their lives on their hooves. The cave does have many writing tables where the lord has written down and added to the book of Centaur Laws. The lord has also recollected many of the adventures he and his warriors have endured over the millions of seasons long ago when he was recognized by the three kingdoms as one of the bravest soldiers who was then celebrated throughout the supercontinent for his valor during the Great War of the Second Age.

Then as the two Centaurs approach the lord, they bow their heads in respect for Lord Khamael, for he is millions of seasons in age. Though elderly even for a Centaur, his mind is that of a colt. His movements are assisted with a cane in each hand.

"My lord, we have seen the origins of the meteors and have witnessed the stirrings within the realm," Ormarath states.

The lord looks from one to the other and says to the warrior, "Go ahead tell me what you have seen."

Ormarath then tells his story to the lord. "We have seen Malakai and Neanderthals formed as one army standing side by side. We have witnessed the one who sits on the left side of Evil crucify innocent Tehrans and has said he is ready to declare war on the known world."

Lord Khamael then begins to slowly pace the room, then stops in front of the two warriors. "The war you speak of which will soon be upon us will be fought on the plains and the forests thousands of meters below us, for we are the forgotten warriors, and I predict this war will not affect our village. Therefore we will do what we have done for two million seasons, we will just go on with our lives in isolation like we always have."

"With all due respect, my lord, even though we are the forgotten species, we are still a part of this world and owe it to the other species we share with them our allegiance. For without an alliance of all living things in this world, the world will fall into shadow and perish right before our eyes," Ormarath answers the lord.

"It is not our problem," Lord Khamael answers him.

Lika then states to the Lord, "The end of the world is everyone's problem."

Before Lord Khamael can continue to speak, his thoughts are interrupted by harrowing screams coming from the village itself. Screams of horror echo within the lord's cave. Ormarath and Lika immediately turn and gallop toward the cave's exit. As they exit the cave, they notice the sentries posted to protect Lord Khamael are missing. They look up and they see standing in the middle of the village square a Malakai with a nail-laden club in hand; its protruding nails are impaled with arms, legs, and torsos, which are all pieces of Centaur body parts for that is what is left of four Centaur warriors the beast has slayed. Their tattered bodies lay in pieces covering the snow-covered ground in their blood and guts. They have died a warrior's death, attempting to protect their village from invaders. Fillies and colts gallop frantically away from the beasts. Alongside the Malakai with spears in hand are ten Neanderthals which are now running after the Centaur fillies and colts attempting to slay the vulnerable, for they are easier prey than the warriors themselves.

Then running out of their caves, the Centaur warriors gallop toward the intruders, most with bow and arrows cocked in their shooting position while some have their swords pointed toward their foes. Ormarath and Lika join the fray and charge the intruders. The Neanderthals then charge the oncoming Centaurs, then the foes begin to clash in battle.

Sword versus spear versus a nail-laden club.

Centaur against Neanderthal and Malakai . . . The swiftness of the Centaurs and the skills they have adapted with their weapons easily cut down the smaller and clumsy Neanderthals, whose appendages are separated from their bodies by the sword skill of the hoofed warriors.

The primitive beasts' body parts lie scattered throughout the town square. The Neanderthals, who have not been slayed and who are missing limbs, scream in agony and are left to die a slow death of pain and torture, as blood pours out of their hacked bodies, turning the snow-covered ground red from their open wounds. Then the Centaurs surround the giant Malakai, for he stands more than seven meters tall and is furiously swinging his massive nail-laden club, still with the body parts of the Centaurs he killed impaled into it at the circle of Centaurs surrounding him. At least forty warriors in total hail arrow after arrow at the massive beast. He has endured more than two hundred arrows penetrating his entire body, but he continues to attack the advancing Centaurs. The arrows do not penetrate past the outer layer of skin; the wounds are superficial to the massive cyclops, so he continues to swing his club at the hoofed warriors.

Ormarath, sword in hand, gallops up behind the Malakai, then scales the beast. He then leaps into the air, then plunges his sword into the top of the head of the Malakai. It penetrates the beast all the way to its handle, sending the blade of the club through the beast's head and down to its shoulders, splitting the Malakai's head in half, and killing the cyclops instantly. The beast falls forward on its face, dead. The Centaurs cheer in unison, for they have slayed all the intruders. But the Centaurs have paid a heavy price in the invasion, for they have lost ten warriors themselves, many of which were husbands and fathers and brothers in arms. The fillies and colts of the fallen weep and mourn the losses of their loved ones.

Ormarath walks toward Lord Khamael and then whispers in his ear, "I guess we are not the forgotten warriors, after all, for death has come on swift wings, my lord."

Lika, wounded, walks up to Ormarath and says to him, "They must have followed our hoof prints in the snow. We led them straight to us!"

"How could I not have realized that?" Ormarath says in a disgusted tone.

Lika puts his hand on Ormarath's shoulder and says, "It's not your fault. You did what you had to do. Don't blame yourself."

"Lika, I am in command. It's my fault," Ormarath retorts.

"We make decisions by following our gut instincts which are usually right, but sometimes things go wrong which we can't control. This is one of those times," Lika philosophizes.

Ormarath looks at his companion and says, "Thank you, my friend, for always being there for me."

"Brothers till the end," Lika adds.

"Brothers till the end," Ormarath responds.

Ormarath turns to *Juda*, his sergeant at arms, and orders him, "Take your squad and surround the village to keep a watchful eye if any other beasts are in pursuit. Sound the alarm if you spot anything moving toward us."

Juda salutes his commander, he then shouts, "Third company fall in and follow me!"

The squad under Juda's command quickly falls in line, then together they gallop out of the village to take up their positions around the settlement.

Ormarath then turns to one of his corporals and says to him, "Nigel, take these beasts, pile their bodies in a heap, and burn them, but drag them outside the village for they don't deserve any honor."

Nigel salutes Ormarath, then carries out his order.

"He is going to have to listen to reason," Lika states to Ormarath.

"I don't think the lord has the stomach for war anymore, but *we* swore an oath to protect our village and its inhabitants, and we will fulfill our oath with or without Lord Khamael's blessing," Ormarath answers.

Lika then says to his commander, "Well, first things first, we need to prepare our brothers for the Rising Ceremony. I will take care of it."

Ormarath nods his head in agreement and bows his head in thanks.

As the dimindark settles in over the realm, the village prepares for the Rising Ceremony of their honored dead. Wooden logs were tied together in pallets and placed in the village square where the ceremony will soon commence. The square is surrounded by many torches to illuminate the ritual. The logs are being soaked in oil to entice the flames to complete the ritual, then the fallen will be laid on the logs and set aflame as is in the Centaur tradition practiced for over three million seasons. The honored dead are dressed in their battle armor. Once their bodies are set aflame, their souls will ascend unto the Spirit World in all their virtuous glory, while their deeds will be enshrined in the writings of Centaur history.

Lord Khamael takes his place in front of the fallen heroes. he then addresses the masses, "Brothers and sisters, we stand here today to bless and to free the souls of our honored warriors as they have paid the ultimate price. They have laid down their lives so we may continue ours. Their deeds will never be forgotten, for they will always be remembered in our hearts. Their deeds are recorded in our history, so the memories of their deeds will never be forgotten, for when the memories of the fallen are forgotten, then they are truly dead."

Lord Khamael turns to the fallen, raises his hand, and continues, "I bless thee and commend your souls to eternal rest. May the Ancient of Days welcome you to the afterlife to be among your fathers and your fathers' fathers, and may you all dwell in their mighty company forever."

Then as Lord Khamael finishes his invocation, the loved ones of the fallen slowly approach the oil-soaked logs and place their torches against them. As they do, the logs become immersed with flames soaring ten meters high which ignites the corpses. Then as the fire spreads on the many wooden pallets, the deceased warriors become engulfed in their flames. The onlookers watch as the souls of the fallen, glistening in the luminescence of the twin moons, begin to rise from the lifeless bodies and ascend unto the Spirit World where eternal rest is waiting for them.

As the ten souls find their way home, they are remembered by the mourners as husbands, fathers, brothers, and friends who will never again, as flesh and blood, see the sunrise of a new day.

Once the ceremony is complete, Ormarath and Lika follow Lord Khamael back to his cave and walk behind him into the lord's library. Ormarath then addresses the lord, "My lord, we are now part of this war, for the forces of Evil have now attacked our village and have killed our brothers. Thus, you know as well as I the carnage will continue. We must prepare for what is to follow, for it will not stop here. It will spread throughout the world which we are all a part of."

Lika then chimes in, "My lord, we swore an oath to protect our species to the death, and to fight and destroy all that is evil."

Lord Khamael looks from one to the other and says to them, "My worst fear is now realized. Ormarath, you are right. We are a part of this world, and we must protect our species. I entrust in you the power to lead our warriors into battle and to protect our homeland, for you are now the general and the protector of Frostford. May all of your decisions always be the right ones."

Ormarath and Lika bow to the lord, then back away. They then turn and walk out of the lord's cave. Ormarath then says to Lika, "At the dawn of twilight, assemble the troops for it is time to prepare for the upcoming storm."

"What's the plan?" Lika asks.

Ormarath looks at his companion. "We will go forth to the Dark Tower and destroy everything in our path!"

Lika stops and stares at Ormarath. He shakes his head and says, "Attack them? Let me remind you, my friend, that they outnumber us a thousand to one."

Ormarath then says, "That is exactly the point. That is why this plan should work. They would never expect us to make that move, would you?"

Lika answers, "Not me . . . Then again, you might have a point."

"Either that or it will be the shortest invasion of all time," Ormarath answers.

CHAPTER XIV

The Daughters of Shayla

"When the Kingdoms align as one, Evil will be driven back from whence it came." – Elisheba, Queen of the Alicorns

Queen Lazuli has decided to send forth from the Castle of the Rising Sun the Daughters of Shayla on a quest to enter the dark realm before the Gathering of the Kingdoms commences. A gathering of this magnitude of all the recognized kingdoms has not taken place since before the Great War began over two million seasons ago. Back then, it was organized to unite the world to fight for the survival of their races against the Demon of Fire. Circumstances once again have arisen to call for a united army to face a more perilous foe. It will take place at the fortress of Ravens Rock on the southern edge of the Dark Forest. It will commence on the evening of the twin full moons at the height of the Season of Harvest. Strategically, the fortress of Ravens Rock is positioned close to the Dark Forest, located between to borders of the Northern and Western Realms on the Plains of Auria but situated far enough away from the Dark Tower so as to not arise the suspicion of their foes. Hopefully, Harlee Antonia will lead her secret squad the length of Snake River up past the fortress of Ravens Rock and into the Dark Forest. Well, that is the plan anyway.

The covert squad of twelve will leave before the dawn of twilight begins its ascent over the realm, for under the cover of darkness is where the assassins thrive. The warriors now prepare their steeds and themselves for the perilous journey to the most northern end of the supercontinent where the climate will change from tropical to arctic. Time is of the essence so they must be as swift as their steeds are, who are the fastest and most rugged breed known in the Tehran world.

The breed of Lambos is considered a divine breed, as legend would have it, created by the Ancient of Days himself who conceived them to be the messengers for the Watchers to carry their tales between one another. They are bred by only one—the allusive dwarf, *Artemis of Mandrake*. He is a hermit who dwells in a hidden valley within the Corona Mountains where it is said he breeds the only surviving few of this midnight black breed. Their color is so deep that they can blend in into the dimindark without being seen. It is said that they have not been seen in the wild since the continents were separated, then only in legend. The Lambos are bred only for the Daughters of Shayla as per Queen Lazuli's decree in which Artemis has done in the service of the queen for many a millennium, as he is a free dwarf. He was awarded his freedom by the queen because of the bond he developed between himself and this endangered species.

"Ivy, is the squad ready to go? The dawn of twilight will soon be upon us," asks Harlee.

"We are ready when you are," Ivy retorts.

A stable hand swings open the barn doors where the Lambos are kept. Then the twelve gallop their steeds furiously out into the bleakness of the dimindark past the citadel, then head north on the *Going to the Sea Road*. Their entire journey will be a perilous one which will take them through the wilds of the supercontinent. Once the squad passes to the west of the town of Ronin, there will be no cities, towns or settlements, nor will there be any trails or paths to follow. The only encounters the squad will come across will be the untamed beasts that roam free throughout the land.

As the dawn of twilight rises over the Southern Realm, the Daughters of Shayla reach the outlay of the Westin Peninsula where the supercontinent then widens its expanse. The topography in this tropical zone is mostly flat, resembling a savannah, though it is abundant with fruit-bearing palm and citrus trees, along with flowering bushes attracting many species of birds, reptiles, small mammals, and, of course, the predators who prey on them. It's a vicious cycle of eat or be eaten.

As the dwarf sun climbs higher in the sky, the heavens are filled with flocks of parrots and birds of prey of many species, both large and small, filling the sky above and flying toward their food sources whose aromas fill the air with a sweet crisp scent. On the horizon, as the squad continues at a steady gallop, they gaze at herds of *white albino deer* foraging on the tall grasses, unaware of a pack of raptor dinosaurs are stalking the heedless deer as they patiently await their opportunity to pounce on their prey.

After almost half a day in the saddle, the twelve warriors stop to take a needed rest at the crossroads where the Going to the Sea Road intersects with the *Sea of Palms Way*. The latter is named for the abundance of palm trees that are amassed in thick groves entrenched all throughout the coast. The different species of trees produce many varieties of fruits which are the staple of life for the wild creatures who call this tropical zone home. The Sea of Palms Way continues east for about 400 kilometers, gradually becoming hilly. Then as the trail gets closer to the mountain chain, the trail steepens while its incline becomes arduous as it gradually levels off between the mountain peaks of the Corona Mountain Chain.

In all the trail, winds upward of 1000 meters and ceases at the town of Mandrake which houses the Dwarfs who work the most infamous of mines located deep in the bowels of said mountains. East of Mandrake, there are no marked trails, no towns, but scattered villages, consisting mostly of exiled dwarfs and Tehran marauders. It is just wild lands where the barbaric nomads and giant creatures of all kinds rule with no laws or morals, for they live each day by instinct, intuition and luck; such is life on the supercontinent of Pangea.

"Ivy, have the squad cool the horses down and let them rest in the shade of the trees" Harlee commands.

Ivy then places small pieces of wood in a pile. She lights it with her flints, which ignite a fire, then places a tea pot over the burning wood to boil water for tea. The warriors then reach into their packs which are filled abundantly with bison jerky, which is their food of choice whilst eating on the run, as it does not require any means of cooking.

"Harlee, you have been so quiet this whole journey. What's bothering you?" asks Ivy.

Harlee walks away from the rest of the squad. Ivy follows her. The general then sits on a large rock, she then takes out a cigar, she lights it with wooden matches and closes her eyes as she exhales the smoke into the air.

"Feel better?" Ivy asks

Harlee just shakes her head from side to side.

"We are the only hope for the kingdoms, for no others possess our skills. If we fail, so does the world. We have a long journey ahead of us filled with obstacles and perils, and when we reach the journey's end . . . That's where it all begins," Harlee surmises.

"That's why we are who we are because we are the best. Harlee you are my general and my best friend. You are way too uptight. A word of advice," Ivy states.

"You are going to give *me* advice?" Harlee retorts.

"Sister, when this is all over and done with . . . you really need to get laid!" Ivy states

Both women laugh out loud and shake their heads in agreement. Harlee then says to Ivy, "Truer words were never spoken!"

The two then make their way back to the squad who are now sitting in the shade in the middle of a grove of palm trees.

Josie then says to the two, "What's so funny?"

Harlee and Ivy look toward one another, then Harlee answers Josie's question, "Ivy thinks I need to get laid."

The female squad all burst out laughing, and Josie then says, "Hey, we all need to get laid. . . . . . big time!"

Then all twelve raise their cups of tea into the air, and Josie declares a toast, "To getting laid!"

"To getting laid!" all the squad repeats, then they all laugh together.

"Ladies, I needed that!" retorts Harlee.

As the squad sits around the fire, sipping their tea, and eating their bison jerky, General Harlee Antonia addresses her squad, "Listen up, everyone." Harlee takes a map out of her pack and places it in the middle of the circle in which her squad has surrounded her. Pointing to the map, Harlee continues, "We will follow this road past the town of *Barre* which will eventually leads to Ronin. Just west of Ronin before we come upon the town, we will come across Snake River. We will then follow the river north until it intersects with the *Holgren River.* Once we arrive there, then we will have to make some big decisions. I feel in the meantime we will need to stay on the west side of the river to avoid entering Wildwood. For if we enter that realm, the dangers we face increase drastically as that realm is truly untamed and mostly unexplored, except if you're a Warrow."

The squad looks around at one another at the mention of the tiny warriors.

"Warrows! I completely forgot about them. You don't think we will come across them, do you, general?" asks Ivy

"If we avoid Wildwood, we should avoid the Warrows,", Harlee answers. She then continues, "We will need to travel swiftly but cautiously."

"Yes, cautiously. There have been rumors that packs of Wolfen have been spotted roaming the woods near Ronin," Ivy adds.

"Wolfen . . . truly?" outbursts *Sergeant Antoinette Bourgeois.*

Harlee then turns to two of her squad. "Josie, Wilma, when we reach the river, I want you two to ride point to keep a watchful eye on the surrounding landscape, just in case."

"Good idea," answers Ivy.

"All right, let's get a move on. We will need to travel as far as we can while in the twilight. it is now midday. We will need to make camp and be settled in before the twilight sets and the dimindark rises upon the realm, for it is not safe to travel in these parts in the dimindark, especially now," Harlee concludes.

As the Daughters of Shayla continue their northward trek on the Going to the Sea Road, their journey takes them just east of the isolated town of Barre, which is sparsely populated with maybe a hundred inhabitants, including about twenty Dwarfs. These Dwarfs live side by side with their Tehran masters and are slaves of the queen. As slaves, they assist the Tehrans in their royal duties or what other commands they are given, for they are compelled to obey or face the consequences of their disobedience. These townsfolk, as well as their dwarf slaves, for generation upon generation have made the armor and the weapons for the queen's army which have been used in battle by the soldiers of past wars, thus they are still being forged in this day and age in the same manner as ages ago in preparation for future engagements. These Tehrans are master swordsmiths and blacksmiths. Therefore, the queen, as a reward to her loyal subjects, has established a small outpost at the edge of town. As a result, twenty-five soldiers live among the townspeople and serve as their personal guards in case of an invasion from the many nomadic tribes who roam the wilds of the supercontinent. The presence of these nomads, though elusive, is prevalent throughout all the realms, for they are known for their barbarism and cruelty which is legendary and feared throughout Pangea.

Once past the town of Barre, the squad have their Lambo steeds running mightily. The horses, while small in stature, have the most endurance of any horses known to Tehrans. Then as the squad approaches Snake River near the town of Ronin, the dwarf sun begins its retreat over the horizon.

"We need to make camp now." Harlee commands her squad, "Set up camp near the banks of the river."

Ivy then appoints two warriors to guard the camp and they will be rotated throughout the night so all can get the rest needed to continue on their journey.

"The river is raging. The water is high. Look at the bridge that crosses it, it is almost up to the deck," Ivy points out to Harlee.

"And it is quite loud. The guards must be on high alert as they may not hear anything approaching the camp," Harlee answers.

"There must have been a lot of rain and snow in the mountain peaks upriver during the Summer Season which melted and is now finding its way downriver," Ivy surmises to Harlee.

{Snake River is a fast-flowing estuary with many rapids along its course. It is a tributary of the Holgren River and flows south furiously throughout the entire length of the supercontinent. At its widest point, it is more than five kilometers across. Then again at the location that the Daughters of Shayla are at, it is about ten meters wide. It's delta then empties into the Southern Ocean just east of the Palace of the Rising Sun at the beginning of the Westin Peninsula. It is a treacherous river with many varieties of fish and sea creatures of all sizes and temperaments that are found throughout its entire length.}

As the dimindark begins to cover the realm, the twin moons begin to rise over the horizon. They begin their ascent as the new moon is barely visible in the heavens and projecting very little illumination over the landscape.

As Harlee gazes at the moons rising over the eastern edge of the Southern Realm, she turns to Ivy and mutters to her out loud, "We don't have much time. The Gathering of the Kingdoms at Ravens Rock is on the evening of the first day of the twin full moons. We need to keep pushing ahead, for the kingdoms will need our intelligence report on how to take on Abaddon before they advance onto war."

"Heading into the Dark Forest, we can only hope we survive the mission to give that report at the gathering," Ivy answers.

Ivy turns to Jilly. "Jilly, start the evening meal. We are all starving."

"Yes, captain. Grilled tyrannosaurus ribs and boiled potatoes, how does that sound?"

"Like a feast," Harlee answers.

"I'll get the water to boil the potatoes from the river," Jilly says.

Jilly then grabs a pot out of her pack and walks the five or so meters to the river's edge. As she bends down to scoop the water into the pot, she looks up to the opposite side of the river. It is like she is staring into a black empty void. Suddenly, the forest becomes silent. The hair on her neck begins to stand up. She gets a feeling like she is being watched. She continues to stare across the river. She then notices pairs of large orange eyes staring back at her; at least six pairs of eyes in all.

"What the—" Jilly says out loud. Then before she can react, a large black figure leaps from the riverbank from the opposite side of the river. Jilly watches as it leaps toward her, but she is frozen in place and not able to react in time. The figure pounces on her, then knocks her to the ground. Jilly lets out a life-threatening scream which pierces through the dimindark. The horrifying scream can be heard for many kilometers beyond the campsite on both sides of the river. The beast grabs her by the neck and clamps down, purging her carotid artery and sending a gush of blood spraying five meters into the air, killing Jilly instantly. Then from the darkness a shout can be heard above the frenzy of the carnage.

Wolfen

As the Wolfen stands atop the lifeless body of Jilly, it lets out a ferocious howl which calls out to the other canines of its pack, thus it ignites them to follow in their leader's footsteps. Five more Wolfen leap across the riverbank and land alongside their pack leader, guarding him and their prey. The Daughters of Shayla are quick to react. Immediately, a barrage of arrows flies in the Wolfens' direction; multiple arrows strike two of the large beasts, killing them dead in their tracks. The leader then grabs Jilly's lifeless body in its mouth, turns, and with the other three surviving companions, leaps over the river and lands on to the opposite bank. The female warriors run to the river's edge and continue their barrage of arrows on the large carnivores. The Wolfen turn and begin to run away from the river into the dense thickets of Wildwood. Harlee and her squad watch with frustration as the Wolfen begin their retreat into the black void of the untamed forest.

Then out of the darkness from the treetops arrows hurl through the air in the Wolfens' direction, striking all four of the surviving beasts as multiple arrows pierce their bodies. The Wolfen scream in agonizing pain as the arrows continue to rain down on them, piercing all four from head to toe. Two of the remaining four, including the leader, fall dead. The leader then releases the body of Jilly from its jaws, while the other two who are badly hurt limp off in the darkness of Wildwood.

The Daughters of Shayla immediately take cover behind the large trees and boulders which line the river as they anticipate that they are next to be attacked, for they know not who rained their arrows on the black beasts. Then a small figure steps out behind a large pine tree and walks up to the lifeless body of Jilly. It kneels, then grabs her hand to feel for a pulse. It then shakes his head, indicating that there is none. The squad then realizes that they are looking at the Warrow warrior. A golden-haired Warrow of the Southern Wildwood.

The Warrow then stands and walks up to the water's edge and calls across the river to the Daughters of Shayla. He then says to the female squad, "I'm sorry. She's dead."

The Tehrans can't believe their eyes. It is a golden-haired Warrow; a warrior of the Southern Wildwood who hail from the Warrow city of Southold.

Harlee steps out from behind a large boulder, then she slowly makes her way to the water's edge directly opposite to where the Warrow is standing. Two commanders stare at one another, separated by the flow of the river. Then Harlee begins to speak to the Warrow. "Thank you for intervening. At least she will have a proper burial instead of being a Wolfen meal."

"I wish we could have done more, but only by her screams were we alerted of your presence, and then the attack on her . . . My warriors and I will bring her body across the bridge to you," answers the Warrow.

"Much appreciated, Master Warrow," Harlee answers him.

Then the rest of the squad of Warrows reveal themselves as they begin their descent down from the cluster of trees which appears like a never-ending wall, for one cannot peer more than five meters into the bleakness of Wildwood.

The squad of Warrows gently picks up Jilly's body, then, respectfully, they carry her across the bridge which is the only safe passage over Snake River for many kilometers. The Warrows then place her gently on the ground at the edge of the campsite. Ten Warrows in total are now standing at the Daughters of Shayla's campsite. The female warriors rush to Jilly's lifeless body and caress their companion as a sister and a friend who lost her life for the cause of saving the world.

Josie, kneeling by Jilly's side, weeping, gazes at the Warrow leader and thanks him for his and his squad's courage. Harlee walks up to the leader and bows to him in respect.

"I am Harlee Antonia, commander of the Daughters of Shayla. I wish you welcome to our campsite, and many thanks for your actions against the Wolfen, and recovering the body of one of our fallen."

"Harlee Antonia . . . Your reputation precedes you. I am *Lucic*, a commander in the Warrow ranks."

Lucic then bows back to Harlee out of mutual respect for a fellow warrior.

"Jilly was planning on making the evening meal," Harlee begins to say to Lucic, then Lucic interrupts her, "If you don't mind, my squad will cook the evening meal. It will give us both an opportunity to break bread together, then to discuss what the Daughters of Shayla are doing camping at Wildwood's edge."

"Fair enough," Harlee answers Lucic.

The Warrows butcher the fallen Wolfen and place the cut steaks on the grill set up by Jilly. The Daughters of Shayla have placed a pile of logs on the edge of the campsite. The logs are then tied together by rope made of hemp. Once the platform is completed, they then place Jilly's body on top of the logs. The Tehrans will perform their own version of the Rising Ceremony which will commence after the evening meal. Once the steaks are cooked, the Tehrans, along with the Warrows, sit amongst one another around the fires, eating Wolfen steaks and potatoes while discussing the current state of the goings-on around the supercontinent.

"Harlee Antonia, you are traveling at a time when the world appears to be upside down. Wolfen in - Wildwood . . . raptors in packs with such large numbers never before seen in the forest . . . Queen Lazuli must have much trust in you to send you into this untamed world in uncertain times," Lucic states.

"Master Warrow, as you know, the Gathering of the Kingdoms will be held at Ravens Rock on the first night of the twin full moons," Harlee states.

"I am aware of that. My king will be in attendance," Lucic answers.

"My squad and I are on a quest to enter the Dark Forest and to gather intel for the inevitable war which will soon be upon us all," Harlee then states.

Lucic then stands and approaches the Lambos eating grass on the campsite's edge. He pets one of them and says to Harlee, "The legend is true then . . . Lambos, are they not?"

"Yes, Master Warrow, they are."

"Magnificent horses. I have never seen anything like them in all of Pangea," Lucic states.

"And you won't again," Harlee answers him.

Lucic then walks back to Harlee. "My lady, your quest is a noble one. One worthy of the cause, but it is one of suicide, for the dark lord will surely see you coming. Let's face it, you are the most feared assassins throughout the continent. You are part of the darkness, but Abaddon is the one who sits on the left side of Evil, and you are now eleven, much too large in number to zip in and out of the dark realm without being seen, especially by his minions who I am sure are heavily patrolling all parts of the realm," Lucic concludes.

"Then what do you suggest, Lucic of Southold?" Harlee asks.

"Take five of us along with you, for *we* can zip in and out of the Dark Forest like the wind without being seen, we are small and wiry, and the greatest swordsmen and archers the Warrows have ever produced. As we are now allies in this upcoming war, we must fight together. And if it must . . . Die together. As we are now one people, one army, with one common goal—survival," Lucic states.

"Master Warrow, you bring comfort to us all, as we will gladly join forces with you and your warriors, for the world, at this moment in history needs allies, not foes," Harlee responds.

Once the evening meal is concluded, Harlee begins the Rising Ceremony. The Daughters of Shayla stand alongside the Warrows who have gathered in a circle surrounding Jilly's lifeless body. All in attendance hold a lighted torch in their hand to ignite her body and release her soul to rest alongside the Ancient of Days and to join him in the Spirit World.

Then Harlee begins an invocation. "Sisters and honored guests, tonight we release the soul of our fallen comrade who gave her life in the midst of war. With these torches, we will set ablaze her body. It will allow her soul to be freed to dwell alongside the Ancient of Days in the Realm of the Spirit World. Her memories will always live within us in our hearts and in our minds . . . Rest in peace, my dear sister, for one day soon we will all be together again, for all eternity."

"Amen" is said by all.

Then all who have taken part in the ceremony place their torches on the logs in which Jilly's body is resting on. As the wooden logs begin to ignite, the flames slowly spread onto Jilly's lifeless body. Then as her body is engulfed by the flames, her soul is released; its white iridescence illuminates, blinding to one's eyes as all must look away as it quickly soars up to the heavens to eternal rest. Then as her soul climbs higher and higher, it begins to ascend into the Spirit World. Jilly's soul begins to disappear into the heavens. The onlookers at the ceremony are overcome with emotions as they will never have the privilege of sharing another moment with their friend as she now has been given eternal rest.

"She is now at peace," Ivy states to Harlee.

Harlee, with tears in her eyes, says, "The only winners are the dead. Their sufferings done. Ours lies ahead."

As the flames of the cremation light up the night sky and the surrounding landscape, the mood of the mourners is somber and bleak. With heavy hearts, Harlee realizes they must move forward, for in war there will be many casualties; that is the nature of it. Harlee looks around at the new alliance they have formed between themselves, the Daughters of Shayla, and the Warrow warriors and realizes that the survival of this world might depend on the actions of the few. Not a word is spoken between all, and both squads begin to take their rest after such a day. After a while, the flames begin to dissipate and once again darkness covers the realm.

A restless sleep overtakes the warriors as they dream of a life of peace and quiet and wonder to themselves, *Is there such a place that exists in this untamed world or is it just a dream?*

Chapter XV

The Hunt for Answers

While the dimindark is still hovering over the Realm, *Issa*, the Warrow sergeant at arms, takes command of the squad as ordered by her captain, Lucic. They depart quietly in the middle of the dimindark, as most of the warriors, except those on guard duty, are still in a deep restless slumber. Lucic has ordered all but four of his best warriors to return to the Warrow city of Southold to inform the king of their *new alliance* with the Tehrans and what their quest has now become. Lucic has given Issa a letter to give to the king explaining the latter, and to also inform him that he will meet up with him at the Gathering of the Kingdoms at the fortress of Ravens Rock at the appointed date and time.

As the dawn of twilight gives birth to a new day, the newly formed alliance begins to prepare for the long journey ahead. Together, their trek will eventually lead them into the dark lands, thus all of the warriors realize that there will be many perils along the way. No one has enjoyed a peaceful night's sleep, as the death of Jilly weighted heavily on their minds and in their souls, along with the added anxiety of what is yet to come. The mood of all is still somber; with the Gathering of the Kingdoms getting closer every day, time is of the essence to obtain answers on the movements of their enemy so their combined army can stand a chance to survive the outcome.

Harlee turns to Lucic. "Lucic, climb aboard *Hanna* and sit behind me, have your warriors do the same with my squad, then we will ride like the wind."

Eleven Tehrans and five Warrows start their quest on a hunt to find the answers to their questions which could lead the way on a crusade to save this world.

The endurance of the Lambo ponies is extraordinary, as they appear to never reach a point of fatigue. Though they are considered small in stature compared to the other species of horses found throughout the continent such as the draft horses used by the Tehran armies which are double their size, the Lambos can endure more weight and travel farther distances at twice the speed as their larger cousins. The alliance begins their travels heading northward parallel to Snake River. As Josie keeps pace ahead of the moving alliance, she serves as the front line of the small moving army; should she encounter trouble, the rest of the alliance will be forewarned. The boundary of Wildwood which adjoins them is just on the other side of the river and is so dense one cannot see deep into the forest, as the foliage seems almost impenetrable with many varieties of tall trees covered with brambles sharp enough to cut deeply into one's body. The plains on which the alliance is riding parallel to appear to be hilly with tall grasses with some cluster of tall pine and oak trees. The sound of the horses' hooves pounding the ground as they gallop at their apex echo through the landscape, sending a trail of dust in their wake which can be seen from great distances that could alert many a nomadic tribe or any of the large predators who lurk in the shadows.

At about midmorning, Harlee realizes that the horses need a break, for they have been running hard since the dawn of twilight. She then turns to Ivy. "Ivy, ride ahead and tell Josie to join us as the horses need a break."

Ivy nods her head. "I think we all need a break," she answers.

Harlee then orders the squad to feed the horses for the second time today, for they have expelled much energy in such a short period of time.

"My lady, the river has a large bend in it which, if we follow its course, we will be taking the long way. I suggest we ride straight north to save time and energy," Lucic states.

"Master Warrow, you are our guide as this is your territory. We are outsiders and will heed to your directions," Harlee answers him, showing much respect to their new ally.

Ivy, riding hard now, has Josie in her sights. She calls out to her in a loud voice which catches Josie's attention. Josie turns and begins to ride toward Ivy. As they meet up in the middle of a large clearing surrounded by tall trees, Ivy and Josie greet each other and both dismount their steeds.

"We have stopped to feed and water the horses," Ivy declares.

"Good, I'm starving, too," Josie states.

Then all at once the horses appear to become agitated; they begin to whinny and seem clearly upset at something.

"Easy boy," Ivy says to *Ringo*, her Lambo steed, as she grabs ahold of his reigns to try to calm and settle him down; Josie does the same with her steed.

"Something's not right," Josie says with a tone in her voice expressing deep concern, as she keeps glancing from side to side. Both warriors grab their bows, then reach into their quivers to fill them with arrows. They then stand back-to-back, covering all angles in a defensive posture anticipating an attack.

"I don't see anything," Josie states.

"Sshhhh, just listen for movement," Ivy whispers.

The two stand back-to-back for moments on end listening, their heads spinning like a top trying to figure out exactly where the movement is coming from. They can hear the crackling of dried leaves on the forest floor being trampled by feet or by hooves, for they cannot differentiate between the sounds. But the sounds appear to be all around, surrounding the two, hidden just inside the tree line.

"Don't shoot until you see something," Ivy commands.

Then rocks begin to be hurled at the two warriors from all angles; rocks of all sizes, from the size of a Tehran's hand to larger sized boulders coming from the surrounding tree line. The two are sitting ducks being caught out in the open. The horses are now clearly spooked, for they have also been pounded by the rocks. The Lambos have begun to bolt toward the surrounding forest as fast as they can gallop and soon disappear into the tree line. The two warriors are now on their own with nowhere to hide, no horses for protection, and no way to escape an imminent attack.

Then a rock hits Josie on the side of her head. She falls to the ground, knocked unconscious. Ivy stands fast alongside her companion, hurling arrows aimlessly into the tree line, though even with her large eyes she cannot see who is attacking them. Then Ivy gets hit with a large rock in the small of her back. She falls to the ground, writhing in pain with the large rock now lying on top of her. As Ivy falls to the ground, she lets go of her bow, for she is now defenseless and semiconscious.

As Ivy lays on the ground clutching her back, trying to relieve the wrenching pain she is feeling, she gazes over at Josie. Her vision is blurry from the impact her body felt on contact with the hard ground. Ivy can just make out her outline. She then calls to her, but Josie is unconscious and doesn't respond to her pleas. Josie's head is bleeding profusely from where the rock had struck her. Ivy looks up and gazes all around her. Though her vision is now clouded, she can see many figures coming out of the tree line . . . Bipedal figures walking toward her and Josie.

As Ivy struggles to focus on the attackers walking toward the two, she attempts to reach for her bow even though she is unable to move with the weight of the rock on top of her. Ivy's bow lies on the ground just outside her grasp. She screams in pain as she tries to crawl toward it, but the weight of the large rock and the pain she is suffering from is too intense. She continues to attempt to retrieve her bow, but it now appears to be futile. She then gives up. She lets out a sigh, then closes her large eyes. Her head slumps to the ground. Ivy then falls unconscious.

When Ivy awakens, she feels the constant pain in which she attributes to the impact of the large rock which struck her in her back. She is bound with hemp rope which encompasses her entire body, curled around her like a serpent constricting her in preparation for her to be its next meal. She gazes next to her and sees Josie also bound in the same fashion, but it appears that Josie is still unconscious. She gazes all around her and realizes she is in a dense forest, for they were moved from the clearing from where the two were attacked. But by who? The scarlet hue of the dwarf sun appears to be heading toward the horizon, so she feels that she and Josie has been unconscious for a period of time. Ivy catches the scent of a fire which seems to be close, for the dark smoke it's emitting is billowing overhead. She is bound tightly and unable to move.

She calls out to Josie in a loud whisper, "Josie . . . Josie!"

But Josie is nonreactive and still unconscious.

Ivy then manages to roll like a wagon wheel the two meters that her and Josie are separated by. Ivy looks around. They are alone, but where and who are the assailants who attacked them?

Ivy, now laying alongside Josie, whispers in her ear, "Josie . . . Wake up . . . Wake up, Josie."

Ivy then nudges Josie with her body, and as she does, she again calls out to her in a whisper, "Josie . . . Wake up!"

Finally, Josie responds. "Ivy . . . Where are we? What happened?" Josie says in a whisper, barely able to talk.

"I don't know. . . We were attacked, but by whom? No one has shown themselves yet," Ivy answers.

"My throat is so dry, and my head is killing me," Josie responds in a whisper.

"Don't talk. Save your strength," Ivy answers.

Then all at once the two can hear the sound of leaves crunching and footsteps advancing toward them, getting louder with each step. The two can feel the ground vibrate with every step taken.

"What is it?" Josie asks.

Then Ivy looks up. Now standing above the two warriors is a Malakai The beast is staring down at them with authority. The Malakai is enormous in stature; its large cycloptic eye is almost black in color with no sclera. Its blackness encompasses its entire feature. As it stares down at the two, its drool is expectorating all over the bound warriors, covering their bodies in its salivation. Ivy and Josie squirm, trying to avoid the slime seeping out of the beast's mouth. Then the Malakai lifts its nail-laden club high into the air, showing his dissatisfaction in their behavior. The two then freeze. Both warriors then lay perfectly still, for the beast can crush them both with its enormous foot or be maimed by its nail-laden club, which can split their bodies in half with one blow.

The Malakai then stands there for a moment, staring at the two incapacitated captives. His breath can be felt by the two seven meters below its cavity. Both Ivy and Josie turn their heads in disgust, for the odor its breath is emitting is enough to make one heave. They then hear additional rustling of the leaves on the forest floor in the distance. Ivy turns her head toward the sounds. Walking toward them are five more Malakai. The two warriors now begin to fear the worst. The five beasts walk up to the two surrounding them in a circle. The two warriors begin to shake in fear that their lives will soon cease to exist. The Malakais then begin to use some sort of a sign language since they are mute, but the symbols one of the beasts is executing appear to be understood by the other five.

Ivy assumes that one is the leader of this tribe. Ivy thinks to herself, *They have their own language. I don't think anyone has ever realized that or have seen anything like that before.*

Then after the six Malakai have completed communicating with one another, they turn and walk of in different directions.

Then after a few moments, once again, Ivy and Josie are alone in the middle of the forest.

"Josie . . . Josie did you see that?" Ivy whispers.

"See what?" she answers.

Josie appears to be unable to focus her eyes.

Ivy then realizes that her injuries are far worse than she originally thought. They have to get outta there. *But how?* Ivy contemplates to herself.

The dwarf sun is fading lower in the sky. The twilight, which is dusky in appearance at its zenith, is now emanating a burgundy hue as it begins to fade over the horizon. Soon the dimindark will set upon the land, thus the two, if they can escape, will not be able to tell which direction will lead them to their companions.

"I can't break these bonds," Ivy whispers to herself.

As the dimindark begins to rise, Ivy can now see the outline of the fire the Malakai have made. She then realizes that all six of the Malakai are standing around it. She can see the outline of their shadows from the glow of the fire. "I have a bad feeling about this," Ivy whispers to herself.

"A bad feeling about what?" Josie asks.

Ivy looks toward Josie. "I have a feeling that fire is for us," Ivy answers.

"What?" Josie says in a confused tone.

"They made the fire to cook us over it. We are to be their evening meal," Ivy answers.

"Ivy, we need to get out of here, but I don't think I can walk," Josie states.

Ivy then begins to try to undo the ropes that is binding her, but she cannot loosen them at all.

"Damn, I can't budge them at all. The more I struggle the tighter they appear to get," Ivy says, huffing and puffing.

Then from behind her, a hand covers her mouth.

"Shhhhhh," says a voice.

Ivy turns her head, her large eyes open wide. "Lucic . . . Harlee . . . How did you find us?"

"Sshhhh . . . I'll explain later. Right now we need to get both of you out of here," Harlee whispers.

"These ropes are really thick. It's gonna take a few to cut them off," says Lucic.

"Harlee, Josie is hurt badly. I don't think she can walk," Ivy states in a whisper.

Then silently creeping up behind Harlee are the Daughters of Shayla. "Don't worry, Ivy, we are all here," a voice says.

"Where are the Warrows?" Ivy asks.

"They are ready to give the Malakai a surprise . . . on our cue," Harlee says.

"Okay, they are both free. Let's get the fuck out of here before we all become the Malakai's evening meal," Lucic whispers.

Quietly whispers Harlee..

The Daughters of Shayla carry Josie deeper into the forest in the opposite direction of the Malakai and place her on Frida, her Lambo pony.

"Frida," Josie says.

Ivy then turns to Harlee. "Ringo? But how?"

"When Ringo and Frida galloped into camp without you and Josie, we knew that something had gone awry. They then led us straight to you, and here you are," Harlee answers.

"What are you thinking, Ivy? You have that expression on your face."

"I think I really need to get laid after this," Ivy answers.

"Don't make me laugh, smartass," Harlee retorts.

"Well, if you want to get laid . . . Honey, you need a bath 'cause you stink!" *Shirley* states.

"Malakai drool," Ivy says.

"Ew, that's gross," Harlee and Shirley say simultaneously.

Harlee then makes a cooing noise to alert the Warrows that they have the two and that they are safe. Then the remaining warriors mount their steeds.

"What do we do now?" Ivy asks Harlee.

"We wait," Harlee answers.

"For what?" Ivy asks.

Then from out of the darkness, lingering in the shadows and out of the light cast from the fire, a barrage of arrows is hurled toward the six Malakai. The four Warrows aim for the cycloptic eye of the huge beasts to blind them, then to finish them off with their golden swords if need be. Arrow after arrow flies true, blinding the beasts. With the velocity they have undertaken, most of the arrows penetrate the beasts' brain cavity, killing four of them on contact.

Though now blinded by the arrows that have penetrated their eye cavities, two Malakai have managed to survive the attack. Though now blinded by the arrows stuck in their eyes, the beasts swing their nail-laden clubs aimlessly in circles. Though they cannot see their assailants, they will not go down without a fight. The Malakai stagger from side to side, swinging their clubs, hoping to make contact with their foes. One of the Malakai falls to the ground, writhing in pain, which gives two of the Warrows an opportunity to finish the beast. Within an instant, they are upon it; one Warrow drives his swords deep into its head, while the other Warrow thrusts his sword deep into the beast's chest cavity. The beast then gasps his last breath, then its body goes limp. It now lies there dead from the final blows.

The last remaining Malakai struggle to stay on its feet. It collapses to its knees, trying to remove the arrow which penetrated its large eye. Then as the Malakai pulls the arrow out, its eye stays attached to the point of the arrow as well as some of its brain. The beast then falls forward, collapses, then falls over dead.

The four Warrows stand there stunned at the sight of Malakai roaming free in Wildwood.

"What are Malakai doing this far south?" *Shanti*, one of the Warrow warriors, ask.

"Good question. I have never heard of them traveling this far south, for they are known to stay above the Plains of Auria, usually staying with the boundaries of the Dark Forest," *Mali*, another warrior answers.

"We have to burn their bodies. Let the only trace of them being in our realm be their ashes," Shanti concludes.

The other three warriors shake their heads in agreement.

The Warrows then cover all of the Malakai's bodies with the dried leaves which are covering the ground of the forest, leaving the beasts where they lie. Mali takes a burning log out of the fire and lights the leaf-covered bodies of the dead Malakai, which ignite immediately.

"Let's get out of here and join the others," Shanti states.

Lucic and the female warriors can now see a large maze of fires in the area where the Malakai were. Its glow is lighting up the vastness of the dimindark which has now expanded its presence throughout the realm.

"I assume Shanti's squad completed their mission," Harlee glancing over at Lucic surmises.

"They are the best of the best," Lucic answers, glancing back at Harlee.

Then after a few moments, Shanti and company appear at where the rest of the group is waiting for them. Shanti then sits on a fallen tree and looks up toward the rest of the group. "The Malakai are all dead. But somebody tell me, what are they doing here in Wildwood?" he asks with concern.

"Evil has spread his reach to all corners of the supercontinent in preparation for his attempt to take it over and either enslave or murder all that walk upon it. That's why our mission is vital, for if Evil succeeds, then the world as we know it will be unrecognizable," Harlee states.

"Excuse me for interrupting, but we need to get a move on, for the fires will surely attract unfriendly beasts looking for an easy meal. We've had enough heartache for one day," Ivy retorts, looking over at Josie who appears to still be in a daze.

"Ivy's right. We need to get outta here," as Lucic agrees with the captain.

The Daughters of Shayla mount their steeds, and three of the Warrows sit behind three warriors as they have done on this journey together.

Harlee looks toward Lucic. "Here, take Sundance. This was Jilly's steed. He will serve you well. Consider it a gift from Jilly for your courage, your loyalty, and your cherished friendship to us all."

"A thousand thanks, my lady, for I could never repay such a generous gift," Lucic says, as he bows to Harlee and the Daughters of Shayla.

"You already have," Ivy says.

The group then heads across the waters of Snake River which has shallowed and narrowed enough at this point to cross it on horseback. Once across, they are out of Wildwood, but the forest is still abundant all around them though it is beginning to thin out as the Grassy Plains begin just three meters to their west. The group decides to stay within the boundaries of the forest, for it is much safer than riding out in the open plains, especially with this many traveling together. The twin moons are barely visible through the treetops and are only a sliver of the moons is visible to their large eyes, which is just two days after the phase the new moon.

After a short while of riding, the visibility is almost nonexistent, so the group decides to make camp for the night while still at the edge of the forest and again by the water's edge. Harlee, Ivy, and the squad bandage and clean out Josie's wound and settle her down for a night's rest, periodically checking on her progress.

Just before the dawn of twilight, Ivy awakens suddenly. She sits up and looks around the camp and all seems to be quiet. The rest of the group is still asleep, except the warriors guarding the camp. She figures while she's awake she would check on Josie. She moseys over to her and stares at her for a moment. She then leans over and strokes her head, but she feels cold to the touch. Ivy lifts her arm to look for a pulse, but she cannot find one. Ivy then calls out, "Harlee! Harlee! Quick, come here!"

Harlee, half asleep, sits up and calls out to Ivy. "Ivy, what's the matter?" Harlee says, half annoyed.

Startled, the rest of the group now awake by the shouting of Ivy begin rush in her direction.

Josie looks over at Harlee with tears in her eyes. She begins to cry. "Josie's gone!"

"What?"

Harlee jumps out of her sleeping bag, as the rest of the group sees Ivy crying, leaning over Josie's stretched out body. Then they begin to run toward her. They then surround Josie.

Lucic rushes to her. He stops and leans over and feels Josie's head, then turns to the women and speaks, "I'm sorry, she's gone. The blow to the head must have done more damage to her than we all thought."

"That's two of us in two days. We have never lost any of us before," Ivy says out loud.

Harlee turns to Ivy. "We are assassins, not regular army. We are out of our comfort zone. We will need to adjust or we will all join Jilly and Josie," Harlee states.

"Either that or we need to revert back to our old ways, which is who we are," Ivy retorts.

"I get your point. It makes sense," Harlee answers her.

She then turns to the others. "Let us gather wood for the Rising Ceremony. Once completed, then we will be on our way, for there is nothing else we can do for Josie now. She deserves eternal rest," Harlee concludes with a somber heart.

As the dawn of twilight begins to show its shadow over the horizon, the warriors complete the Rising Ceremony. Thus, as the fire ignites and rises into the predawn sky, Josie's soul is released and ascends to the heavens and into the Spirit World. All who are gathered say their last goodbyes to their fallen comrade.

"Are you hungry?" Ivy asks Harlee.

"No, depressed. We have lost two sisters, and we've only just begun this quest," Harlee answers.

"No one ever said war was fun . . . No one ever," Ivy retorts.

"Somehow, I'd rather be a live assassin then a dead courageous soldier on the frontlines," Harlee responds. She goes on. "Our strategy has to change. We have to revert to our old ways, if we are to survive this upcoming war, especially with the foes we will be facing in the upcoming battles," Harlee theorizes.

"Lurk in the shadows, then attack from their blind side, never to be seen," Ivy states.

"Exactly!" Harlee answers.

"The Daughters of Shayla are back," Ivy" surmises

"Have the girls saddle the horses. The dawn is rising. We need to be on the move," Harlee orders Ivy.

Once the horses are fed and saddled, the ten remaining assassins and the five Warrows begin the second leg of their journey, heading straight to the direction of the Northern Realm. But their journey is just getting started.

CHAPTER XVI

The March to the Gathering

The ruling kingdoms of Pangea begin their preparation for the journey north where the free kingdoms of Pangea will decide the fate of the world. The gathering will be the summit to plan for the upcoming invasion of the Dark Forest against the Evil Lord Abaddon. This gathering will occur at the fortress of Ravens Rock on the border of the Dark Forest. It will commence on the evening of the first night of the twin full moons. The fortress is under the control of King Galen, ruler of the Northern Realm, who will be the host of this historic meeting with the rulers of all the recognized kingdoms being assembled in the same place at the same time. Ravens Rock, being strategically located on the border of the Dark Forest, will allow the decisions of this war council to be carried out in a timely manner. The armies of the Tehran kingdoms will travel with their long columns of soldiers, along with their wagons to carry their wares on the dusty roads which connect the realms as communal realm ways.

Queen Lazuli's army will have the most prolonged journey, as the Palace of the Rising Sun is almost twenty-five thousand kilometers away from the fortress at the southernmost tip of the supercontinent. Because of the long treacherous journey ahead, her army has already begun their trek north, led by the commander of her army, General Levi Wult, with some six hundred troops on horseback with another one hundred soldiers on foot. King Baltazar will lead his army of five hundred soldiers and be accompanied by his sorceress and confidant, Ursula, and his son, Prince Vale, the commander of his army and his naval armada. The kingdoms of the Warrows will have to navigate through the untamed forest of Wildwood, then be exposed out in the open, as their journey continues through the treacherous terrain of the Grassy Plains.

As the armies begin their trek northward, the winter season has already began to take its grasp on the northland, with temperatures beginning to plummet below freezing when the dwarf sun settles below the horizon as the dimindark settles in over the realm, as is common for the temperatures during the winter season this far north to dip below 238 Kelvins. Temperatures at twilight at that point will not rise much further as the winter season will be nearing its peak once the armies arrive at their destination. Thus, the bleakness of the dimindark will abound until the Season of Awakening springs forth upon the land and the twilight once again appears in the sky to show it has not forgotten to bring forth new life throughout the world.

By the time the troops reach the fortress, the Sea of Storms, which lies above the supercontinent on the arctic circle, will be frozen over, making it impossible for ships to navigate its waters. The entire northland will be in a deep freeze, making it almost impossible to survive long-term out in the open air for long periods of time without shelter to survive the extreme frozen overnights.

With the armies marching en masse toward Ravens Rock, their large numbers will not be able to conceal their presence from the allies of their enemy. This will open a window for the spies of Evil which come in many forms to report to their master as to what they will be witnessing and will allow Evil to prepare for the imminent invasion of his fortress. It will also allow the Evil Lord Abaddon to anticipate and respond to future confrontations with his enemies by confronting their movements with his army of foul beasts in kind.

Queen Lazuli, remaining at the Palace of the Rising Sun while her army heads north to the gathering, is preparing for her journey, along with her sorceress, Aveline. They will fly to the gathering on the back of her pterodactyl, Samael, along with Samael's flock which will accompany the two as their personal guards on their journey north.

"I hope Harlee, Ivy, and their sisters in arms will be victorious in their quest," Aveline says to her queen.

Lazuli glances back at her sorceress. "They are the best at what they do which is to sneak up on their target and kill them dead in their tracks without ever being seen, then disappearing like a ghost," Lazuli answers.

"I would agree under normal circumstances, your majesty, but this is not an unsuspecting assassination. They are walking into a well-guarded fortress, guarded by an army of beasts. They may be a little out of their league," Aveline retorts.

"They will be successful in their quest. If not, we have others waiting in the wings to take their place," Lazuli answers Aveline.

Aveline stands there gazing at the queen. She cannot believe what she has just heard from Lazuli. She would let them walk into a trap and not show a bit of concern or remorse. Aveline thinks to herself, *What a bitch. I have served her since she inherited her position from her father, and each and every day I despise her more and more.*

She then continues her conversation with Lazuli. "Where do you think our soldiers are along their route?" Aveline asks.

"Somewhere along the Southern Highway. Ultimately, they will rendezvous with King Baltazar and his army where the Southern Highway intersects with the Great Western Road. It is there they will travel as one army to the fortress of Ravens Rock where *we* shall meet them by way of my flock of pterodactyls," Lazuli concludes, as she gives a smirk to Aveline at what she had just said to her.

Aveline walks to the rails on the balcony of the queen's porch. She gazes out on the Southern Ocean. The radiance of the dwarf sun is gleaming down upon the sea; its scarlet hues turning the color of its blue water to a dark lavender, making the sea appear almost black, similar to the waters which illuminate off the Black Lake near the eastern shore of the supercontinent.

Aveline then speaks in a concerned tone, "The waters have become very dark as of late and extremely turbulent. It is as if a darkness is seeping into their depths, stirring the life that exists there into chaos, driving them out of their historical ranges, thus upsetting the balance of nature that exists throughout the world."

"I have witnessed firsthand the goings-on in the oceans. It is not a normal cycle. It is driven by an unseen force, for the shroud of Evil is covering the land. It is accelerating now throughout the vast oceans. It's blanketing the world at a brisk pace, bending the will of the lesser species to its own desires," Lazuli retorts.

Aveline exhales with a big sigh, looks up to the heavens, then says out loud, "Let us hope we are not too late!"

The Southern Highway is a long barren stretch of a dirt trail whose terrain is flat with a lack of trees, except some clusters of Pindar trees do appear every now and then where a water source is found, such as a meandering brook or where water accumulates after a heavy rain, allowing a temporary small lake to occur. It is an infertile land of short grasses, and its soil is composed of a rock-hard compound known as caliche, which makes it impossible to till for crops, as its soil is as tough as dinosaur's scales. The openness of its landscape gives forth to a steady current of air blowing up from the Southern Ocean which sometimes increases to a harrowing gale and usually occurs in the winter season when the warm southern current meets the frigid airflow which plunges down from the northern platitudes. And as one travels closer to the Plains of Auria, one can see fifty kilometers in every direction without any obstructions to bar their view. That is the hazard of traveling such long distances out on the open terrain, as this is the territorial range of many a large dinosaur species, as well as a number of large feline species; some of whom hunt in packs and can run twice the speed of the army's large draft horses.

"Keep the column moving, sergeant," orders General Levi.

The General sits upon his horse alongside the trail as he watches the column move past him. Alongside the general sitting atop his draft horse is the general's second in command, Captain Christopher William.

"Aye, aye, general," one of the many sergeants in the brigade responds.

The general then turns to Captain Christopher William. "We have thousands of kilometers to go, and I am a little worried about the predators we can stumble across out here in the open," General Levi says to Christopher.

"General, we have many troops marching in close quarters. We should be able to fend off most anything that attacks us," the captain responds.

"In the twilight, captain, I would agree. It's in the dimindark that worries me. Even with our ability to see somewhat in the dark, our troops may not have the instinct to react quick enough to an attack," the general interjects.

"I will post sentries all along the boundaries of our campsite to give our troops fair warning if anything comes close to the encampment," the captain answers.

"Double the guards you would normally place, captain, for out here its double the trouble if we get attacked," responds the general.

Two days and about 550 kilometers later, General Levi's column has made steady progress on their trek northward, moving at an even pace along the Southern Highway. The troops have not seen a single lifeform in the two days they have been traveling, except for an occasional flock of pterosaurs riding the thermals up high on the warm currents of the troposphere.

As twilight begins to set on the western horizon, General Levi orders Captain Christopher William to set up camp alongside a cluster of Pindar trees.

"Get the campfires started and start cooking the evening meal," the captain orders.

The assigned troops begin to set up the tents for their fellow soldiers, as the ones assigned to feed the horses begin their task. As the fires are fed, their fiery glow lights up the bleakness of the dimindark, sending their brilliance out to the surrounding landscape out about one hundred meters at least.

Wheat ale is drunk by the troops, as that beverage is their libation of choice above all other. Bison meat chopped and ground, then simmered in a kettle with a small bit of rainwater is the evening meal for this day. Though not home cooking, it will suffice to give the protein needed to survive the endless grind of continuous riding and marching as the column continues into the bitterness of winter which lies directly in their path.

Large barn fires surround the edge of the encampment as the sentries walk their posts between them, always peering out into the blackness of the dimindark for any and all unwanted visitors who may stray into their line of sight.

The encampment is set up around the tree cluster which partially blocks the steady blow of the wind pushing up from the south. But being upwind, their scent is carried on the molecules of air, pushing their aroma in the direction in which they are heading. This is especially cognoscente to Captain Christopher William who triples the guard facing the north.

Lightning is seen to their south, streaking across the sky, as the steady blow of the wind begins to pick up and begins to increase in intensity.

"Looks like we are in the path of the upcoming storm," a sergeant says to the captain.

The captain stares at the lightning lighting up the night sky and says to the sergeant, "Make sure everything is secured. It looks like we're in for a doozy."

A short time later, the rain begins to fall. It starts out as a light drizzle. Within a short period of time, its velocity begins to intensify and becomes mixed with hail the size of small pebbles. The lightning is getting closer to the camp, as the wind in the upper troposphere pushes it northward. It appears that the camped army is directly in the storm's path. Tents begin to blow over as the wind intensifies and the stakes, which hold the tents in position and were driven into the hard soil, give way to the developing gale and the now water-soaked ground. The ferocity of the rain falling from the sky extinguishes the fires which was keeping the encampment lit as protection from any roaming beasts that can detect movement in the dimindark. The sentries then abandon their posts, as they cannot continue to do their duty as the storm impedes their ability to serve, which allows the encampment to become vulnerable to the roaming beasts which inhabit this region and to *Mother Nature* itself. Lightning cracks all around them, lighting up the bleakness of the dimindark.

Many of the soldiers' tents have been destroyed by the hail accompanying the rain which have increased in size to about fifty millimeters round. Many soldiers scamper into the cluster of Pindar trees for cover to escape the deluge and destruction.

Then a tremendous bolt of lightning strikes one of the larger trees in the center of the tree cluster, splitting the tree in half. As the split tree breaks apart, many pieces of it break off and tumble to the ground, killing ten soldiers, at least, and injuring many more in its wake. Then a few moments later, another lightning strike directly hits another tree, sending it aflame, which begins to spread throughout the tree cluster.

Lightning Bolt after lightning bolt continue to strike the cluster of trees continuously, as if they are striking on command, starting a chain reaction throughout and setting aflame the forest located in the middle of nowhere. Many soldiers have been killed or knocked unconscious by the falling debris, while some have been trapped under the larger fallen tree limbs. Their screams shout out into the night and can be heard above the howling gale. A scream for help. Their bones shattered, while some have lost limbs in the carnage.

General Levi crawls over to the captain and shouts to him over the blowing gale, "What is happening?"

The captain grabs hold of the general's arm and shouts above the noise, "I don't know, general, bit this isn't a natural occurrence! Look at the concentration of the lightning strikes. They are all occurring around us in the tree cluster. It is as if they are directed specifically at us."

The general seems bewildered by the captain's explanation. "What do you mean, captain?"

The lightning continues to strike at the trees. The fires created by the lightning bolts are becoming larger and spreading through the clustered forest with each passing moment. The soldiers who were not injured in the tree cluster attempt to scramble out into the openness of the plains. running or crawling for their lives.

"Run! Run!" screams Captain Christopher William to his soldiers who entered the cluster of trees looking for refuge.

Then, all of a sudden, the wind dissipates, the rain come to an abrupt halt, and the lightning ceases. The air is filled with smoke as dense as a thick fog creeping over the landscape. The night then becomes silent. The only sounds being heard are the screams of the burning bodies of the soldiers trapped under the burning brush and the crackling of the intense flames shooting fifty meters into the night sky, engulfing the entire line of trees.

Captain Christopher William looks up to the sky. Above the soaring flames, he sees many figures hovering above the treetops which appear, in size and body configuration, to look like Tehrans . . . but with enormous wings; wings whose appearance look like the wings of a bat but have a span of over three meters wide.

"Winged Tehrans," the captain says out loud to himself.

General Levi, standing next to him, puts his hand on the captain's shoulder, then says, "Shadow Demons."

The captain looks at the General with sort of a bewildered expression. "What are they?" the captain asks.

"They are the *Jinn-do* . . . the Shadow Demons. They are guardians of the Underworld and the conjurers of evil spells."

"So what you are saying is that they brought the storm?" the captain remarks.

"My boy, they are the storm!" the general replies.

The general goes on to explain to the captain the legend of the Jinn-do which he sees before him. "Legend has it they were created from the dust of meteors that plummeted the planet at the creation of the world. Evil whose lust for power over his brother who is the Ancient of Days. Yes, the two deities were brothers who came into being at the same time from the huge explosion that created the universe. This endless dark matter that exists all around us."

The General points up to space. "Jealously and a lust for power separated the two. Evil was never named, though if he had, his true name has never been uttered anywhere. Evil became adversarial with his brother because his brother developed his powers faster and became more powerful than Evil, who wanted nothing more than to rule over everything in the universe including his brother whom he wanted to make a slave to serve him. The Ancient of Days, feeling betrayed by his brother, banished him to the Underworld which was created as punishment for Evil for his treachery, allowing him to only rule over all that is unclean and unholy. Evil then created the Jinn-do, who are the freethinkers of Evil and the Spellbinders who take on their adversaries through *Black magic*, such as conjuring the storm we have just witnessed and killing all that stands and fights for good through their evil spells of creating havoc and destruction throughout the world. Only the Watchers are their equal. That is why they must be set free from the dungeons below the Dark Tower, for they are the only ones who can combat the Jinn-do head-on and send them back to the Underworld. Until then, the Jinn-do are free do Evil's bidding without any restraints. This is the legend that was told to me by my father which has been passed down from generation to generation over millions of seasons."

The captain is speechless; he has no other explanation for what he has just heard. He glances away from the general and again gazes up above the burning forest in front of him and stares at the figures hovering above it.

The figures are shrouded in deep ebony whose iridescence has always been associated with Evil. Their eyes glow a piercing yellow which penetrates the night sky with a malevolent stare and whose grasp seems to permeate into one's soul.

"What are they waiting for?" asks the captain, as the two continue to stare at the black figures.

"They are assessing the casualties they have inflicted, or so it would seem, to see if they have made a difference in reducing our numbers and to assess what other methods they can use to inflict more death and destruction over their enemies . . . us! For that is Evil's way!"

"Are we in for a second wave?" asks the captain.

"I don't know. I have never encountered them before. No one in our lifetime has. Well, since the creation of the Watchers, that is."

The Watchers have kept them from exiting the Underworld since the Great War when they fought alongside the Necromancer as he tried to take over the world and was defeated after Naamah was incinerated by Isolde, the White Witch. Isolde opened a portal in the crust of the planet, which appeared like an earthquake of an enormous magnitude, then with a wave of her staff, sent his body to rot in the Underworld. The Jinn-do were sent back alongside him. She then, with another wave of her staff, closed the portal and sealed it using the magic of the Alicorns.

"Where is Isolde now?" asks the captain.

The general gazes into the captain's large eyes. "I don't know. I have not seen her in millions of seasons, for she is not a fan of our Queen and avoids any contact with her unless the situation is dire. But without her, we may not have a chance against Abaddon, for she is a much more powerful Sorcerer than Naamah could have ever been. She may be our only hope, for the divine magic of the Alicorns flows through her veins. Only the all-powerful Ancient of Days is more celestial than the magic of the Alicorns."

One of the sergeants runs over to the two officers. "General, we have lost more than fifty soldiers, and we have just as many in need of medical attention."

"Do what you can for them, sergeant, and prepare the dead for the Rising Ceremony," answers the general.

"Yes, general," the sergeant answers. He then salutes the two officers and scurries way back to the injured troops.

"This is not going to sit well with the queen, general."

"I will deal with her when the time comes, captain," the general answers.

Again, the two look up above the burning forest; the mysterious black figures are gone. The two officers look toward one another; not a word is spoken between them, for they know even though Evil is not visible to their large eyes they can feel its presence all around them, waiting to strike when all the world is at its most vulnerable.

At the dawn of twilight, the dwarf sun begins its ascent over the landscape. Its rays are emanating a dark burgundy hue due to the grey smog brought forth by the burning cinders, smoldering, which lay on the forest floor; its incandescence barely penetrates through to the ground. The air is now stagnant, the breeze is absent, and the smell of charred wood and burnt bodies fill one's nostrils with the foulest of odors.

The bodies of the dead are cremated according to Tehran tradition following the ancient ceremony handed down for millions of generations, as each species has their own version of the Rising Ceremony in preparing their dead for the afterlife. It is their beliefs and traditions which are akin to all the critical thinking beings on Pangea. It is this tradition that is the common element of their intertwined civilizations.

It is midmorning by the time the wounded have been attended to and placed on the medical wagons. They will be transported alongside the column, as the moving army begins to continue their trek north for their rendezvous with King Baltazar and his army where they will continue as a single brigade as they march toward the fortress of Ravens Rock to attend the historic gathering of the recognized kingdoms.

"The wounded are going to slow us down, big time," states the captain.

"We will meet our rendezvous date, barring any more unexpected encounters, that is," answers the general.

"Many horses scattered because of the storm and the fires, but we have gathered most of them up. The ones we couldn't find were probably a hearty meal for one of the many predators that roam this open land," states the captain.

"If that's the case, have the riders on point be extra careful. As a matter of fact, double the point guards, just in case," orders the general.

"Yes, sir," the captain replies.

"Line the column up, and let's get the fuck out of here. We still have a long way to go," states the general.

By the time the battered column begins their trek, the dwarf sun is at its zenith, the farther north they travel the shorter the twilight will prevail in the sky as each day they wander northward brings them closer to the winter season. Soon darkness will cover the land both by day and night as the bleakness of the dimindark follows its seasonal path, contributing to the deep freeze that will prevail throughout the upcoming war, adding many casualties to an already crippling climate which will be the alternate enemy for both sides of the conflict.

Chapter XVII

Ravens Rock

It has been many days and nights since the Daughters of Shayla began their trek northward over the length of the entire supercontinent. They have overcome a multitude of hardships which included the loss of two of their sister warriors. Along with their Warrow companions, the remaining troop has survived the rigors and challenges that the wilds of Pangea has put forth in front of them. The troop has ridden the length of Snake River as it has guided their trajectory. Then they reached the great divide where Snake River and Holgren River converge, whose confluence is more than a kilometer wide with riptides of unparalleled turbulence, pushing wave heights that could challenge the hostility of the open sea. The troop then turns their forward momentum eastward. They guide their ponies over the *Twin Rivers Bridge* and continue their trek over Holgren River whose headwaters begin at the Sea of Storms. At the river's headwaters the fortress of Ravens Rock stands tall just to its eastern boundary as the highest tower stands on cliffs 50 meters above its shoreline, whose heights gaze into the sky overlooking the Sea of Storms. The fortress is positioned so it can allow its sentries to peer out into the depths of what appears to be an endless wasteland of water and ice.

Winter has set its grip firmly on the Northern Realm, with temperatures during the twilight seem to be hovering around 272 Kelvins.

Winter attire is adorned by all, though it is still in the midst of Season of Harvest. In the northern latitudes, the winter season is an early arrival.

The troop must push forward as they fight the clock to the countdown to the Gathering, as the twin full moons is still a ways away. The warriors now walk their steeds on what appears to be a well-marked trail for the first time since their sad encounter with the pack of Wolfen many days ago. This trail appears to be the main route heading northeast, as it is a well-worn path ten meters wide with hoof prints and wagon impressions throughout its length so far.

The Holgren River is behind them now as they prod along this trail. The river is raging with the force of a bully taking on a weaker foe with intimidation and brute strength, and its intensity can be heard as if they were still standing alongside of it. The path now begins to turn directly eastward, moving away from the raging river as the terrain has a slight incline that has been a constant for some time now. The cloud cover fills the entire sky with the rays of the dwarf sun casting shadows as it tries to penetrate the overhanging branches of the large pine, oak, and maple trees adorning both sides of the trail, thus making the visibility harder to distinguish the goings-on within the neighboring vestibule of trees.

"Can you smell the sea air?" Ivy says out loud to all.

"Smells like home. How I miss the sea. We must be getting close to the coast," remarks Harlee.

"It is so quiet. No bird sounds, no animals of any kind wandering through the brush," Lucic observes.

Then Harlee stops the column. She then just stares out into the abyss. Then after a moment, she says to all, "I don't know how we did it, but we appear to be on the *Great Western Road*."

"Are you sure?" Ivy asks.

Harlee then turns to all and points to the north, then says, "Behold . . . Ravens Rock."

A silence comes over the troop, with everyone just staring at the fortress sitting high on a hillside cliff.

"That's a big fortress," Ivy blurts out.

"For sure, we have all have heard of it. Legends speak of it, but never in all my days did I think I would ever see it with my own eyes," Lucic states.

"Wildwood is very far away from here, Master Lucic. Under normal circumstances, you would have never traveled this far from your home. At least, you get to see it with friends," Harlee answers.

Lucic smiles at his companions and nods his head in agreement.

The troop then moves on.

The trail then comes to a fork in the road. The warriors steer their Lambo ponies to the left, as it appears to head straight to the fortress itself. The trail then narrows to about five meters wide. The tree cover begins to subside. Then all at once, after about a half of a kilometer on the trail, the trees are no more and the landscape ahead is barren. Then the fortress comes into full view of the warriors.

Harlee sighs, then says, "We need a short rest."

"Fuck that. I need a bath," Ivy then says.

All shake their heads in agreement with Ivy.

As the Daughters of Shayla, along with their Warrow companions, ride toward the Iron Gate of the fortress, in the distance, the troop can see what appears to be soldiers on horseback riding its perimeter as to guard against any enemies that might threaten their existence.

The movement of the Lambos on the narrow trail is stirring up a cloud of dust which alerts the soldiers patrolling outside the fortress.

An ear-piercing horn blast echoes through the surrounding landscape originating from the walls of the fortress itself, as a lookout has spotted the oncoming column alerting all of the soldiers inside and outside the fortress of an approaching group of riders. The fortress begins to stir, with soldiers appearing to go on high alert and with many being directed to what posts they are to cover as they prepare for the unknown riders heading directly to the Iron Gate. The stone walkways between the towers of the fortress begin to fill up with archers. The approaching riders can witness that the many archers lined shoulder to shoulder have bow and arrows in hand, pointed directly at them. The soldiers on horseback guarding the outside of the fortress begin to gallop their steeds directly at Harlee and her companions; their swords removed from their sheaths and pointing toward the riders heading toward the fortress.

Harlee motions to her companions to come to an abrupt halt.

"We have a welcoming committee. No one make any sudden moves, everyone, understand?" Harlee insists.

"Good idea. I don't want to die by the ones we are supposedly aligned with," Ivy remarks.

The Daughters of Shayla and their Warrow companions stop their forward motion and sit atop their steeds and cease any movements so as not to provoke an attack on themselves. Ten riders donning the armor of the Northern Realm gallop up to them and begin to circle the troop with their swords drawn and their sharp edges pointing directly at them.

Once positioned around the troop, a sergeant approaches the column. He stops directly in front of Harlee who is at the front of the procession. His expression is one of confusion. He thinks to himself, *Female Warriors? Together With Warrows? Both dressed in battle armor.* He appears lost for words, for he stares at the troop without saying a word.

Harlee then begins to speak to the sergeant. "Sergeant, I am Harlee Antonia. A general in the army of the Southern Realm on orders given directly to me from Queen Lazuli. We are on a mission of great urgency. I need to speak to your commanding officer immediately."

The sergeant doesn't immediately say anything. He continues to survey the riders, for he is still in disbelief of what he is seeing. "Follow me, general" are the only words he can muster.

The sergeant turns and begins to lead the troop of female Tehrans and their Warrow companions on the narrow trail in the direction of the fortress. As the riders begin their forward motion, they are surrounded by the other nine soldiers of the Northern Realm. Harlee and company slowly walk their steeds toward the fortress.

Ivy leans toward Harlee and whispers, "Very talkative, isn't he?"

Harlee smiles at Ivy and whispers back to her, "This should be an interesting meeting."

As they approach the Iron Gate of the fortress of Ravens Rock, the sergeant shouts up to the soldiers standing on the walkways, "Open the gate!"

The Iron Gate begins to slowly swing open, and as it does, the procession enters the fortress.

Once they are all inside, the Iron Gate begins to close behind them.

"Wait here," insists the sergeant.

Harlee and company dismount their steeds, and as they do, many soldiers seem to surround them, not in an aggressive way but in an awe-inspiring way as many have never seen Warrows, let alone female warriors or Lambo ponies. The soldiers just stand there, staring at the companions.

Within a few moments, the sergeant returns; this time with a captain of the guard. The captain approaches Harlee. He then bows to her and says, "Welcome, general, to Ravens Rock. I am Captain *Skol Sevverson.*"

"Thank you, captain, for receiving us. I am General Harlee Antonia on a mission directed by Queen Lazuli. My companions and I and our horses are in need of a good meal and a night of rest, and we will continue at the dawn of twilight to continue our mission."

"Harlee Antonia . . . Your reputation precedes you. And your companions, very unusual," the captain says, as he stares at the Warrows.

"Follow me. We can talk in our meeting hall on how my soldiers and I can assist you," the captain concludes. He then turns to the sergeant and orders him, "Sergeant, escort the general's warriors to the mess hall and tend to their horses. Put the ponies in the stables and have our men tend to their needs."

Harlee bows to the captain. "Thank you, captain, for your hospitality."

Harlee then turns to Ivy and Lucic. "Accompany me, as you two are commanders in our company and my trusted companions," she insists.

The three follow Captain Skol Sevverson across the compound to a large building in which they assume the Gathering will take place on the evening of the first night of the twin full moons.

As the four sit at a large table in the meeting hall, Harlee begins to tell the captain the tale of their quest and what they look to accomplish on their venture in the Dark Forest.

The captain then says something that shocks the three! "General, I have to tell you. Isolde, Prince Quill, two Warrows, a Centaur, and a Wiki are on their way here. I received a message attached to an ivory eagle yesterday. It was sent from Prince Quill to prepare for their arrival. They should arrive here sometime evening venturing from Lions Gate. They appear to be on a quest similar to yours. I recommend you meet with them when they arrive."

Harlee looks toward her companions and says to them, "Great minds think alike."

As the dimindark settles in over the fortress, the Daughters of Shayla and the five Warrows are guests of the soldiers of the Northern Realm. The cooks in the fortress have prepared a meal of elk steaks grilled over a large spit, with a side dish of green potatoes boiled and smothered in goat cheese. Wheat ale is abundant and flowing throughout the evening, as all off-duty soldiers, along with their guests, partake in this feast.

At about the midnight hour, the feast has not seemed to slow down. Then a private, who was on guard duty, rushes into the mess hall and runs directly to Captain Sevverson. He salutes his superior, then leans over and whispers in his ear.

The captain turns to General Harlee and leans over whispers in her ear, "They have arrived."

Harlee nods her head in acknowledgment.

Captain Sevverson then says to her, "They are in their guest quarters cleaning up after their long journey. They have been informed of your presence and will meet with you and your commanders in the meeting hall."

Harlee then leans over to Ivy and Lucic and informs them on Isolde and her companions' arrival at the fortress. The three then finish their mugs of ale with a long gulp. Harlee walks over to her troop of warriors, both Tehran and Warrow, then informs them on the upcoming meeting. The three then walk out of the mess hall and head straight to the meeting hall.

As the three companions walk into the meeting hall, they realize that the hall is empty of their counterparts. Its four long walls are adorned with lighted torches every five meters or so, brightly lighting up the large room. Ten pitchers of wheat ale adorn the large table which are scattered about throughout it.

"Well, at least we can wet our whistle while we wait," remarks Lucic.

"I have had enough. Anymore and I won't be myself. I have a tendency to fall over, and my legs have a mind of their own when I drink too much," says Ivy.

"Then what happens?" inquires Harlee.

"Well, my legs then have a tendency to spread when I fall over, but in a good way," Ivy insists.

Harlee and Lucic double over in laughter.

"You are just a fuckin' slut," Harlee laughs.

"I most certainly am," Ivy boasts in a proud, loud, and drunk tone.

Again, the three laugh, as Lucic fills his mug to the top with ale.

Then the door to the meeting hall swings open. Isolde, followed by Prince Quill; two Warrows, Turak and Philo; their Wiki scout, Amolo; and Galgaliel the Centaur enter into the meeting hall.

The three awaiting warriors quickly stand, as the six companions approach Harlee, Ivy, and Lucic. As the five approach, the three awaiting warriors bow in unison to the five in respect, especially of being in the presence of royalty.

Turak and Philo notice Lucic standing there and scream in delight, for Turak and Lucic are distantly related on their mothers' side; their hair colors—golden-colored hair of the Southern Wildwood from the city of Southold and jet-black-colored hair of the Warrows of the city of Wildwind—differentiate them as to what clan they are associated with. The three Warrows embrace each other as they have not set eyes on one another in thousands of seasons.

The rest of the warriors smile at a reunion of the Warrows and clap in unison; a reunion that all wished could have been done in more peaceful times under less stressful circumstances.

"Harlee Antonia," Isolde calls out loud, followed by a huge smile as she embraces the warrior.

"My Lady Isolde, it is a pleasure to see you again. How long has it been . . . two thousand seasons, at least. Maybe more," Harlee surmises.

"At least. My lady, you look well. By the way, how is your . . . queen?" Isolde inquires.

"She hasn't changed a bit, my lady," Harlee answers.

"I'm sorry to hear that," Isolde retorts.

Then all chuckle at Isolde's remark. Once the sorceress and the general have completed their greetings, Isolde and Harlee do the formal introductions to each other's companions.

The eight warriors then sit at one end of the large table clustered together and begin their meeting, which is to be a prelude to the Gathering upcoming in the near future. Pitchers of wheat ale are distributed to all sitting in on the meeting. Then four soldiers enter the room bringing forth bowls of fruit, cheeses, and vegetables for the companions to pick on as they start their meeting, then the soldiers leave the room as quickly as they entered.

Prince Quill begins to speak to start the meeting. "So, tell me, general, about your mission."

"My Lord, I am here with nine more of my sisters. We are known as the Daughters of Shayla, along our allies of five Warrow warriors led by Lucic, a captain in the Warrow ranks. The Warrows have traveled along with us almost our entire journey and have been indispensable to us and our mission. They may be small in stature, but what they lack in size, they make up in heart and courage."

Prince Quill nods his head in agreement. "They are formidable allies who have proved their worth many times as far back as the Great War when our two species fought shoulder to shoulder against the evil Naamah," Prince Quill adds.

Harlee continues, "We will enter the Dark Forest as we were ordered to by my queen. We will gather information on our enemy and report back here before the Gathering of the Kingdoms commences."

"Is that all you intend to do?" Isolde questions.

Harlee looks to the prince, then to Isolde with a curious look in her eyes. "What do you mean, my lady?" Harlee answers her as to evade her question.

"Well, I will tell you a story, Harlee Antonia. Myself and my Warrow companions entered the dungeons of the Dark Tower. We saw the Watchers shackled and chained in that foul place. I spoke with Oriel. I know the size of Abaddon's army, but we are here for another reason," Isolde states.

"What is your mission, my lady?" Harlee asks Isolde with a bit of apprehension.

Isolde stands, then states to Harlee what their mission will be, "We will use the armies of the Free Kingdoms as a diversion. We will sneak into the castle in stealth by way of the Sea of Storms. Abaddon and his army will be concentrating on the battle ensuing on the plains where the attack will happen. Then I will face Abaddon alone, just he and I—one on one. Then I will destroy him once and for all," Isolde concludes.

A hush comes over the room; not a word is spoken, not a breath is breathed, as all the large eyes of both species open even wider.

"That is an undertaking of epic proportions, my lady," Harlee states.

"I can see no other way of defeating the Evil Lord. If we can avoid the massive slaughter of our armies' soldiers, then our personal sacrifices will not be in vain," Isolde states.

"Excuse me, my lady, but I think our chances of victory will be slim. Even if you can defeat Abaddon, we know not what other powers Evil may have planned or what other evil lord is standing in the wings," Ivy states to Isolde.

"I can understand your feelings, captain, but we will last longer with our plan than facing ten thousand Malakai and Neanderthals on the battlefield straight up," Galgaliel states.

"Ten thousand?" Harlee says, gasping.

"The Gathering begins in four days," Prince Quill says to all in the room.

"Four days. I thought we had at least fourteen days," Harlee states loudly.

"I'm sorry, general, but your calculation in time is incorrect. We haven't much time. We need to leave at the dawn of twilight. Can we count on you and your associates?" the prince asks Harlee.

Harlee then turns to Ivy and Lucic, who both at the same time shake their heads up and down, indicating they are in if Harlee agrees. Harlee then turns to the prince and Isolde. "Your highness, my Lady Isolde, my dear Warrows, Wiki of Wildwind, and, of course, my lord Galgaliel, it will be our honor to fight and die beside you, for we will fight with honor and courage to defend this world with our last breath," Harlee states to the five.

Then all in the room stand and raise their mugs of ale, while cheering on their new alliance.

Prince Quill then walks over to Harlee. He then asks her to sit with him at one end of the large table. "General, we will be a platoon of twenty-one. I figure, we will take four of the longboats. We can sail along the coast where the sea is still yet to freeze over. If we are lucky, the weather and the wind will cooperate with us. We should reach the shore by the Dark Tower in a day and a half, give or take," explains Prince Quill.

"Sounds about right, your highness," Harlee confirms.

"My dear Harlee, we are comrades in arms. No more 'Your highness' by anyone. My name is Quill, plain and simple. Please call me by my name, okay?" reiterates the prince.

"As you wish, your highness . . . I mean, Quill," Harlee answers.

"That's better," answers the prince.

The warriors then retire to the guest quarters provided for them by the prince, as they ready themselves for the journey to war.

Throughout the night the soldiers of the Northern Realm load supplies on the four longboats which will carry the platoon of twenty on their quest to reach the Dark Tower. Each warrior carries their own sword, but the prince's soldiers have placed may quills filled with arrows which have been stored on all four of the boats, along with enough food to support twenty warriors for five days as they will need additional food and drink as they trek through the bleakness of the dark lands. With only a few days to complete their mission, time is of the essence, as the armies move toward Ravens Rock for the gathering of the free kingdoms to decide the future of all of Pangea, or just maybe it's just the beginning of the end.

Chapter XVIII

An Endless Wasteland of Water and Ice

As the dimindark is past its pinnacle, its dysphoria, as well as a thick, thick fog as concentrated as a bowl of cheese soup, appears to have spread like a sickness over the realm. Its vapor seems to have expanded its proliferation upon the Sea of Storms, for its concentration has advanced far out into the Northern Ocean and appears as an impenetrable wall, as one can only see a few meters in any direction.

Harlee, Ivy, and Isolde are standing on the rocky beach; a mist, plus a dry snow, swirls through the air produced by excess flakes blowing up from ice floes just twenty meters from the shore. The three are dressed in their winter gear so as to not freeze in this arctic blast. The temperature is hovering around 266 Kelvins and doesn't appear it will climb any higher as the day progresses and as the thick fog will not allow the scarlet rays of the dwarf sun to penetrate past its density. The base of the fortress is towering high above the three on the edge of the cliffs, sending its beacon out into the night sky like a tall lighthouse overlooking the mostly frozen sea.

"I hope the visibility improves or we're all fucked," Ivy states.

"We need to leave soon, for the sea is rapidly freezing over and soon it will encompass the shoreline itself. Then we will have to travel by foot, instead of by boat," Harlee surmises.

"Then our timeline will put the armies of the kingdoms at an even higher risk if we cannot get to the Dark Tower in a timely manner," Isolde states. She then continues, "It will be a slow go if this fog doesn't lift soon, for sure, for we definitely need to be able to keep a watchful eye on the large predators that swim in these frigid waters, for these waters are as black as the dimindark itself, which is a perfect camouflage for an unprovoked attack."

Harlee and Ivy look toward one another.

"Predators, what predators? What the fuck are you talking about, Isolde?" Ivy asks with a deep concern in her voice.

"My dear Ivy, just because the waters are very cold and dark doesn't mean that it doesn't abound with life," Isolde answers.

"Well then, isn't that something you could have told us before we decided on this path?" Ivy reiterates in a loud voice.

"Every path has its risks, captain, you know that, especially in your line of work," Isolde answers.

"She has a point, Ivy," Harlee says.

"I guess," Ivy reluctantly agrees.

The rest of the platoon walks together down to the water's edge and gathers around the three already there.

"Holy shit is it cold!" says Lucic.

"Welcome to the northern latitudes, Master Warrow. It will get much colder as the winter season gets closer with each day," interjects the prince.

"You mean it gets colder than this?" Philo asks the prince.

"Cold? This is just the beginning!" He then asks Isolde, "Are the boats packed and ready to go?"

"Yes, they are. We need to leave soon before the rest of the sea freezes over."

"I agree. Then let's be off," orders the prince.

The band of companions board the four longboats, as the Daughters of Shayla, who comprise of the largest independent squad, spread themselves out between all the boats, as they have deemed themselves the protectors of the mission.

Then before the dawn of twilight begins to rise over the realm, the platoon raises their sails, then pushes off the rocky coast. With the wind at their backs, Prince Quill leads the warriors comprised of Tehrans, Warrows, a Centaur, and a Wiki on a suicide mission for all Pangea into a wasteland of water and ice.

A thick fog surrounds the four boats as they slowly are pushed by the cold winter wind toward east. They move offshore about thirty meters from the shoreline, which is about halfway between the frozen sea and the rocky coast, so as to freely navigate the turbulent northern waters. The longboats are similar to large canoes, with an overall length of 6.1 meters and a width of two meters. Their sails are fixed to a pole 7.6 meters high which holds a single sail.

The wind is blowing at about twenty knots, sending wave heights soaring above a meter, then crashing into one another without any symmetry, which is tossing the longboats around like a very drunk Tehran trying to ride a horse at a full gallop without falling off.

"I think I'm going to be sick!" shouts *Sally*, one of the female Tehrans and a warrior in the Daughters of Shayla, as she leans over the side of the boat and throws up her breakfast into the turbulent sea, which sets off a chain reaction with some other companions on her boat.

"What a waste of a breakfast!" Turak says in Harlee's direction.

"Gee, Turak, thanks for the sympathy," Harlee invokes, as Sally continues tossing her breakfast over the side of the boat.

"Is it ever going to calm down?" Sally shouts to anyone who will listen in between heaves.

"Nothing lasts forever, Sally, like life itself. There's a beginning, a middle, and an end," Quill states.

"Right now, I wish it would end already," Sally states.

As Sally continues to lean over the side of the boat, she stares down at the tempestuous black water, trying to catch her breath in between sending her breakfast into the sea. She notices dark shadows moving rapidly all around the boat. She tries to stare underneath the waves as many shadowy figures rapidly swim alongside them. Sally then backs away from the side of the boat and falls on her back toward its middle. She turns to Isolde and yells, "There's something down there!"

"Where?" Isolde asks.

"In the water, all around the boat!" Sally yells in fear.

The prince, standing next to Isolde, motions to the other boats for them to move closer to the shoreline, for they are too far away for him to give them verbal orders, plus they couldn't hear him over the crashing waves and the blowing wind. Then the other three boats follow the prince's lead and follow his maneuvers to steer closer to the shore. Hopefully, they can see his change of course through the thick fog. The prince points to his eyes, then he points to the sea, then moves his arms in a motion which expresses the word "No."

"I hope the others understand what you are trying to tell them," Isolde says to the prince. "Me too, I hope they can make it out through this pea soup fog," he answers.

As the four boats turn their trajectory starboard toward the shore, the waves appear to increase in size, as if they are being manipulated to do so.

Galgaliel turns to Philo and says, "Why is Quill changing our course?"

"Maybe 'cause the sea is getting rougher by the minute?"

Then *Lilly*, one of Harlee's warriors standing next to Philo, leans over the side of the boat and notices figures swimming swiftly under the waves next to the boat. She leans a little closer to the turbulent sea to get a closer look, and as she does, she screams.

Tentacles.

Many of them grab ahold of Lilly, encompassing her body from head to feet. This is unfolding right before the eyes of the other warriors on board the longboat. Then within a flash, she is whooshed over the side of the boat and taken down underneath the waves.

Philo screams, "Did you see that?"

All on board rush to where Lilly was standing and peer into the turbulent black waters.

"I don't see anything!" Philo screams.

"Where did she go?" screams *Nina*, another warrior of Harlee's squad.

Nina stands holding on to the sides of the boat, trying not to be the next one overboard and holding her sword straight out in front of her in case another attack happens.

She gazes from front to back in a hysterical fashion, then from her flank, a figure leaps out of the water toward Nina.

This figure appears to have the body of a Tehran with arms that fall below its waist. On its head, instead of hair, is tentacles without adhesive cups that come to a point which then fall below its shoulders; yellow eyes aglow to help it peer into the blackness of the Sea of Storms. Instead of legs, there appear to be at least ten tentacles with adhesive cups throughout their length, while they appear that each tentacle is about three meters long.

The figure grabs Nina with its two arms, then wraps its tentacles around her entire body, and as it does, it sinks its huge fangs into the Nina's neck, rupturing her jugular artery and sending a stream of blood four meters into the air. The gushing blood covers the others on the longboat. The two entangled bodies fall into the boat. Nina screams in agony, but she cannot resist her capture, as her body is engulfed by the beast's tentacles but she tries to resist with all her might.

"Cecelia!" yells Galgaliel.

The others on the boat lunge forward to attack the beast, attempting to plunge their swords into it, but the swords cannot penetrate its body and just bounce off. Its outer skin looks like a hard protective shell similar to the exoskeleton of an insect.

The beast scowls at her attackers with a high-pitched squeal whose decibels send a shock wave penetrating the eardrums of all on the boat. The warriors drop their weapons and cover their ears, as they fall to the deck of the boat from the sounds put forth by the beast. This gives the beast the distraction it needed, so it moves its body with Nina entangled in its tentacles. It then throws itself into the sea, plunging below the waves and out of sight of all on the longboat.

"Lilly, Nina, they're both gone!" Philo cries out hysterically.

Galgaliel is just standing there in shock, staring out into the empty turbulent water. Then after a long moment, Galgaliel comes to his senses and continues following the other three boats toward the shore. The four longboats finally make their way to the shore. Once they are affixed to the shoreline, the warriors from the other boats run to the distressed survivors who has just lost two of their own.

"What was that . . . thing?" Philo asks out loud.

He then looks toward Galgaliel. "You yelled Cecelia? What does that mean?"

Galgaliel swallows hard and answers him, "That is the only name I know of to describe what we saw . . . A name handed down from legends told to me by my forefathers about a creature who dominates the Sea of Storms. This creature survives by ravaging all life that exists in these frozen waters, but I have never seen one before until this day."

Quill then begins to speak, "It is known in the common Tehran tongue as the Sea Witch, and Galgaliel is correct, it ravages on all sea creatures for survival in these waters. It is an ancient species, one that roamed the seas as far back when the continents were separated. The waters flowed back then between the continents with no obstructions and all the sea was warm then. As the continents converged to create Pangea, the temperature of the waters changed with the seasons, thus the Sea Witch adapted to the frigid waters of the north where it exists today, never traveling out of the frozen zone. It appears to have the body of a Tehran with tentacles that grab and adhere to anything it attaches to. They are all female, except for one."

"The mighty *Horak*," Isolde says.

"Horak? Who is that?" Turak asks.

"Horak, King of the Cecelia," Isolde answers him. She then continues, "The Sea Witches are his harem. They carry his seed and only give birth to females. That decree was promised to him by Evil itself, so he alone would rule over the Sea of Storms to prevent being challenged to his harem by his offspring. All this to pledge his allegiance to Evil itself."

"It's a dangerous world we live in," Quill answers

"Death at every turn," Isolde concludes.

Quill then turns and canvasses the landscape. The snow is coming down hard, the sea has continued its turbulence, and the group still has a way to travel to reach their destination.

"Let us travel by foot until the dimindark fully encompasses the realm, for it is too dangerous to travel by boat. Then we will set up camp and rest for a short time," Quill surmises, as he addresses the group.

The group then travels by foot along the shoreline in the direction of the Dark Forest, and as luck would have it, the wind is at their back.

The group travels deep into the dimindark. Then on the horizon the night sky begins to brighten. The twin moons begin their ascension over the Sea of Storms.

Harlee stops and turns to Ivy and says to her, "Look, the twin moons are almost full."

"The Gathering will commence on the evening of the second day, for that is all the time we will have to reach the Dark Tower," Isolde interjects.

Harlee and Ivy nod their heads in agreement with Isolde.

Isolde turns to the prince. "We need to make camp here, for there is a path between the mountains which will lead straight to the Dark Tower itself. But we need to be vigilant, for the path will be cluttered with our enemy."

"Okay then, let us move away from the shore," Quill orders.

"There are many caves along the route we will travel. We can make camp in one of them. I will take the lead from here and guide us to the Dark Tower," Isolde states.

As the travelers stand on the shore facing the edge of the most northern point of the Dark Forest, they all stare at a wall of enormous trees towering sixty meters into the sky. Their presence appears to be deformed and misshapen, almost as if they are diseased, or their growth has been deformed by the harsh weather which prevails year-round in this frozen realm, or just maybe it may have been done on purpose by an evil entity to discourage travelers of all forms of life from entering this evil place of their own free will.

"Do not despair, for I will light our path before us," Isolde insists.

The group turns south and begins to head inland. The mountains are tightly clustered together, and the forest begins at the shoreline's edge. Their steep inclines jut high into the sky which protects the northern flank of the dark realm, for what seems almost impenetrable to the naked eye. The power of the Alicorns guide Isolde directly to the hidden path which winds in between the spires. It is a narrow path about two meters wide whose foliage covers their ability to see the night sky.

At its entrance, Isolde addresses the group, "This is the secret entrance into the Dark Forest. It is called the 'Dutha de nero,' the Dark Path. It is long, hilly, and narrow. There is danger at every turn. Beware, there are many caves along its route where our enemy can hide and attack unseen out of the darkness. Silence is our friend and will extend our lives, if we are lucky enough. Remember that! I will lead the way. Now follow me."

Isolde closes her large eyes, then whispers in the language of the Alicorns. Then slowly the end of her staff begins to brighten until it has a steady glow to it. Its brightness is just enough to see three to four meters ahead of her, but not too bright that it may attract their enemy who may be lurking in the not so far distance. The group walks in a single file as the path is indeed narrow. Galgaliel takes up the last position of the squad, with Amolo on his back facing backward as sort of a sentry of sorts; all four arms filled with two bows and two arrows each just in case. The Centaur is the largest figure of all of them and best suited with his riding companion to be able to fend off an attack from the rear flank.

It is a slow go along this narrow path with blowing snow covering the ground in front of them. The hanging branches of the large pine and ash trees in their deformed state hang down, covering the sides of the Dark Path and insulating the many caves along its route hidden behind them. Isolde notices footprints darting in irregular patterns all along the path heading into the forest itself. They are almost miniature in size but appear to be fresh, as the blowing snow has not covered them as of yet.

Isolde says nothing to her companions, as they might just be some form of rodent scurrying about the forest floor foraging for food of some sort. The forest is dead silent, the patter of the travelers' footsteps making a dull thud with each step taken is the only sound which echoes throughout the narrow path. Then ahead of the travelers, Isolde sees a glow in the distance; a bright glow indicating a torch being held high to see the path ahead. The glow of the torch appears to be getting larger and brighter with each passing moment. Isolde realizes that whatever is holding the torch is moving quickly and heading in their direction. Isolde stands there, frozen, not sure what to do. She thinks to herself, *Does our enemy know we have entered this land? Do we stand and fight which could potentially bring forth the army of Abaddon down on us? Do we retreat back onto the shoreline which would cause a stir and again bring forth our enemy unto us?*

Then from behind the covering branches along the path, Isolde witnesses a stir by the base of the path stirring the branches on her right begin to move from side to side.

"This way! This way!" a high-pitched squeaky voice calls out to them.

Isolde looks down along the ground and sees a figure standing bipedal, waving its arms to come in its direction. A figure about thirty centimeters in height who is waving to her continuously!

"Well . . . Come on!" it says with authority.

Isolde is startled, for she has never witnessed such a figure before and has never heard of anything like she is seeing, not even in legend. With no other option, Isolde turns to her companions and whispers to them, "Follow me. Quickly!"

Isolde separates the branches which reveals a massive cave entrance. She turns to her companions and waves them on to follow her through the hanging branches covering the cave entrance. One by one the companions move quickly into the secret cave until Galgaliel, with Amolo on his back, are the last in line to enter the cave. Then all are safe now, hidden away.

"How did you know this was here?" Turak whispers.

Isolde points to the tiny figure standing in front of the group. "He told me," Isolde answers.

"Sssshhh . . . quiet!" says the tiny figure.

The tiny figure runs to the cave entrance and disappears in between the branches. The warriors stare at one another with confused expressions on their faces, like "What the fuck was that?" Outside the cave entrance the companions can hear the thuds of massive footsteps walking past them;

not a word is spoken between them, as they all unsheathed their swords and are ready in case of a sudden attack.

After a few moments have passed, the tiny figure walks through the branches and stands in front of the companions. He looks them over one at a time. He then turns to Isolde and begins to address her in a high squeaky voice. "You are the White Witch, yes?" it asks.

Isolde bends down on one knee so as to bring her closer to the tiny figure and to not intimidate him. She then answers him, "Yes, I am Isolde, daughter of Elisheba."

"I thought so," says the tiny figure.

"You are lucky I came along. Malakai, three of them, have just past our home," the tiny figure says to them all.

"Thank you for your assistance, but who are you?" Isolde asks.

"What are you?" Prince Quill interjects.

The tiny figure looks from Isolde, then to the prince, and smiles. He then says to them, "Excuse me for not introducing myself, that was rude of me. I am *Gobi*, the king down under."

"Under where?" asks Philo.

"Over there," Gobi answers. He then points to a hole about sixty centimeters around about three meters from where they are all standing.

"King of who?" Isolde asks.

"The *Dokka*, of course."

"There are more of you?" asks Harlee Antonia.

"That's a silly question. Of course there are more of me. Many, many more," Gobi answers.

He then calls out to the other Dokka to reveal themselves to their guests. "Come out, come out, my fellow Dokkans. Lookie what I have found roaming in the forest."

With that, the tiny hole where Gobi has pointed to begins to fill with many tiny figures who look like him. They begin to walk out of the tiny hole in single file—Dokkas, one after the other, hundreds of them. They appear like tiny Tehrans, although their heads are flat on top. They have very large eyes for such tiny creatures. Their ears are pointed, like the Warrows, and each of their hands are adorned with four fingers. They are dressed in winter attire, which appears to be made out of fur made from mice or rat as the tails are still attached to the bottom of their clothing, as this land is frozen throughout all of the seasons, especially underground where the temperatures are colder than on the surface and where the dwarf sun never appears.

Prince Quill turns to Isolde and says to her, "Have you ever heard of them?"

Isolde shakes her head, "I can't say that I have, not even in legend. It is like they have slipped unnoticed through time and space. Then, again, I have not spent much time this far north in many, many millions of seasons," she answers him.

"Malakai are such foul beasts. The Neanderthals trap and eat Dokka. We hate them both," Gobi states. He then goes on. "We have heard many tales of you, my Lady Isolde. My kin have observed you for many millions of seasons throughout your travels," Gobi says to her.

Isolde looks confused. "How have you . . . observed me, may I ask?" Isolde asks Gobi.

"The Dokka have many tribes scattered through the land, my lady. We see many things. Things you could never witness. We are small and can conceal ourselves, that's why you have never heard of us . . . see."

"I see, Gobi . . . I see," Isolde answers.

The Dokka scatter around the visitors in mass and talk amongst themselves in their high pitch murmur, as they have never revealed themselves to Tehrans in their entire history of existence out of a non-trust of anything other than other tribes of Dokka.

"There are so many of you, King Gobi!" Isolde states.

"We make many offspring, as I have twenty-one wives myself, and about one hundred thirty offspring, as do many other Dokka families."

"I guess there's not much else to do in the darkness underground in the frozen north land," Philo states.

"Twenty-one wives . . . Can you imagine? I'd run away . . . far, far away," Turak says.

"For sure, and I'd go with you," Philo interjects, then both laugh.

"How well do you know the surrounding land, Gobi"?" Isolde asks.

"The Dokka know every centimeter of the forest," Gobi states.

"Isolde, do you think they can help us navigate through the Dark Forest in secret to the castle?" asks Prince Quill.

"I will ask him," Isolde answers. She then goes on. "Gobi, a dark lord has taken over the Dark Tower and we have come to confront him before he tries to destroy our world, do you understand?" Isolde says.

"The Dokka know of the goings-on in and around that evil place. We have seen it. But we are too small and not enough Dokka to do anything about it," Gobi states.

"An army is coming and will be here in a couple of days, but we need to get inside the castle before they arrive. Can you and your tribe help us get inside the castle?" Isolde asks.

Gobi looks toward his tribe for a moment, then back to Isolde and says to her, "Then the Dokka will help the White Witch and her friends."

With that said, the rest of the Dokka tribe screams out with approval. The Dokka then approach the warriors and embrace them as one of their own, for as of now they are all part of the tribe.

Chapter XIX

The Gathering of the Kingdoms

The twin moons shine full in all their glory, illuminating the dimindark. As with all full moons, they signal a new beginning; as in this instance, a new season, the winter season. Or maybe in this case, it signals the end of times. Only the days ahead will give way to the answer. The evening of the Gathering of the known kingdoms of Pangea has finally arrived. One by one their armies begin to fill the surrounding landscape encompassing the fortress.

Thousands upon thousands of the five kingdoms' armies camp on the surrounding plains of Ravens Rock. Their campfires stretch well into the surrounding forest, as they can be seen from high atop the fortress walls.

Many of the warriors of the different kingdoms have never set their large eyes upon one another, as many were not yet born when the Great War, which ended the Second Age, was fought. Also, all the kingdoms command their warriors stay within its own boundaries for their own protection, as well as protecting the citadels of their royal family, as traveling between the realms is always perilous journey. Though the battle now appears that it will be fought once again in a familiar place—the plains encompassing the Dark Tower; only with a different adversary. Evil seems compelled to destroy every living thing that exists in this world, and those that survive are to be enslaved to serve Evil's messiah, the Demon Abaddon. The overall stature in the eyes of Evil suggests holding Abaddon in a higher regard then Naamah ever was, even though the Necromancer was of his own seed. Abaddon alone sits on the left side of Evil itself and he has done so ever since the deity began its rule of the Underworld, which was its banishment from the Spirit Realm for the betrayal of his brother—the more powerful and righteous Ancient of Days.

The two deities know each other as well as two brothers can, as each is familiar with the other's tactics, strategies, and beliefs, and most of all, the divine powers each other possesses. One, whose desires is the preservation of all life, as well as to maintain the worlds inner and outer beauty. While the other is to instill its dark powers by procuring the enslavement or death on all who defy its will. Good versus Evil, as it was written in the ancient texts of the Watchers authored by Oriel, as he foresaw the future of life on this world; a world identified by its single supercontinent; a world which within itself has no name.

As the five monarchs of the recognized kingdoms begin to gather in the meeting hall, the security to protect them is overwhelming. The meeting hall is wall to wall with soldiers representing all the kingdoms.

Captain Skol Sevverson, the commander of the fortress, calls out to all in attendance as each king enters the room as a sign of respect to the emperors who have traveled so far to attend this meeting. At the head of the table is its host and ruler of the Northern Realm, King Galen Emor. Seated next to him is Giselle, his sorceress and counsel.

To King Galen's right is King Baltazar, ruler of the Western Realm; the general of his army and navy and son, Prince Vale; along with Ursula, his sorceress. Opposite them are the two Warrow kings, King Leo the Just of the Northern Wildwood and *King Alastair* of the Southern Wildwood.

King Galen begins to address the monarchs. He then stands and looks over the gathered. "It seems we are missing one . . . Queen Lazuli..

"Excuse me, your majesty, we met the other day with one of Queen Lazuli's generals. She assured me the queen was en route," Captain Sevverson cites.

"We?" asks King Baltazar.

"Yes, your majesty. Prince Quill, Isolde, Galgaliel the Centaur lord, and their traveling companions met with me," answers the captain.

Then a stirring appears to be happening outside the meeting room. The sound of soldiers' footsteps appears to be running to and fro, which can be heard by all in the meeting room.

"What is happening, captain?" asks King Galen.

Captain Sevverson exits the meeting room to see what is taking place in and around the fortress. He enters the courtyard and sees a stirring in the sky above the fortress, large winged figures casting their shadows in the night sky.

One soldier begins to yell, "Pterosaurs! Oh, my lord!"

Captain Sevverson runs to the middle of the courtyard and commands to his troops, "Stand down. Do not draw on them." He knows the legend of the queen and how she likes to make an entrance.

Twelve pterodactyls in all are circling the fortress in a line. They then break off from formation and the twelve lands equally on all four sides of the fortress. The sentries cower at the sight of these large reptile dinosaurs.

Then one of the pterosaurs descends into the middle of the fortress and lands in the courtyard.

This pterodactyl is twice the size of the others, thus upon its back are two figures. The pterodactyl which upon the two figures are sitting begins a harrowing scream, which is emulated by the others situated upon the fortress walls. All of the soldiers in the vicinity cover their ears and fall to their knees, for their screams are piercing to all of their senses.

The pterodactyl then lowers itself close to the ground, and the figure in front throws one of her legs over the beast and descends to the ground, followed by the second figure.

The figure in front throws back her red hood, then pulls out from inside the hood her long flowing black hair which falls to the small of her back. The second figure just stands there and pulls back her black hood to let her long hair flow down, also. Queen Lazuli, accompanied by Aveline, her sorceress, has arrived at the Gathering.

Queen Lazuli then walks up to her pterodactyl's face and embraces it. She then kisses it on its snout and whispers to him, "My boy, Samael, find sanctuary in the forest. I will call on you again, soon."

With that, Samael flaps his wings, creating a hurricanelike force stirring the air and swirling the snow-covered ground, and lets out a loud screech. He then lunges forward and takes to the air. As he ascends to the sky, the other pterodactyls scream as they follow Samael into the night sky of the dimindark; their shadows fade out of sight and head east into the surrounding wilderness of the Dark Forest.

Captain Sevverson approaches Queen Lazuli. He bows to her, then says "Queen Lazuli, welcome to Ravens Rock."

"Thank you, captain," she replies.

"If you would follow me, your majesty, the meeting is just getting started."

"Lead the way, captain," Lazuli answers.

Captain Sevverson turns, then briskly leads Lazuli and Aveline across the frozen compound as the arctic wind is blowing fiercely from the north. Moments later, the three enter the building where the meeting is located. The captain leads the two up to the door where the meeting is taking place. The captain opens the door, then steps inside. He stands at attention as he announces the two to the rest of the Gathering, "Hear ye, hear ye! Presenting Queen Lazuli, Empress of the Southern Realm."

Lazuli enters the meeting room, followed by Aveline, who walks two steps behind her queen. All the participants in the room stand as they do when any sort of royalty come into their presence.

Lazuli walks up to two empty chairs at the table. She then stands behind them and acknowledges each king individually out of respect for their title.

"Queen Lazuli, thank you for accepting my offer to be at this most perilous Gathering. Please, take a seat at the table so we can begin," states King Galen.

Lazuli and Aveline both bow to Galen, then take their places at the table among the rulers of the five recognized kingdoms.

Giselle speaks to Aveline, "My lady, by what means do pterodactyls have the ability to brave this frozen realm?"

"My Lady Giselle, their ability is through the spells I concoct over millions of seasons of trials and tribulations," Aveline retorts.

Giselle nods her head in awe of the sorceress.

King Galen then stands and begins to address the rulers. "My fellow rulers of Pangea, we are gathered here today because of a great peril which is stirring in the Dark Tower and now is upon us which threatens our existence. It deems to enslave or extinguish all life on Pangea by thrusting our world into shadow which will converge Pangea with the Underworld, where the two will become one. Imagine a world where dimindark will be a constant. A world of bleakness, ash, and fire, thus twilight will never rise over the world again. A world where Shadow Demons will be the taskmasters to carry out the will of Abaddon the Destroyer.

"Behind this madness is Evil itself. Though we have faced his minion before, never have we faced an affliction of this magnitude. My brother, Quill, along with the White Witch, with warriors of Southold and

Wildwind, a Centaur lord, and the Daughters of Shayla led by General Harlee Antonia, are, as we speak, on a mission, one that they have taken upon themselves to do. They plan to secretly enter the Dark Forest and face evil head-on. A suicide mission to save all life on Pangea, and to preserve our world and all its resources. Resources which provide sustenance and life-giving qualities to each and every lifeform on the planet. And to once and for all vanquish the evil whose presence abounds in the shadows of our world."

King Galen then continues to describe their mission in detail and how the armies gathered at Ravens Rock will assist them in creating a diversion; one which will cost many lives of all the species involved in the attack.

After explaining the plan which takes much time, King Galen stops, then looks around the table for additional answers or comments from all gathered. No one in the room says a word. The silence is deafening!

After a few moments of quiet, Queen Lazuli breaks the silence. "This is an unexpected turn of events, but a logical one, no less. One that can save many lives, overall. Those who have now entered the dark realm are the best we could hope for, and their mission shall not be entered in vain."

Once again, the silence is deafening. Not a single soul disputes the plan.

"Has no one anything else to say?" Galen asks in a controlled tone.

After a moment, a voice is heard from the table. "Queen Lazuli has said all there is to say," retorts King Leo the Just.

"So let it be deemed this night, the night of the twin full moons in the Fourth Age of our world, that the five kingdoms of Pangea are united as one, and as one, we shall form a single army to do battle against the ultimate Evil and his underling," King Galen concludes.

Then all the rulers of Pangea stand in unison. They all then raise their glasses of ale together high above their heads as one, and hail the upcoming war for the survival of their world.

"Then let us feast this night, for at the dawn of twilight, we shall lead our armies into the Dark Forest to do battle," King Galen announces.

After much time in conference, planning their attack, without considering a retreat for this war will be for the survival of all of Pangea, thus there is no turning back once this war begins. In the middle of dimindark many hours later, the meeting of the recognized kingdoms finally adjourns. The attendees walk together and exit the building as a group to stretch their legs and get a breath of fresh air. The temperature has dropped to about an icy 255.4 Kelvins, with the wind howling at the force of a gale.

The landscape surrounding the fortress is abound with the many tents of the armies of the five kingdoms. Each tent carries the colors of the army it represents, with the Warrow tents being half the size of that of the Tehrans'. The temporary housing of the armies has spread beyond the boundaries of the Northern Realm and have penetrated the Dark Forest, as more space was needed to accommodate the mass amount of the soldiers of both Tehran and Warrow alike. The many fires spread throughout the landscape are now in a smolder as the logs placed in their hearths glow as their fires have burnt themselves into cinders as the dimindark has progressed. Their glow lights up the campsite and the night sky above the settlement. There is a quiet within the campsite, as the soldiers take their rest, for in a short while the campsite will be abustle with the movements of all the warriors preparing for the final battle. But as for now, the only sounds heard are the blowing wind and the crackling of the cinders slowly burning as the snow continues to fall silently while accumulating on the frozen ground.

Chapter XX

A March to War

As the dawn of twilight begins its ascension over the landscape, its antecedent rays begin to purge the morning sky, signaling that the dawn of a new day is beginning to emerge out of the blackness of night. The scarlet hues it projects blends with the obscurity of the dimindark, giving it an incandescent aura of an unnatural shade of a dark burgundy filling the sky from end to end, which makes an already skittish army preparing for war even more suspicious of what may lie ahead. Already, the armies of the five kingdoms are abuzz, as they are beginning to assemble and line up by the kingdom that they represent. The army of the Northern Realm leads the column, with Captain William in command, followed by Queen Lazuli's army led by her commander General Levi. The main army of the two kingdoms of Warrows are scattered throughout the ranks, thus all are well armed with their bows and arrows in hand, accompanied by their golden swords which hang from their hips. Being small in stature, the Warrows can blend into the landscape without being seen by their enemy. The Centaurs of Galgaliel's tribe have formed just in front of the soldiers of the King Baltazar's army, as his army representing the Western Realm take up the last position of the column, while Prince Vale places his men in the order in which he seems fit.

Prince Vale approaches the kings, as Queen Lazuli will ride with her flock of pterosaurs into the Dark Forest and attack the castle from above.

"Your Majesties, the army is assembled and awaiting your command."

The monarchs gaze unto one another. They then ride through the ranks, walking their steeds the length of the long column. Once they see that all are assembled, the five slowly gallop their steeds in the direction from which they came. At about halfway through their return, the monarchs come to a halt. Once stopped, the monarchs turn and face the column of soldiers.

King Galen then nudges his steed forward and begins to address the army. "Soldiers of Pangea, today we march straight into the dark lands to do battle with the one who sits on the left side of Evil for the survival of our way of life. We will destroy its armies and take back control of our world."

The armies cheer loudly and raise their swords in approval.

King Galen continues. "We will fight until their army is destroyed and are never able again to breathe Pangean air. Let us go forward . . . to *war!*" King Galen concludes.

The monarchs ride up to the head of the column among the cheers of their soldiers. Once at its lead, King Galen unsheathes his sword and points forward while sitting on top of his steed. He leads an army of fifty thousand Tehrans and their Warrow and Centaur allies toward the Dark Forest for the final battle.

Meanwhile in the cave at the northern tip of the Dark Forest

Isolde turns to Gobi. "Gobi, we need to get into the Dark Tower unseen, can you help us?"

"Gobi can lead you through the caves which go straight into the catacombs then the dungeons," he answers. "There is only one problem, my lady," Gobi adds.

"What is that?" Isolde inquires.

"The *Milldok*, my lady. The Milldok," Gobi answers in a frightened manner.

"What is the Milldok, Gobi?" asks Prince Quill.

"How do you say it in the Tehran Language?" Gobi mutters to himself, then turns to some of his kin, and for a moment they talk among themselves. He then turns to Isolde and says, "The Milldok. The scorpions in your language, my lady," Gobi answers.

"*Not again!*" Turak and Philo say together.

Then another Dokka leans over the Gobi and, in a squeaky whisper, she speaks into Gobi's ear opening. Gobi then mutters, "I forgot about them."

"Forgot about what?" asks Harlee Antonia.

"I forgot about the arachnids," Gobi answers.

"Arachnids?" Philo bursts out.

"You gotta be fucking kidding me! Scorpions and giant spiders!" Ivy interjects.

"No, no kidding, my lady," Gobi answers in a serious manner.

"Well, it's either that or we make our way overland which would increase our chance of being seen by the minions of our enemy and there goes our surprise attack. Either way is not good," Quill states.

"We need to get through the catacombs and into the dungeons and free the Watchers. We will need their help if we are to defeat Abaddon," Isolde states.

"How? Only the power of the Alicorns can free them. Remember that's what Oriel said to us," Turak reiterates the words of the Watcher.

"I know, Turak. I'm working on that. I was taught the ways of the Alicorn. I will figure it out, I hope," Isolde answers him.

"Gobi, we will go through the caves. Are you ready to lead the way?" Isolde asks him.

Gobi nods his head, "Yes."

Isolde then bends down and extends her hand to the ground, and Gobi steps on her hand. Isolde then places the Dokka on her shoulder and says to him, "Hold on."

Isolde then closes her large eyes and whispers in the language of the Alicorns. Then magically, the end of her staff slowly illuminates into a bright white light that illuminates the entire cave in which all are standing.

Gobi turns to Isolde. "Wow, Gobi can see far!" the Dokka says. He then points to his left and says to Isolde, "That way! That way!"

The entourage of warriors begin their journey through the underground maze of tunnels, forging ahead to reach the dungeons of the Dark Tower.

The tunnel they are traveling through is completely dark. It appears to be about two meters wide and about four meters high. The scarlet rays of the dwarf sun have never penetrated them, ever. It is suspected that the scorpions have forged them over millions of seasons that the vile pests have existed in this environment.

Isolde's staff has created quite an illumination which enhances their way like a barn fire lighting up the night sky. The warriors travel with much caution as there appear to be many offshoots that they will be coming upon on their perilous journey.

"Careful . . . Careful . . ." Gobi whispers to Isolde, as he points to an offshoot tunnel that the group is approaching which appears to be about five meters ahead of them on their right side. As they inch closer, there appears to be an echo of movement within the tunnel.

Tick, tick, tick, tick echoes through the labyrinth.

"Scorpions," Isolde whispers out loud.

The group becomes very uneasy, as they point their weapons in front of them in anticipation of an attack. The group continues to approach very slowly the offshoot tunnel. Then a tip of a scorpion claw protrudes from inside the offshoot, giving away its whereabouts; thus, at the same time the movement within the offshoot becomes more active. The activity increases in volume which turns into a frenzy within the offshoot tunnel. Then lunging from the offshoot is a large black scorpion which lands directly in front of Isolde. The scorpion seems to be about four meters long. Its body arched, with its back legs full extended, while its claws are opened as wide as they can be, anticipating capturing the White Witch in them. Isolde quickly points the end of her staff directly at the large predator. Isolde then whispers in the language of the Alicorns, "Eman eman e la luna ze furro."

The end of Isolde's staff immediately pulses with a light so bright that all in the company must look away out of fear of losing their sight, for the light is brighter than the brightest flash of light any of them has ever witnessed before; a blinding light of tremendous power and intensity. It creates a pulse, then this pulse of light shoots fiercely into the scorpion, sending it aglow, while the heat it transcends is hotter than the hottest fire felt above the Underworld. The scorpion is frozen in its tracks. It lets out a high-pitched whine, then it immediately begins to slowly dissolve into the ground where it stood, turning its exoskeleton into liquid muck. Then after a long moment, all that is left of the beast is a puddle of goo and guts.

"Ew, you melted it. Very cool, but smelly," Gobi says in his squeaky voice, showing satisfaction of Isolde's deed while waving his little hand in front of his rectangle face to push away the smell.

"How did you do that?" Harlee Antonia asks Isolde.

"I'm not sure. The words just came to me," Isolde answers.

"The power of the Alicorns lies within you, Oriel said. Remember? I guess he was right," Turak states, staring at the White Witch.

Isolde turns to Turak and shakes her head in agreement with a startled look in her large eyes. Isolde then slowly walks up to the offshoot and points the end of the illuminated staff into the tunnel. A cluster of scorpions waiting for the warriors to show themselves scurry away into the darkness and quickly move deep within the tunnel out of the bright light of Isolde's staff. The group just stands there, waiting to see what will happen next. Then all goes quiet; no other movement is detected by any of the group, neither fore nor aft.

Gobi then says to Isolde, "Straight ahead! Straight ahead!"

Isolde then turns to the entourage and speaks directly to Galgaliel, who is the last in line, then says to him, "Galgaliel, Amolo, keep an eye out behind us, for that is where we are most vulnerable."

Amolo, who has seemed to take up a permanent position on Galgaliel's back, turns around and faces backward. His large eyes are open to their max, with his bow and arrows cocked. He then readies himself, just in case an attack commences.

The group then continues its forward momentum, though moving at a snail's pace.

Rodents scurry about the tunnel floor in mass numbers, freaking out the Tehran assassins.

"I hate rodents," Ivy says out loud to anyone who will listen.

"Quiet! We need to be silent in our movements," Isolde says, as she turns her head back to look at Ivy.

As the moments build, Isolde notices that the tunnel ahead seems to expand and appears to open into a very large chamber. The White Witch leading moves forward with extreme caution. Then after a few moments, Isolde leads the group up to the chamber entrance. She just stands there unsure of how to proceed, though she realizes that there is no turning back.

Then from the middle of the line of warriors, Lucic calls out in a loud whisper, "Why have we stopped?"

Isolde turns to face the entourage, and in a loud whisper says to all, "We have just come across a very large chamber or a cavern."

"What do we do?" asks Philo.

"Do? We move forward, cautiously. Very cautiously," Isolde states, for she can only imagine what they will encounter once they enter this chamber.

Isolde, leading the company, steps into the chamber, and as she does, her body feels a coldness that engulfs her inner being, chilling her to the bone. A sensation of both evil and death surrounds her. It is as if she has willingly walked into the Underworld itself of her own free will. Isolde tries to compose herself for a moment. She then points the illuminated end of her staff high above her head and clenches her teeth, then closes her large eyes as tight as she can, directing more of the magic of the Alicorns into the staff to extend its glow even more to get a clear look at what they are walking into.

As the chamber is now fully illuminated, Isolde looks up to the top of the large chamber. She calculates that the chamber is about twenty meters high, as well as about twenty meters wide. The top of the chamber is covered with arachnid webs which continue to extend onto the chamber walls about midway to the floor. It is dead silent. The only sound heard is an echoing of the continuous dripping of liquid hitting the chamber floor.

Drip . . . Drip . . . Drip . . . Drip.

Isolde scans the chamber from top to bottom. She notices a puddle on her right side about ten meters from where she stands. She points her staff in its direction. The puddle is about a meter round. She realizes that it is not water, for it has a dark contour to it.

"Blood," she says out loud to herself, wearily in a whisper.

Isolde looks up toward the ceiling of the large cavern. She then notices a large figure enclosed in a huge web; a large ball of white that is fully encased in a cocoonlike enclosure. *It must be some kind of animal because it is dripping blood,* she surmises to herself. As she looks closer at the wrapped figure, she notices part of an arm protruding from inside the cocoon. It is a Tehran arm, a fresh kill, as it is still purging its fluids onto the chamber floor.

The all at once the, ceiling begins to move.

Large arachnids emerge from behind the thickness of the web structure high above the heads of the intruders.

Isolde quickly looks toward the opposite side of the cavern and notices another opening which appears to lead away from the cavern itself. All in her entourage are now standing alongside her, staring up at the ceiling in disbelief of what they are witnessing high above their heads.

The arachnids begin to quickly move toward the walls of the cavern as if to begin their descent on the intruders. Twenty, thirty, the numbers of the large beasts begin to grow, as more and more emerge from behind the massive web structure.

"Run!" yells Isolde. "Run as fast as you can!"

The group immediately begin to run with all they can muster. Isolde grabs Gobi and holds him tight in her arms. Galgaliel grabs Turak and Philo, one in each hand, then pulls them close to him as he gallops as fast as he can. He yells to Amolo to hang on to his back. The Tehran warriors shoot their arrows into the air in hopes of taking out some of the beasts as they run as fast as they can across the chamber.

Many arachnids descend from their position from the middle of the chamber ceiling to attempt to pounce directly on their victims and a few are successful in their quest.

As the group runs to the exit, no one looks back, for looking back is a bad habit. As they continue to sprint across the cavern, they can hear the screams of their comrades who have been accosted by the large harvestmen. Their cries echo loudly throughout the chamber in a desperate call for help, as their bodies are being torn apart by several arachnids acting in concert. Their blood and organs splatter across the chamber covering some of the group with their body parts, fluids, and blood. As the last of the survivors reach the opening on the opposite side of the chamber, standing by the exit is Isolde. She turns, facing the crowded chamber, and witnesses a mass number of the arachnids charging toward them. The entire chamber is now filled with the filthy beasts. She realizes they cannot outrun them, for their quickness and sheer numbers can easily overcome them instantaneously. Again, she speaks in the language of the Alicorns and sends a pulse of light and heat directly into the chamber filled with the beasts. The surviving members of the group are still running for their lives. The pulse of light and heat fills the chamber, burning everything in the room which succumbs the large arachnids to their death as their bodies dissolve slowly onto the chamber floor. All that is now left of the beasts are puddles of goo and slime.

Isolde stands at the exit, gazing at the mass death she has initiated. The odor of the burnt arachnids fills the air with their stench. She turns to look behind her and realizes she and Gobi are all alone. The survivors have fled into the safety of the long tunnel, but what other terrors may they come across in their escape? Isolde quickly sprints to find her companions, for she fears for their lives as they are without any light to lead their way in the blackness of this labyrinth.

Isolde calls out to her companions as she runs through the tunnel. She then hears a return call to her. It is Harlee Antonia responding to her cries. As Isolde approaches the group, she gazes at Harlee, who is waiting alone for her about five meters from the rest of the group.

Harlee, her large eyes filled with tears, looks at Isolde, then says to her, "Claire, Lizzy, and Pia didn't make it." Harlee then falls to the tunnel floor. She looks up at Isolde and says, "Lucic." She can barely talk through the tears. "Lucic and Moe were killed, also."

Isolde then says, "Five companions . . ." She hangs her head, then begins to sob uncontrollably, which is then followed by the rest of the group.

After a few moments, it is Galgaliel who then tries to appear to be the voice of reason. He turns to Isolde. "My lady, as much as it all hurts, we need to move on. It's too dangerous to stay here. Our mission . . . Remember the mission."

Isolde lifts her head and looks at the Centaur, then nods her head in agreement. The White Witch slowly stands up and looks at the remaining companions. She then says, "Come on. We need to go. Galgaliel's right. Gobi, lead the way."

Gobi then points into the blackness of the tunnel ahead and says, "This way! This way!"

The group then slowly begins to follow Isolde and Gobi. Galgaliel and Amolo once again take the position at the rear of the column, with the Wiki facing backward on the back of the Centaur in case of an attack from their flank.

After a short time, the group wanders upon an opening with a maze of tunnels clustered around a circular room. Seven tunnels in all, clustered alongside one another. Isolde turns to Gobi and asks him, "What do you think?"

Gobi stares from tunnel to tunnel for a long moment, then says to Isolde, "I was here more than ten thousand seasons ago before the scorpions and the arachnids infested this dark place." He then points to one of the tunnels. "The third tunnel from the left is the one we need to go through. I am sure of it. Mostly, the others will just lead to our death."

As Isolde's staff lights up the room, the group stares at the floor of this circular entranceway and notices that there are bones of many species of animals, both large and small, as well as Tehran bones and pieces of their body parts scattered throughout the floor. Many, many rats and baby scorpions forty-five centimeters long are feasting on the discarded body parts left behind by their predators. The deeper the group travels within this labyrinth the damper the air has become, while the smell of death increases in intensity with every step they move forward.

Again, the travelers can hear movement from the other tunnels echoing throughout the labyrinth.

Tick, tick, tick, tick.

"Remember, we are not alone. Not by any means. Keep alert!" whispers Prince Quill.

"Alright, Gobi. We will take the third tunnel from the left as you have indicated. I hope you're right," remarks Isolde.

"Trust Gobi. Gobi knows," remarks the Dokka, as he looks to the heavens for reassurance.

Isolde's staff has emitted quite a bright beam of white light, as the remainder of the companions begin to enter the designated tunnel. Baby arachnids thirty centimeters round scurry along the walls and the ceiling of the tunnel, running from the light as it captures their presence, as do the vermins which appear to be everywhere within the labyrinth. Then Isolde spots an insect she has never seen before. It is long, yellow, and has a multitude of tiny legs which move in unison like a wave on the ocean as it moves along the tunnel. It is about a meter long.

Isolde grabs ahold of Gobi. "Gobi, what is that?" Isolde asks in a panic.

"Damn . . . A beast of a thousand legs. A baby at that!" Gobi remarks in his startled squeaky voice.

"That's a . . . baby?" Isolde asks in a panicked voice.

"Yes, my lady, that's a baby. Adults are five meters long and have fangs at least thirty centimeters in length. They are a horrid creature and fast. They can outrun one of your draft horses easily. That might have been the noises we heard just before or maybe not," the Dokka insists.

"Let's hope we don't come across any of them," Isolde whispers to the Dokka.

"It would be unpleasant if we did, my lady," Gobi answers her.

"The tunnel is straight and does not have any offshoots, so far," Prince Quill, walking directly behind Isolde, whispers to her. He continues, "This is not good, for if we are attacked either fore and aft, we have nowhere to retreat, we would be trapped."

"Don't worry, don't worry! We are almost at the end," answers Gobi.

"Well, what comes after this?" Quill asks the Dokka.

"Why, the catacombs, of course," Gobi answers.

After what seems like many long moments, Gobi points ahead of him and whispers to all, "The catacombs."

As the companions walk up to its entrance, they stand clustered together, gazing at its round opening. They all can feel a cold but steady breeze of stale air pushing against them, making a hollow noise as the escaping stale air swooshes past where they all stand. The entrance is five meters round with ruins etched, encircling the opening. Isolde stares at the ruins and mutters to herself. "Mal A buddr, ahn il la rok," Isolde then says out loud.

"What does that mean?" Prince Quill asks.

"It is in the language of the Underworld, which is the oldest language ever spoken, translated into the Tehran tongue. It means 'Death to all who enter.'"

The companions gaze at one another; a look of terror has encompassed all their faces. Isolde peeks past the entrance and see many torches lit which line the catacomb walls about every five meters or so.

"The catacombs seem to be well traveled. There appears to be torches lit throughout," Isolde whispers to all.

"At least that light will keep the scorpions at bay," Harlee Antonia remarks.

"Yes, but the army of Abaddon is surely about within these walls. We need to be on high alert, everyone, understand?"

All shake their heads in acknowledgment.

"Okay then, let's move," Isolde says.

Philo turns to Turak, and says to him "It's not the scorpions I'm worried about, it's that Beast of a Thousand Legs that scares the shit out of me."

Turak answers him, "Well, the scorpions scare the shit out of me too."

Both nod their heads in agreement at one another.

"My lady, Gobi has not been in this chamber since before the Great War, but I still remember my way around, I think. We used to play here as small Dokka before Evil claimed this place as its own," Gobi tells Isolde.

"Gobi, we need to find the Great Chamber inside the dungeon. That's where the Watchers are being held," Isolde tells the Dokka.

"We will face many perils along the way, my lady, for we must survive the catacombs before we enter the dungeon, and that will be no easy task. It will be a full day's journey from where we are to reach the dungeon," Gobi answers her.

"Then we better get started," Isolde retorts.

The remaining warriors begin their trek to get through the catacombs. The way is not silent, for the travelers can hear the sounds and grunts of Malakai and Neanderthals scurrying about in the distance. Silence and stealth in movement are the only way they will survive this journey, and a little luck would be appreciated by all. There appear to be many offshoots as that is what the catacombs are known for; some with torches revealing their secrets but many are without, leaving those passages in total darkness where any number of beasts or the minions of Abaddon could potentially linger unseen and attack without warning. Without Gobi's guidance, one could potentially wander in this endless maze for thousands of seasons, lost, which will only end in eat or be eaten.

Then up ahead of the travelers they can hear the sounds of large footsteps coming straight in their direction. Isolde turns to her companions and whispers, "Quickly! Up ahead! Everyone into that dark tunnel!"

The group hurries in a single file into the darkness, but Galgaliel's hooves make the sound of a scurrying horse on the rock floor. The group stands out of the light of the lit torches of the tunnel they were just traveling.

Then all goes silent.

The warriors stand tall; all with their bows cocked full of arrows and patiently wait for their enemy or enemies to pass them by.

Moments pass and still nothing is heard, only silence prevails; no movement can be detected.

Could Galgaliel's clanking hooves have given them away? Isolde could only assume.

The group continues to wait patiently in silence.

Then moments later, they hear the footsteps again, advancing closer to their location. The footsteps become louder and louder. Then all at once a group of five Neanderthals begin to strut past the dark tunnel where the companions have hidden themselves. Two of the beasts are holding torches high above their heads. As they begin to pass the dark tunnel, the last beast in line who is holding a torch stands at the dark tunnel entrance and waves the lit torch into it, as the beasts must have suspected someone or something is also moving about within the catacombs. To its surprise, he sees the group of travelers standing there in the shadow of its light. Before he can alert the others, he is struck in the head with five arrows, killing him instantaneously.

The lit torch the beast was carrying falls to the floor, causing a loud crackling of the lit torch and falling and bouncing on the rock floor which echoes throughout the catacombs. Prince Quill, with the aid of Harlee and Ivy, quickly drags the dead beast out of the light of the tunnel and pull him back into the darkness of where they are standing.

Isolde quickly snuffs out the lit torch with her feet and moves back into the darkness. Then the forward motion of the remaining four Neanderthals quickly stops. Isolde, as well as the others, can hear the grunts of the Neanderthal language as the beasts communicate with one another. Startled by the sound they all heard, they turn and move back to where the companions are hiding. The beasts move cautiously as they have not moved far from the dark tunnel.

Turak and Philo look toward one another. Turak then says to Philo, "Fuck this!"

The two Warrows leap out into the lit tunnel and fire their arrows, three arrows each at a time, thus killing the remaining four Neanderthals in an instant before any of their companions can even move to assist them.

The remaining companions are awestruck at the lightning speed of the small warriors.

Isolde sticks her head out into the light tunnel and looks at the two Warrows and whispers, "Nice shootin', boys."

"I thought so," answers Turak.

"What do you mean you thought so? I'm the one who shot them!" remarks Philo.

"You . . . you missed every shot. That was all me!" Turak retorts.

Philo gives Turak a look of disbelief. "Nice try, but you couldn't hit a tyrannosaur if he was biting you in the ass," Philo fired back.

"Boys . . . Boys, you both did good," Isolde interjects.

Then Turak and Philo high five each other in satisfaction.

"Yes, Turak you did good . . . but I did better," Philo remarks.

Then both Warrows laugh together and embrace each other as brothers.

"Are we done?" asks Quill.

"We're done," both Warrows say in unison.

"Good. Then let's drag these beasts into the darkness of the tunnel," orders Quill. "Good idea," answers the two Warrows in unison.

The five dead Neanderthals are dragged by the warriors into the darkness of the tunnel in which they were hiding.

Ivy then turns to Harlee. "Do these things ever bathe? Boy, do they smell!"

"Yeah, they remind me of an old flame of yours. Remember *Richard*, the sergeant you used to see?" Harlee reminisces.

"You have to bring that up now," Ivy answers her back.

"Sorry, but it does remind me of him," Harlee answers.

"Yeah, you're right. I'm glad I dumped his sorry ass," Ivy answers.

Then everyone in the group chuckles at the two females.

Gobi, standing on Isolde's shoulder, shakes his head from side to side.

"What?" Ivy whispers to Gobi.

"Nothing.... nothing" as the Dokka smiles at Ivy.

The warriors once again begin the slow trek through the catacombs, as Gobi leads Isolde in the direction of the Great Chamber where the Watchers are being held captive.

The main passageways of the catacombs are aglow with torches every five meters or so, as they are the main thoroughfare of the minions of Abaddon moving about through the catacombs, while the many, many offshoots which are less traveled remain in complete darkness. The catacombs are cold, damp, and abounding with the stench of the foul beasts of Evil. It is not silent by any means as the warriors can hear the *tick, tick, tick* of the large insects and the patter of the numerous vermin moving about in the total blackness of the less-traveled passageways.

"This way. This way," Gobi instructs Isolde, as the Dokka points to his right toward a passageway which is in total darkness.

Isolde grabs a lit torch off the tunnel wall and holds it in front of her to light the way ahead. As she turns the corner to enter the unlit tunnel, the torch's glow lights up the passageway. She is then face to face with a Beast of a Thousand Legs which is lurking three meters in front of her and the group.

Isolde then gasps, for this beast is fully grown and appears to be five meters long and a meter tall, at least. At once, many arrows fly toward the huge insect drawn from her companions' bows, but they just bounce off the beast and fall scattered throughout the tunnel, for its exoskeleton is thick and impenetrable by the warriors' arrows. The large insect just gazes at the intruders in what appears to be a hundred eyes staring back at them. Flexing its thirty-centimeter protruding fangs at the intruders, it then begins to arch the sections of its body as to prepare for an attack. Isolde freezes in her tracks. Then without any sudden moves, she let's go of lit torch. It falls to the rock floor, releasing many sparks which flutter about the tunnel. Then with both hands she grips her staff as if holding on for dear life.

A malevolent rage fills the soul of the White Witch. She begins to growl like a wild beast; the irises of her large eyes turn a fiery red. Then all at once the beast lunges toward Isolde. The White Witch leans forward. Then as she does, she lowers her staff, plunging it into the mouth of the large insect. Then Isolde closes her large eyes and growls even louder. Her staff then shoots a bolt of lightning into the belly of the beast. The lightning bolt travels throughout the beast's five-meter body. The force of the bolt then explodes inside of it, turning the Beast of a Thousand Legs into a *beast of a thousand fragments.*

The explosion echoes throughout the catacombs.

Isolde is still standing, her staff extended and encased with the head of the beast. The group is now covered in blood and guts, but they have survived . . . so far.

Quill grabs Isolde by her shoulders and asks her, "My lady, are you okay?"

Isolde, covered in blood and guts, answers, "Do I look okay?"

"No, you look gross," Quill answers.

"Well, my prince, that's exactly how I feel. Yuck! But I am not injured." Isolde turns to her companions and asks them, "Is anyone hurt?"

Everyone is covered with blood and guts and just stare at her and shake their heads, indicating that they are not injured, but all appear to be in shock, staring at one another and covered in insect guts.

Gobi taps on Isoldes head and says to her, "We need to go."

Suddenly, movement can be heard throughout the catacombs; footsteps which appear to be heading in their direction are getting louder and louder as each moment passes.

"Quick, follow me," Isolde says to her companions.

Isolde quickly sets the end of her staff aglow in a bright white light and moves quickly down the tunnel, followed closely by her companions.

When they reach the tunnel's end, it intersects with another tunnel which runs perpendicular to the one they are exiting. Gobi points to the left and says, "This way. This way."

The companions turn the corner into another completely dark tunnel; the floors and walls are covered with vermin scattering from the companions as the light of Isolde's staff captures them in its beam. In the distance the warriors can hear *tick, tick, tick, tick,* indicating they are not alone as the many large insects infested in these tunnels are now aware of their presence, thus they appear to be in pursuit of them. The travelers are now moving at an accelerated pace. They hear the footsteps of the minions of Abaddon echoing throughout the catacombs and appear to come from the other tunnels surrounding the warriors.

Isolde realizes their quest is in jeopardy.

As the tunnel comes to an end, it concludes at an intersection of three other tunnels which encase a circular room. Isolde instructs her other companions to follow her into its center. The companions then stand in the center, forming a circle around Isolde and facing all four exits. Neanderthals and Malakai fill two of the tunnels and rush to where the companions are standing. The beasts stop at the tunnels' exits at the edge of the circular room. The Neanderthals are grunting and yelling in the sounds of their primitive language. The Malakai, who are mute and dumb, stand there with their nail-laden clubs being held up above their heads. The sound of *tick, tick, tick* are getting closer with every passing moment. The warriors are all armed, with their swords drawn and pointed at their attackers.

Isolde then drops to one knee. She lifts her staff to the heavens, closes her large eyes, then mutters under her breath in the language of the Alicorns. She then screams as loud as she can, then pounds the end of her staff on the rock floor as hard as she can muster, which sends a shock wave throughout the tunnels like a 10.5 magnitude earthquake pulsating throughout the catacombs. Then after a few moments the ground stops shaking. All then goes quiet; only silence surrounds the warriors. The minions of Abaddon and all the beasts and vermin that roam the catacombs are knocked unconscious where they stood, covering the floors of the many passageways.

The warriors just stand there in silence, not sure of what just happened. Isolde turns to her companions, "We need to make haste. I only rendered them unconscious, for there were too many of them to deal with."

"Through this tunnel," Gobi tell Isolde, as he points to the last tunnel on the left.

Then quickly the group of warriors begin to navigate around the unconscious bodies lying throughout the passageways. Their pace is now quickened as they still have a ways to go to get to where the Watchers are imprisoned. Gobi guides the warriors through the many passageways; some are lit and many are not. The catacombs are an endless maze in which one wrong turn and one can be lost forever, never to find the way out, and where one would perish in the blackness of evil; only their skeletons would be left for one to contemplate the fate of the deceased.

Then after many kilometers of traveling within the confines of the catacombs, the company finally comes upon the Great Chamber where the Watchers are imprisoned. The warriors stand at its grand entrance and gaze upon the greatness and size of the chamber itself. The glow being emitted by the lit torches within chamber is brighter than what the dwarf sun emits at its zenith.

The call to war is near, as the army of the five kingdoms continue their march in the Dark Forest. They are about to enter the Valley of Lost Souls—the narrow passageway which leads up to the Great Plains which surround the evil castle where the Great War of the Second Age was fought. They will soon be in the shadows of the Dark Tower itself. Thus, with that, the War of the Fourth Age will soon commence.

Chapter XXI

The March through the Valley of Lost Souls

The army of the five kingdoms approach the hidden entrance where they will enter the hidden valley. Giselle dismounts her steed. She walks to the drapery of vines, which lies between the mountain walls, hanging to the ground like a window covering to block the scarlet hues of the dwarf sun from entering a room. She then pulls the vines to the side, uncovering the secret entrance, thus revealing the forest corridor known as the Valley of Lost Souls to all. Before moving forward, she begins to speak to the kings to warn them of the perils that they may face as they march forward.

"Your majesties, this part of the journey will be filled with many perils—huge arachnids, whose webs will be many, cave bears, antler bats, and many other foul beasts that survive in this environment. We must stay alert, for the darkness of the winter season is now upon us. The dwarf sun will be hidden from us until the Season of Awakening sprouts new life many, many days from now. The snow has piled high, as high as a height of a Warrow and is now blanketing the north land."

King Galen turns to the other kings. "Let us move the army inside the valley. There are many caves there where we can all escape this harsh weather. At least, for the time being."

The rest of the kings agree with King Galen's assessment and order their troops to move ahead.

As Giselle enters the valley, she waits at its entrance for Ursula to enter. As Ursula walks into the valley, she spots Giselle standing to one side of the entrance. She approaches her, for she can sense that Giselle wants to discuss the situation at hand

"You seem troubled, my lady," Ursula addresses Giselle.

"The Dark Tower is a little more than a day's march from here. If we can get through the valley without incident sometime tomorrow late in the day, we will arrive on the plains directly alongside the Dark Tower," Giselle states.

Ursula then looks up and gazes at the treetops. She notices the vast amount of arachnid webs covering the thick array of trees which hang over the designated path.

"I think we will have many an incidents between here and the castle. If, for nothing else, the proximity to the Dark Tower will have more of Abaddon's creatures milling about," Ursula answers.

"We have to pass through this valley first, which may be as treacherous as the battlefield we face ahead of us," Giselle retorts.

"What do you suggest?" Ursula asks.

"Let us lead the army through the valley. With our combined magic, we may be able to stop bad things before they happen," Giselle suggests.

"Seems logical," Ursula agrees.

Giselle and Ursula watch as the troops begin to enter the valley through the secret entranceway. Then the troops begin to settle in not far from the entrance, as there is safety in numbers, as to wander too far from one another can lead to an instant death from above or from a darkened cave.

Then once inside, the troops begin to explore the many caves located throughout the narrow valley.

One by one the caves are explored. Each cave is entered by a group of soldiers, with torches in hand lighting up each cave individually, as they are unsure of its inhabitants, if any. So far, the exploration is without incident, as the caves they have explored are empty of any life. All that remains are the many skeletons and scattered individual bones of the prey left behind by the predators who consumed them.

As Giselle looks at the steep inclines of the mountainsides, she notices pairs of glaring red eyes peering out of the caves above the valley floor. She nudges Ursula and points to the upper caves and whispers to her, "Wolfen. Many of them. There must be large packs of them living in the upper caves!"

"With all the troops pouring in, we just rang the dinner bell," Ursula interjects. The two sorceresses glance at one another.

The narrow valley is very still as the icy wind of winter is blocked by the tall spires of the mountain walls. The snow continues to fall in leaps and bounds on the valley floor which continues to accumulate, now piling up taller than an adult Warrow. The temperature feels like around 249.8 Kelvins, which is cold enough to freeze the body of a Tehran to the death if left exposed to the elements for a prolonged period of time.

Giselle motions for King Galen to come over to Ursula and herself. As he approaches the two sorcerers, Giselle points to the treetops and to the caves in the upper mountain walls. Galen stares at both for a moment, then says to the two, "We are not alone, not by any means!"

"No, my king, we are not," answers Giselle.

Then out of a distant cave come the roar of a large predator.

Its screams are echoing off the mountain slopes, sending its wail piercing throughout the valley, reverberating as far as sound would allow it to travel. A mammoth bear exits the cave with two Tehran soldiers locked in its massive jaws. Both soldiers are screaming in agony as their bodies are crushed under the pressure of its powerful jaws and its eighteen-centimeter-long fangs. Hundreds of arrows are flung in its direction by the soldiers of the five armies, many hitting its mark, but the bear runs expeditiously away from the mass of soldiers running toward it. Though covered in many arrows, the large mammal runs with the speed of a Wolfen, or so it seems. It then disappears into the bleakness of the dimindark, fading into the wall of snow fiercely falling from the dark sky; the sounds of its huge feet and claws muffled throughout the deep snow and that of the screaming soldiers, which can be heard fading into the distance.

"I was afraid something like this would happen, but not as quickly as it has," says Giselle, shaking her head.

"This, I fear, is only the beginning of what is yet to come," answers Ursula.

"The loud roar of the bear might have alerted the army of Abaddon. I will place some troops down deep into the valley as a precaution in case of an attack," King Galen says out loud to the sorceresses.

The tribe of Centaurs come forward and approach King Galen. The tribe asks to volunteer to scout ahead of the army to keep the path safe as the soldiers settle in to rest and eat a meal before moving forward, for the kings realize this will be the last meal for many.

The Centaurs, dressed in battle armor, begin to move silently through the deepening snow to venture deep into the valley; thus, within a few moments, are out of sight of Giselle, Ursula, and King Galen.

Galen then speaks under his breath, gazing toward the brave Centaurs, "May the spirits of the Ancient of Days be with you and protect your brave souls." The king says this prayer as he looks up to the heavens for affirmation.

Then large chunks of snow and ice begin falling to the valley floor, most just missing many of the soldiers. But some have struck a few soldiers, disabling them or killing them instantly in their wake by their immense size and shape. Then all in the valley look up to the treetops to see what has shaken them. There appears to be a lot of movement high above their heads. Many, many shadows appear to be moving fast among the thick branches, allowing more chunks of snow and ice to continue falling in vast amounts.

"Arachnids!" screams a soldier in despair.

Then all at once at least twenty giant arachnids, attached to their thick silk, begin to balloon down to the valley floor. They then pounce directly on the soldiers, who stand below them, engulfing them in their more than two-meter-long legs. As they grab onto the soldiers' bodies, the arachnids sink their thirty-centimeter fangs into their victims' necks, their blood gushing in streams four meters into the air. Tehrans and Warrows alike are both the victims of the foul beasts, which turns white snow to red with their spilled blood.

Many arrows are flung at the beasts and when struck the large arachnids' exoskeleton does not allow the arrows to penetrate their hides. But a few of the beasts are caught as they fall to the ground during their attack and are then mounted by many soldiers whose sharpened swords do penetrate deep into the cephalothorax of the beasts. And the continuous plunging into their hide rips apart the arachnids' organs and kills them instantaneously leaving their bodies sprawled on the valley floor; some with their victims still intact in their fangs, both lying dead in a pool of their own blood.

The attack only took seconds for the arachnids to execute. All in all, ten Tehrans and five Warrows have surrendered their bodies and their souls to the foul beasts.

There wasn't time enough for the sorceresses to react, for the attack happened so quickly.

Meanwhile . . .

The Centaurs have moved slowly down the valley, staying off the well-marked path while walking off to the sides near the mountain slopes. As the large eyes of this species allow them to see clearly in the dimindark, the warriors move cautiously in and out of the trees which abound the valley.

Then the warriors can hear the thud of footsteps coming toward them, as they appear to be getting increasingly louder with each step. The Centaurs then hide behind the perspective trees they are closest to. In the shadows of the valley, they spot two large Malakai with an escort of four Neanderthals coming straight at them. The twenty Centaurs then fill their bows with arrows and aim directly at the intruders. The Malakai have their nail-laden clubs resting on their large shoulders, ready to swing into action if needed. The Neanderthals have their sharpened wooden spears out in front of them, ready to plunge into their victims if need be. The foes walk cautiously as they must have heard the screams of the cave bear and have come to investigate the scream that has pierced the entire valley.

Moment by moment the foul beasts stride closer to where the Centaurs are positioned. Then about five meters away from where the Centaurs are waiting in the shadows, a Neanderthal who is in front of the pack stops. The beast sniffs the air around it, then feverously looks from side to side. The beast begins to grunt in its native language which sets the other Neanderthals into a tizzy.

The Neanderthal has picked up the scent of the Centaurs!

Then out of the shadows a barrage of arrows come flying directly at the foul beasts, killing all four Neanderthals in their tracks. The flung arrows have imbedded in the Neanderthals' bodies from head to toe, but barely wounding the large Malakai as their thick skin is almost impervious to the arrows flung by the warriors.

Quickly, the Centaurs spring into action and attack the two large cyclops with their swords, slicing at their limbs, as two Centaurs get cut down by the swinging nail-laden clubs of the Malakai. Two hoofed warriors have been embedded into the huge clubs and are now part of the weapon being used by the seven-meter-high beasts.

Then a multitude of arrows strike each of the beasts in their single eye, blinding them both. The Malakai feverishly swing their clubs in a frenzied manner but know not where their enemy stands. Their screams echo throughout the valley, thus the army of the five kingdoms can hear their screams from their position just inside the valley entrance. The Centaurs then change tactics and attack the Malakai from behind, driving their swords with all their strength deep into their heads and necks of the huge beasts. The blood of the beasts flow from the incisions which have been inflicted upon them. Then slowly each beast falls to the ground while taking their last breaths as they quickly die from their wounds.

The Centaurs, breathing heavily from the battle, just stand their ground, staring at their two dead comrades who are still impaled in the nails of their enemies' weapons.

"We cannot cremate their bodies now. It is too dangerous. We must push ahead. After the final battle, if we are still alive, we will come back and implement the Rising Ceremony properly," a Centaur advises.

"Leave the foul beasts where they lay for all of our enemies to see. They deserve that," another Centaur says.

Then the remaining warriors turn into the bleakness of the dimindark to continue their quest, moving ahead deeper into the Valley of Lost Souls.

Back at the soldier's camp

"What in the fuck was that?" Captain William blurts out, as the entire army stops from what they are doing and stares in the direction of where the screams have just come from.

"Death," answers King Leo.

"But to whom?" asks King Baltazar.

"We shall soon find out," Ursula answers.

Then overhead in the reflection of the twin moons, Giselle and Ursula can make out many shadowy figures flying above the treetops, heading in the direction of the Dark Tower.

The two stand there for a moment, confused at what they have just seen.

"Shadow Demons," Giselle says to Ursula in a startled voice.

"The evil lord must have called for them, for he knows deep in his wretched soulless body we are marching to the Dark Tower," Ursula states.

"He will muster all his strength in the final battle against us," Giselle says, as she turns and looks toward Ursula.

King Galen, as well as the other monarchs, have also spotted the shadowy figures flying across the darkened sky. They now realize that the window of opportunity for the attack is beginning to close. They must continue immediately with their march to the Dark Tower, for they now know deep in their souls that they will need to initiate this battle to begin as soon as possible before more reinforcements come to Abaddon's aid. For if the evil lord's army continues to grow, their chance of success will begin to falter, and quickly.

The kings and the sorceresses converge a meeting in front of a campfire, as they sit on oak logs to keep warm in the icy cold to discuss the ongoing situation which has just escalated.

"We need to move on immediately. We cannot wait another moment," remarks King Galen.

"I agree. We realize the troops need to rest, but if we wait, their rest could be permanent instead of temporary," remarks King Baltazar.

The Warrow kings and the sorceresses shake their heads in agreement.

King Galen then turns to Prince Vale and Captain William. "Get them up and in formation. We need to leave immediately," King Galen commands.

"Your Majesties, allow Ursula and I to lead the column. Our magic could be the difference between success and failure," Giselle states.

"As you wish, my lady," King Galen surmises.

"Do you think that's a good idea?" King Leo asks King Galen.

"They have powers you and I could not even guess to have," Galen answers the Warrow.

"I see your point, Galen. I see your point," Leo answers him.

"My other concern is for the Centaurs. I just hope they're okay after what we heard before," King Baltazar adds.

"Me too," King Galen answers, as the others shake their heads in agreement.

Then after a short while. "Your majesties, the army is in formation and ready for your commands," Prince Vale states to the kings.

The kings mount their steeds, then head to the lead of the column. Giselle and Ursula have placed their steeds five meters ahead of the kings' steeds. Giselle turns to the kings and says to them, "At your command, Your majesties."

King Galen turns to take a look at the column behind him, then he turns to face forward and looks at Giselle. "Forward, my ladies," he commands.

The column of soldiers then begins to move forward.

Captain William shouts out to the troops, "Keep your eyes and ears peeled all around and above you. We are moving into more dangerous territory now."

The campfires are left burning as the army has left in a haste. Their steeds walk at a steady pace as the heavy snow continues to fall on the valley floor creating a blanket of zero visibility ahead of them. The large draft horses make it easier for the Warrow ponies walking behind King Galen's steeds which has packed down the snow with their large hooves to make it easier for the ponies to navigate in the deepening snow

Torches are now carried by many a rider to add to the safety of the movement of the long column.

What's the difference now? Abaddon knows they are coming!

This far north, it's hard to differentiate between twilight and dimindark, for time in this evil realm has no meaning. Thus, the winter season will be bleak and dark for a long time to come, as this season is still in its infancy and will last much longer here as it would have farther south.

Just up the path, the column comes across the Malakai and the Neanderthals which were slayed by the Centaurs. Though two Centaurs remains are also left in the deepening snow, the soldiers realize with every battle there are consequences. The kings dismount their steeds and gaze over what's left of the battle scene. King Galen looks toward his sorceresses and says, "I wonder what else we will find ahead."

The upper caves on the mountain slopes seem alive with many pairs of glowing eyes staring down at the moving column. Occasionally, a loud barrage of howls echo over the valley from high above, keeping the soldiers aware of the danger they may encounter in their travels. The valley is full of body parts scattered along the path. Some appear to be from a fresh kill, while others are just remnants and skeletal parts which have been lying there for some time, or so it would appear from their condition.

After full days' ride, the Valley of Lost Souls makes a sharp right turn. It now heads directly toward the Dark Tower. At the turn, the tribe of Centaurs is waiting with fires burning and pots of tea brewing over them.

"Welcome to the end of the world," says *Trig*, one of the Centaur warriors.

"It does seem like it, doesn't it?" answers Ursula.

"Let us stop for a brief period, then we can move on," King Galen announces to all.

As the soldiers dismount their steeds, the blowing wind has picked and is now blowing at a steady gale with the open valley of the plains twenty kilometers directly ahead of the column.

Some of the warriors enter the many caves, which abound the foot of the mountains to escape the blowing wind and the freezing temperatures, as they drink cups of tea to try to warm themselves.

"We are sorry for your losses. We witnessed their remains on the path northward," King Baltazar says to the tribe of Centaur warriors.

"A thank you" is acknowledged from many of the Centaurs.

"We are on the last leg of our journey. Soon we will be at our destination," Giselle says out loud to anyone who is in earshot of her voice.

Then after a short time, King Galen addresses the troops, "Soldiers of Pangea, let us once again mount our horses and march the final leg of our journey to battle the ultimate evil. Let us ride as brothers, together, one last time."

The column of soldiers once again begins their march, now marching eastward directly toward the Dark Tower itself. A gale force wind is blowing the blizzard of snow directly into their faces, not allowing the soldiers to see more than a meter or so in front of them. The march of the five kingdoms continues steadily through the deepening snow and the howling wind. As they reach the valley's end, the landscape opens to the plains below them, revealing the armies of Abaddon camped throughout the entire landscape. Many fires abound with Evil's minions gathered around them, trying to warm themselves in the blistering cold.

The kings of the five kingdoms gather the troops together for one last time, and King Galen addresses them for the last time, "Tonight, we rest and enjoy a meal, for at the dawn of twilight, we will march to the Dark Tower and annihilate our enemy to claim victory for the freedom of our world."

The kings and the sorceresses then gather to analyze the situation at hand and to lay their plans for the upcoming invasion which is now just a short time away.

Chapter XXII

The Great Chamber

As the warriors enter the Great Chamber of the catacombs, they can feel the divine presence of the Spirit World abounding all around them; an essence of purity penetrating deep within their souls. A calmness permeates their being, for it is a feeling as if the weight of the world they have been carrying has been lifted off their shoulders. The companions move cautiously, heading for the source of the light. As they move, swords are drawn, bows are filled with arrows, their large eyes are opened wide, for they know what lies ahead as war comes closer to all. As the warriors move toward the imprisoned protectors, they gaze upon the next closest beings to the Ancient of Days—the creator of all that is.

"Do not cross into the circle of flames. It is the barrier which keeps the Watchers imprisoned, for you will be set afire and be burnt to a crisp," Isolde instructs the others.

The others back off and stay behind the White Witch.

As the warriors inch closer to the Watchers, a bitter cold pierces their bones, which is then accompanied by a feeling of dread which encroaches deep into their souls, for the evil Abaddon has encased their ambience in an evil spell which exists within the circle of flames that surround the prisoners. The White Witch is becoming more aware of the powers she possesses, for the magic instilled in her by her mother Elisheba has ingrained her powers deep within her subconscious which, after billions of seasons of life, is now finally beginning to surface. She knows now she must first break the evil spell keeping them at bay before she can free them from their chains.

The Watchers, all five of them, appear haggard, thin, and frail, as they all are lying in an inclined position scattered within the circle of flames, still bound by the heavy chains in which Abaddon has placed on each of them. As the warriors approach the Watchers, Oriel looks up at Isolde, and in a whisper, which is all the strength in which he can muster, says, "I see you have returned, Isolde. I have felt your presence for some time now."

"My dear Oriel, I have come to free you and the others from your bondage, for war is about to commence outside these walls in which we all must face together, for only together can we send Evil back to whence it came," Isolde answers him.

"I see you have brought reinforcements, my lady. We will need all the help we can get, for I have felt many souls enter the Spirit World as of late," interjects Raziel in a faint whisper.

"Oriel, Raziel, you will all again gain your strength and powers once the evil spell that surrounds you is broken," Isolde states.

"My lady, you have more powers than you know. Conjure them, then use them to do your bidding. But you must hurry, my lady, for I can feel that the army of Pangea is close and ready to do battle," Oriel whispers.

The companions appear uneasy, as Oriel's words resonate deep within their being.

"They are here?" Prince Quill asks in a startled voice.

Oriel closes his large eyes. He then becomes silent, seeking to acquire a vision of the goings-on in the outside world. Then after a long moment, in deep mediation, he opens his large eyes and looks at the prince and answers him, "The army of the kingdoms of Pangea are gathered at the edge of the valley overlooking the evil plains that surround this unholy citadel. They are gathering their strength and courage, ready to do battle as the dawn emerges from the dimindark. Your brother is with them, leading them in battle. You are the prince of the Northern Realm, are you not?"

"Yes, I am," Quill answers.

"Your brother has regained his strength. His mind is now clear, for he leads the army in memory of Ella, which has given him purpose and drive. For her soul and the souls of all the departed lying in the *Tomb of Eternal Life* are waiting for the day their souls can rise from their lifeless bodies through the ritual of the Rising Ceremony after *Evil is finally destroyed*, and the fear of their souls being stolen by Evil itself upon their ascension is finally extinguished," Raziel answers him.

"I promise, my dear Raziel, if we survive this war I will personally perform the sacred ceremony and send their souls to the Spirit Realm to be with the Ancient of Days," Quill answers him.

"Thank you, my prince. I know you are a Tehran of your word, for their souls seek eternal peace," Raziel answers him.

Then the travelers begin to hear a stirring in the outer chambers of the catacombs. It is as if the unconscious creatures that abound the maze of chambers are beginning to awaken from the spell Isolde has rendered on them.

"Do not fear the stirring in and about the chambers, for we are safe if we stay within the light of this chamber, for darkness is the ally of our enemy," Isolde preaches.

Isolde spreads her arms and commands her companions to retreat to the opposite side of the Great Chamber. And as they do, the White Witch bows her head and places her staff directly in front of her. She then grasps her staff with both hands and begins to speak in the language of the Alicorns, "Un lata, ena miligaan, sy in la kalour. De un ni sonier en haliaba." Translated into the Tehran tongue, "I command thee in the name of the Alicorns to break this barrier of evil."

Isolde then points the end of her staff at the invisible barrier surrounding the Watchers. The end of her staff projects a bolt of lightning so bright and so hot that all in the chamber must look away. The lightning bolt then spreads into many lightning bolts that surround the columns in which the invisible barrier has been placed throughout. The bolts of lightning encompass all around the prisoners, attaching itself to the circle of columns which is the source of the barrier created by the evil Abaddon. Then the bolts of lightning begin to sparkle brightly, then slowly they begin to fade until they are finally extinguished. The columns have disappeared with the sparkle of the fading lightning.

Isolde takes a deep sigh, then appearing exhausted, slowly walks over to Oriel. She then bends down on one knee and places her left hand on the shackles binding the oracle. As she releases her grip, the chains crumble into dust and crumble in a pile of ash on the stone floor. She then goes over to all of the other four oracles and does the same for each of them.

Finally, after ages of being in bondage, the Watchers are now free.

Isolde the walks back to Oriel, bends down, and caresses his face. She then kisses him on his forehead and whispers to him, "My dear Oriel, you are now free from Evil's grip."

"A million thanks, my lady. You have learned much in the short time since we last spoke. Your power is now at their fullest potential which is where they should be. You are a force to be reckoned with and have become an equal to us in the eyes of the Ancient of Days. The Ancient of Days has now appointed you as the *Watcher of Righteousness* and the *Commander of his Heavenly Army*. You are now the *Arc Angel of the Spirit World*. And all who live and breathe in this world, bow to you."

The Watchers all bow to Isolde, followed by her companions.

Then a bright light appears to fill the chamber, yet all can gaze upon it. The white light then becomes a steady pulsating glow. Oriel then speaks directly to Isolde, "Behold, my lady, the *Creator of All That Is*."

Then the *white pulsating light* speaks to Isolde, "Isolde, daughter of Limrath and Mira, thus raised by the mighty Elisheba, I grant to thee Divine Powers. The words you speak will be the words spoken in the *Spirit Realm*. The deeds you do will be with my blessing."

Then a white beam of light engulfs the White Witch which then transforms her into *Spirit* and *Flesh*, thus becoming a divine disciple of the Ancient of Days and his commander of his *Spiritual Army*. She is now truly the *White Witch*.

The bright white light then begins to gradually fade. Isolde then emerges from its eternal glow, revealing her transformation. Isolde's flesh has transformed to a pure white, while the irises of her large eyes are now platinum blonde in color. Her long flowing salt and pepper hair is now pure black with tints of royal purple throughout. Her attire is now a white, sheer, long flowing dress whose train flows a meter behind her, for she is now truly a divine being.

The Ancient of Days now speaks directly to Isolde again, "Isolde, thy staff will now be thy weapon. Use it wisely and use it fiercely against thine enemies. Now, go, for the army of our enemy is gathering its strength to begin their attack."

With that, the white light brought forth by the Ancient of Days slowly fades, taking with him all five of the Watchers. Thus, the Great Chamber reverts to being lit once again by the torches attached to its walls.

As all of this is happening in the Great Chamber, the dark magic shielding the Watchers from any attempt of escape or communication to others through their ability of telepathy has been lifted by the magic of Isolde.

Ursula and Giselle all at once become overwhelmed with a wave of goodness which penetrates deep within their being. Ursula turns to Giselle and blurts out, "Did you feel that?"

"I felt it," Giselle answers. Giselle then closes her large eyes and lifts her head to the heavens and continues to speak, "The Watchers have been set free. Isolde has done it."

"All praise Isolde," Ursula responds.

"We must tell the kings, for this is our advantage in battle," Giselle states.

"I am sure Aveline has felt it, too," Ursula surmises.

"I'm sure she has, for she is what we are," Giselle answers her.

The sorceresses walk to where the kings have congregated. They explain to the kings and the commanders of their armies the feelings they have both experienced and have been overcome with, what it means going forward in the upcoming battle, and how they can use it to their advantage.

In the middle of their conference, Raziel, the Watcher who oversees all life on the world of both animal and flora, appears out of thin air and presents himself to the kings and the sorceresses in conference. He bows to all in the cave, and then he begins to speak, "My lords, the Watchers have been freed from the bondage that the evil Abaddon has placed on us. We will assist you in your quest, for your quest is also ours. We shall use every power instilled in us by the almighty Ancient of Days to defeat the evil Abaddon and his army. Allies to the end."

Raziel then places his right arm across his chest and bows to them once again. With that, said Raziel slowly vanishes.

King Galen the turns to his commanders. "Have the army prepare for battle."

As Isolde turns to face her companions, they all bow in unison to the new Watcher.

Gobi looks up at Isolde and says to her, "Wowser! Wowser! You sure do know how to make a statement, my lady!"

"Thank you, Gobi. Are you ready to lead the way once again?" Isolde asks him.

"Oh yes, my Lady Isolde. I am at your service, of course," Gobi insists.

"Then let us move forward," Isolde interjects.

Gobi points to one of the exits that lead out of the Great Chamber and says, "This way! This way!"

The band of companions then follows Isolde, with Gobi on her shoulder, to the exit he has indicated.

This passageway is lit with torches placed on its walls every five meters or so. Galgaliel grabs one of the torches in the passageway, as he and Amolo are once again defending their flank. This passageway is without any other tunnel intervening with it, therefore there is no other means of escape in case of an attack either fore and aft. This tunnel is free of vermin, for nothing is moving inside it, except the travelers. After about two kilometers, the passageway appears to be getting warmer with each step forward.

"Did somebody turn on the heat?" asks Philo.

"It has gotten unusually hot all at once," interjects Prince Quill.

"Magma," Gobi spurts out.

"Magma?" Harlee Antonia questions.

"There are many volcanic mountains in this chain whose tubes run under the ground, making many caverns. Some have magma running through them, while others don't," Isolde answers.

"It feels like 326 Kelvins," Galgaliel surmises.

"Now we know why nothing lives here. The heat will do it," Ivy interjects.

Then as the passageway comes to an end, it opens up to another large chamber. The heat is now immense; much hotter than the passageway. The travelers can see two rivers of magma flowing freely. The magma is divided by an island about twenty meters round in its center. This island's platform sits about five meters above the magma flow. Many body parts and of different species are scattered throughout the island.

As the companions approach closer from their chosen path, which is cut into the side walls of the large chamber where it continues alongside the flowing magma, they notice an element of torture situated in the middle of this small island—a *pendulum*. An ancient method of torture that has not been used or seen since before the Great War of the Second Age, and then it was only used by Evil himself, for it is the cruelest method of torture ever invented. It then leads to a slow death by slowly cutting a being in half one pendulum swing at a time, which is beyond the pale of any kingdom of any conscience.

"Look! Look!" yells Philo.

The company gazes at the small island from their path and realizes that a Tehran is strapped to a long table in the middle of the island by thick metal chains; he is lying on his back. His hands and feet are spread wide, as if he was being pulled apart and like the process of being drawn and quartered. A pendulum held by a large wooden bracket attached to the table hangs over him swinging furiously back and forth. The swish of its movement can be heard over the sounds of the flowing magma. With each pass, the pendulum descends lower and lower, trickling closer to its victim.

The Tehran strapped to the table is screaming in fear, for he cannot break the chains that have bound him.

"Holy shit, look at that contraption! What the fuck is it?" Ivy asks out loud.

The rest of the companions are dumbfounded by what they are seeing, for they have never witnessed such a method of torture before.

"A pendulum. An ancient form of torture not seen in billions of seasons," Isolde answers Ivy.

"Who would use such a thing?" Philo asks.

"Evil. Only Evil would use this," Isolde retorts.

"We need to help him. But how? I don't see any way to get over to him," Quill remarks.

"Look! Neanderthals guarding him. Four of them," Philo remarks.

"They are too far for our arrows to be accurate," the other Warrows remark.

"We need to help him, now!" Quill insists.

"Look, over there!" Harlee points to a winding staircase.

Looking up, the company notices a stone bridge that is attached to the wall of the cavern which is directly above their heads.

"Let's go!"

Galgaliel then turns, with Amolo on his back, and begins to head to the staircase, followed by Prince Quill and the band of Warrows.

The group ascends the winding staircase, then across the narrow stone bridge, runs as fast as their legs will let them in a single file. The Neanderthals are whooping, hollering, and jumping in the air as to egg on the rescuers to challenge them.

As the group descends the staircase, which leads down to the island, the Neanderthals are waiting at the bottom of the staircase. Galgaliel is in the lead position and can see their wooden spears, peering on the sides of the bottom of the staircase. Before Galgaliel reaches the bottom, he leaps over the top of the Neanderthals, and as he does, he cuts two of them with his swinging sword. As he lands, Amolo shoots two sets arrows into the wounded Neanderthals and kills them both. The Warrows behind the Centaur have their golden swords drawn and attack the two remaining Neanderthals. One of the spears plunges into the shoulder of one of the Warrows, leaving a gash which starts to bleed down his left arm. The other Warrows challenge both beasts and plunge their swords deep into the remaining Neanderthals, killing them both.

Quill, stepping down from the last stair, instantly runs in the direction of the bound Tehran, leaping over the dead Neanderthals as he does.

"Quick we have to free him!" Quill shouts at the others.

As the group approaches the pendulum, the sound of it swinging back and forth give way to the immense force this form of torture instills.

The pendulum is now less than eight centimeters away from cutting the bound Tehran.

"Watch out for the pendulum, for it can kill us if we are in the way when it swings!" Galgaliel yells.

As the half-moon-shaped blade, about sixty centimeters wide, swings back and forth at a furious pace, it keeps getting closer to its victim with each and every swing.

"I can't stop it!" yells Quill, as the pendulum is now about 3.8 centimeters away from cutting into the bound Tehran.

"We have to do something!" Philo yells at Quill.

Then the pendulum begins to make a slash into the Tehran's loose clothing. He screams in terror, but there doesn't appear to have any way to stop the pendulum's momentum.

Galgaliel swings his sword at the pendulum as it passes over the victim, but it doesn't slow it down at all. The next swing begins to cut slightly into the midsection of the bound Tehran. A trail of blood shoots into the air.

"We have to stop this thing!" yells Quill.

The following swing of the pendulum cuts a little deeper, and the Tehran screams in agony as the blade is beginning to pierce his organs.

Quill feverously tries to unclasp the chains, which have bound him, but to no avail, for they are thick and heavy and will not budge. He then tries to pull at them to loosen them, but he cannot. Galgaliel tries to cut them with his sword and swings it again and again, but his attempts go unanswered.

Again, the pendulum swings are cutting deeper into its victim. This time it cuts deep, taking part of his intestines with it as it swings back and forth, sending his insides into the air, then splattering them on the island floor in a pool of blood. The victim's blood is now splattering all around the small island, covering the attempted rescuers from head to toe.

The pendulum swings again now, cutting midway through the Tehran, as more of his insides go splattering all over the island floor. He screams one last time as the blade finally cuts him in half.

The bound Tehran now lies dead under the swinging blade. His body, now cut in half at the waist, and his insides and blood scattered across the stone floor in the middle of the island.

The pendulum then stops swinging as it cuts deep into the side of the table of torture. Then the only sound that can be heard is the stream of magma flowing in their basins on both sides of the soldiers.

"Oh, Lord of the Spirits, how is this allowed to happen?" Philo asks tearfully.

"What a horrible way to die," Galgaliel remarks.

The companions stand there in shock at what they have just witnessed and break down in their mourning of the fallen.

"Who was he?" Philo asks, wiping away his tears.

Quill looks around the island for any signs of where the Tehran might have come from.

Then in a corner of the island, he notices battle armor. He recognizes it as his own. The prince walks over to the discarded pile of armor. He kneels before them. He then turns to his companions. "He was one of my soldiers," he says in a mournful voice.

"Are you sure?" Philo asks him, as he looks to Turak.

"I'm sure. This is the armor of my armies," Quill answers him.

"We are so sorry," Galgaliel says in sympathy.

Quill nods his head in acknowledgment and thanks.

"There is nothing else we can do here. We need to move on, my lord," Turak says to Quill in a respectful tone.

"How many others have also been in his place before, I wonder?" Quill says out loud.

Quill takes a last glance at him, then calls the others to follow him to move on. Before the prince exits the island, he grabs some of the victim's clothing still attached to the discarded armor. He dips a small portion of the clothes into the flowing magma in which the clothes immediately catch fire. He then throws the incinerated clothing onto the pendulum, engulfing the apparatus of torture and the dead Tehran soldier still attached to it. Then the flames suddenly reach ten meters into the air. Quill stares at the blaze, but just for a moment. Then turns to join the others. "Let's go."

As the small group returns to the others waiting for them across the bridge on the other side of the flow of magma, Quill says not a word to anyone but motions to them to move forward.

As the companions move on the passageway in the opposite direction from the flow of magma, the air slowly starts to cool. The torch-lighted pathway is straight without any intersecting tunnels. The group travels about a kilometer or so, then suddenly the tunnel comes to an abrupt end. It is blocked by an iron door encasing the parameter of the tunnel itself.

"On the other side of the door : . . . the Dark Tower," Gobi say in a petrified squeaky voice.

Isolde turns to her companions. "Try to move in the shadows and stay as quiet as you possibly can."

Swords are drawn and bows are filled with multiple arrows in anticipation of the beginning of the encounter of the end of all things.

The companions stand there and gaze at one another, terrified. What will they face once the iron door opens?

As Isolde approaches the iron door, it begins to open from someone or something on the other side of it. Isolde quickly jumps back in a ghast, as the door slowly begins to open.

Neanderthals . . . Six of them, at least.

As the beasts step into the passageway, they spot the intruders.

Before the Neanderthals can react, arrows are flung at their direction, hitting five of them. Unfortunately, one goes untouched and begins to back up out of the passageway. The beast turns and begins to run to alert the other minions of Abaddon.

Quill darts out of the passageway and watches as the surviving Neanderthal clamors away from him, hurling his arms into the air to catch the eyes of one of his comrades. Quill then throws his sword in its direction and hits it at full stride directly in the center of its back. The beast falls onto the cobblestone floor just inside the castle walls, face first. Quill runs up to the fallen beast and to make sure he is dead pulls out his dagger, he then plunges it into the back of the beast's neck, assuring his demise.

Quill then drags the impaled body back into the passageway, then closes the iron door behind him. He then removes the sword from his back and turns to his companions. "The way seems clear now," he insists.

After the group collects their thoughts and calms themselves, Isolde then slowly opens the door. She sticks her head through the opening and looks both ways along the cobblestone walkway. She sees that no other being is in her range of vision. She then turns to her companions and whispers, "Let's go. Quickly!"

One by one the companions follow Isolde's path in a single line out onto the cobblestone walkway.

They are now within the castle walls.

The companions hug the walls as they move forward. Isolde, who has not stepped foot inside this evil tower in over 2 million seasons, for it was then, when she vanquished the evil Naamah, back to the Underworld on these very walls.

"Do you remember the way?" Quill whispers to Isolde.

"Vaguely," she responds.

The group continues to move forward, staying in the shadows. They regroup in a dark out cove so Isolde can get her bearings. Then all at once a shuffling begins. Footsteps, many of them coming from all directions, moving fast, thus, moving about all around the intruders. The companions cluster together, moving to the back of the alcove so as to not be seen by their enemy.

A large horn then blurts its call; a single blaring note rings long and deep from atop the castle walls penetrating throughout the surrounding landscape.

A call to war has begun!

Chapter XXIII

The Longest Day

"When the horns of war sound deep into the forest, the final conflict between righteousness and the damned will change the course of all life on Pangea."
–Isolde, The White Witch, as she prophesied before the final battle of the Great War of the Second Age.

A bedlam has begun throughout the Dark Tower. The cobblestone floors that line the castle vibrate violently with the footstep of many Malakai and their now allies, the Neanderthals—the staple of Abaddon's army. The beasts race vigorously to their assigned positions, being directed by the minions whom Abaddon has adopted as his commanders. In the distance, the companions hiding in the darkened alcove can hear the loud footsteps of the army of Pangea, plunging through the deepened snow. Their steps pound the ground in unison as they march down the forest slopes heading directly toward the plains which surround the Dark Tower.

Isolde shushes her comrades, then says to them in a whisper, "Listen, do you hear that?"

All the hidden warriors listen intently. Then after a moment she whispers again to all, "The army has arrived."

As the kings continue their march down the slope leading onto the plains, in the distance they can see the remnants of a line of X crosses still with skeletons attached to them, standing out above the snow-laden ground.

King Galen, leading the army, suddenly stops their forward motion, as he gazes onto the plains.

"Look!" King Galen says to the other monarchs, as he points to the line of crosses.

"Lord of the Spirits, what has the evil lord done?" King Baltazar says in a gasp.

"He has sent a message to all who look upon his carnage," Giselle answers.

"A message. What message?" asks King Baltazar.

"All who defy his word shall pay with their lives," Giselle retorts.

"That has always been Evil's message," Ursula concludes.

"Yes, Ursula, but this message is directed at us," Giselle concludes.

"He will answer for all his misdeeds to us, for today will be his judgement day, and we will sentence him to the gallows," King Galen states.

Then after a moment of solitude, as all gaze upon the tortured dead in disbelief, King Galen motions for the column to continue.

The plains are adorned with many contained fires which are being used by the army of the dark lord to warm themselves in the frigid cold of the winter season. The beasts camped on the plains begin to come together to regroup to the ready themselves for battle. The snow continues to fall zealously and has been continuous for many, many days, accumulating now up to the bellies of the draft horses, almost two meters high.

The sound of footsteps of the approaching army grows louder and louder in each passing moment, as the mass of five thousand move closer to the castle with every step. The walkways of the castle walls begin to fill with the minions of Abaddon as to protect their lord in case of a breach from the army of his enemy.

The horn of war continues to sound the alarm of an incoming invasion in its one bland tone, blurting into the surrounding landscape and assuring their enemy that the evil army protecting the castle is preparing to defend their domain to the death.

Black shadowy figures resembling Tehrans, adorning batlike wings can be seen flying toward the castle itself.

Ursula catches a glimpse of something moving in the sky above the plains as she looks upward. She sees dark figures flying directly to the Dark Tower.

Ursula gasps and grabs the arm of Giselle. "Shadow Demons," Ursula remarks to Giselle.

Both sorceresses just stare at the flying figures. Then Giselle turns to the kings and points to the sky. "Look!" she says with trepidation.

"What are they?" King Leo gasps.

"Dark warriors created by Evil itself. Shadow Demons as he has called them, conjured in the bowels of the Underworld, answering only to the Great Evil, like a plague beginning to spread throughout the land that will destroy everything in their path," Ursula answers the Warrow king.

The Shadow Demons, as many as twenty in number, land in unison on the top of the turrets of the Dark Tower, shoulder to shoulder. They stand in unison and gaze upon the looming battlefield and at the army of the righteous in despise, as their black batlike wings open wide to project the aura of dominance over all who reject Evil's will.

Then the Iron Gates of the Dark Tower slowly begin to open. The chains pulling the gates open ring loudly in a synchronized fashion which can be heard far onto the far end of the plains. Once fully opened, Neanderthals—alongside the giant cyclops, the Malakai—begin to come forth. The ground shakes with their forward motion. The Neanderthals are adorned with their wooden spears, while the Malakai carry their nail-laden clubs almost as large as the size of an adult Tehran. Shoulder to shoulder, they march onto the plains and moving away from the Dark Tower, encompassing huge numbers with their intimidating size and scope.

The army of Pangea continues their trek onto the plains until the last of the soldiers reach the battlefield.

The five kings and the army of Pangea then come to a halt about five hundred meters from their enemy. Then the army of the five kingdoms lines up behind the kings as one. Both armies come to a standstill and face one another in defiance. The army of the five kingdoms line up as such: the Centaurs stand directly behind the line of kings, some with bow and arrows in hand while others firmly grip their swords; on their flanks, the Warrow army stands fast with their bows filled with arrows; while the Tehran's two thousand on horseback are surrounded by the balance of their brethren on foot. All are adorned with the armor of the kingdoms they represent. The army they face is ten thousand strong.

Malakai and Neanderthals stand side by side, as the huge cyclops, maybe more than a thousand strong, wait alongside their smaller ally for the command from the evil Abaddon to commence their attack.

As the snow continues to fall hard, with the wind blowing steadily at a gale, a deadly silence has fallen over the plains; a standoff of two great armies has commenced—Good versus Evil . . . One last time.

As the thunder of footsteps, which have clamored through the deepening snow, have faded into silence, Isolde realizes that *now* is the time to strike. She motions to her comrades to move forward and follow her, as the passageways of the castle have become eerily silent, for the soldiers of Evil have placed themselves in position to receive their enemies with all their might.

"Quickly, while their attention is focused on our allies! We must get into position and wait for the battle to commence. Then when all their attention is focused on the battle on the plains, we will strike," Isolde whispers to her companions.

The companions move quickly down the hallways and up the staircases that head toward the turrets where the evil lord will position himself to oversee the forthcoming battle. As the group moves higher and higher leading to castle's pinnacle, the sound of footsteps moving around begins to grow louder. Isolde can see the silhouettes of their enemies in the distance, moving about from room to room. As they get closer to where all the movement is appearing to come from, the warriors spread out so as to be able to fight on many fronts.

Isolde points to each warrior to make sure they are far enough apart to assist one another in case of an unexpected attack from out of the darkness and to spare as many lives as she possibly can.

Then a stray pair of Neanderthals cross their path. Galgaliel steps in front of them, now with Amolo, Turak, and Philo on his back. Then the small warriors fill the bodies of the beasts with multiple arrows, killing them dead in their tracks. Then Quill runs up to be alongside the Centaur, as the Daughters of Shayla move to both sides of his flank, followed by the tiny Warrows.

They approach another set of stairs that head upward, and with Isolde again leading the group, the companions move cautiously and slowly up the winding staircase. The closer the companions get to the upcoming floor the murmur of the beasts become louder.

Isolde turns and motions with her finger perpendicular to her lips to remain silent. As the group approaches the top, Isolde peeks out of the staircase and into the adjoining hallway. To her right, she sees the last staircase which leads to the turrets of the Dark Tower. Standing at its base is a Malakai of great stature, guarding its entrance. Isolde backs away and turns toward her companions. "Shit, there is a Malakai guarding the entrance to the staircase that leads to the turrets."

"We need to take it out," Quill states.

"As arrows will not penetrate its thick skin, we will need to plunge our swords into it, preferably into its head," Galgaliel claims.

"It's almost seven meters tall," Harlee states, as she peeks around the corner. "It is one big fucker," she then declares.

"We need to draw him away from the entrance," Isolde whispers.

Turak and Philo look at one another, then Turak whispers to all, "I got an idea!"

"I hate your ideas. Every time you get an idea, I get hurt," Philo answers him.

"Well, this time you may get dead," Turak retorts.

"Well, that would be a pleasant change," Philo answers him.

Gobi turns to Isolde and asks her, "Are they always like this?"

Isolde shakes her head up and down, then rolls her large eyes.

"Listen, Philo and I will draw the Malakai away from the stairs. Then as he chases us, you all kill it. Simple," Turak shares with the group.

Philo peeks around the corner, then turns to Turak and asks him, "Do you see how big it is?"

"Yes."

"Do you see the size of the club it's carrying?"

"Yes."

"And you still think it's a good idea?"

"Yes, yes, and yes," Turak gives his final answer.

"Okay then, let's do this," Philo answers. He then adds, "But if I die, I'm blaming you."

"You always blame me, anyway, for everything," Turak answers him.

Amolo shakes his head and says something in the Wiki language to both Warrows. Both react by saying at the same time, "Shut up, Amolo!"

Turak and Philo tiptoe into the hallway. Turak motions to Philo to move back down the hallway, away from the other companions to draw the beast to them. Both Warrows load their bows with two arrows each and drop their arms by their side to not make the obvious as to not be seen before they are ready. Once positioned where they want to be, both Warrows begin to antagonize the huge beast. They jump up and down, waving their arms and calling it names. The Malakai turns and spots the tiny warriors. He then becomes enraged, being goateed by such tiny things. He begins to snort. His large eyes become enflamed with anger. He lifts his large club above his head, puffs out his chest, and begins to aggressively move toward the Warrows. As the beast comes within four meters of the Warrows, both Turak and Philo lift their bows and take aim at the cycloptic eyes of the beast. All four arrows penetrate directly in the large beast's single eye. The Malakai drops the huge nail-laden club and covers its eye with both hands. It then drops to its knees in writhing pain, letting out a hollow yell which is all it can muster being mute.

Then out of the adjoining hallway, Galgaliel and Prince Quill attack the beast from behind. Galgaliel leaps onto the Malakai's back and plunges his sword deep into the beast's neck which protrudes out its front. Quill leaps over the Centaur, then plunges his sword into the back of the Malakai's head, sending it through its forehead. The Malakai falls forward onto the cobblestone floor in a pool of its own blood, dead on impact.

"Well, that wasn't too bad," Turak remarks.

Philo glares at his companions and remarks, "Wasn't too bad . . . are you kidding?"

Isolde then whispers to all, "We need to move silently up the staircase. We don't know what's up there, so be prepared for anything."

Isolde cautiously walks up to the staircase. She peeks up toward the doorway at the top. The coast is clear, but there appear to be a lot of movement on top of the turret. She sees a bright aura projecting from the landing surrounding the turret, sending its glow down into the hallway where the companions are standing. The aura begins to intensify; thus, its brightness is now blinding to Isolde and her companions. The warriors shade their large eyes so as to not look directly into the blinding light.

Isolde turns to her companions and points up the staircase and says to all, *"Abaddon."*

The two armies stand fast, facing one another and awaiting commands from either commander to begin the assault.

King Galen turns to his army to give inspiration to all. "Soldiers of Pangea, today is the day we take back our world from tyranny, oppression, and evil. It will be written down in the annals of history how we fought for our freedom. Fight and die with honor. And may the Lord of the Spirits bless us all."

Then once again the great horn on the castle wall begins to blow its monotone blare out onto the battlefield. Its sound is long and loud, echoing throughout and sending its projection deep through the plains and into the surrounding forest signaling the beginning of the attack.

Abaddon is now standing on the turret overlooking the battlefield; his large crown sitting on his head, sending a blinding glow of light out into the sky surrounding the evil lord. He lifts his arms to the heavens in defiance of his spiritual brother, the creator of all things. Then flames shoot out, extending from his hands into the heavens above, as the evil lord laughs loudly as if he is invincible to all.

Suddenly, the snow abruptly halts, the clouds begin to separate, and the flames protruding from the evil lord's hands begin to extinguish.

The Watchers have arrived.

The armies begin to charge one another. Their battle cries echo through the plains. Then from above, a flock of pterodactyls begins to swoop down toward the Dark Tower. The Shadow Demons take to the air to do battle with the prehistoric beasts. Queen Lazuli, atop of Samael, leads the attack from the sky, with Aveline atop *Myra*, Samael's mate, flying side by side with her queen.

On the battlefield, the opposing armies' slaughter is spewing all over the plains. Malakai, Neanderthals, Warrows, Centaurs, and Tehrans alike lie either dead or wounded throughout the battlefield which range in the thousands.

Then from behind Abaddon's army, a centenary of Centaurs dash out of the surrounding forest and begin to attack the army of evil, attacking them on their flank. Ormarath and his warriors have answered the call to battle, inflicting the evil army with a great many casualties. The pterodactyls have drawn the Shadow Demons higher into the sky, tearing at their bodies, shredding their flesh, and sending many of them falling to their death. The remaining Shadow Demons scatter and fly away from the battlefield, realizing defeat.

Then Queen Lazuli directs her pterosaurs to attack their enemies on the battlefield. Samael leads the flock down, directing their attack on the huge Malakai, shredding their flesh, and amputating their limbs with their long and sharp beaks.

The army of evil is now surrounded on all sides by the soldiers of Pangea.

Abaddon becomes enraged and his aura intensifies. Isolde and her companions rush up the steps which lead to the turret where Abaddon is located. As Isolde bursts out onto the turret, she is met by the evil lord's protectors who are surrounding him, both Neanderthals and Malakai. The rest of her companions burst out from behind her onto the turret and begin to engage their enemies, swinging their swords and lashing their arrows at their foes.

Abaddon turns to face the White Witch. She and the evil lord now stand five meters apart. Abaddon moves his hands forward with his palms facing the sky, then balls of flames begin to accumulate in his palms then begin to enlarge. Isolde points the end of her staff at the evil lord.

Abaddon blurts out at Isolde, "You, witch! You think you can defeat me? I am the king of this world. You shall be my slave for all eternity!"

Isolde stares at the evil lord and angrily answers him, "Sorry to disappoint you, but you shall die by my hand."

As Abaddon begins to lift his arms with the balls of flames in his palms intensifying, Isolde shoots a whip of lightning out of the end of her staff, which wraps around the evil lord's neck like a lasso. Isolde then flicks the end of the fiery whip, and the end attached to her staff wraps around one of the juts on top of the turret, sending Abaddon flying off the turret to hang from the end of the fiery whip two meters from its end. The evil lord struggles to remove the fiery whip from its neck, and the more he struggles the tighter it becomes, as Oriel levitates five meters in front of him, assuring that he will not succeed.

Isolde then steps onto the edge of the turret, staring down at the evil lord struggling to free himself. She leans over the side and speaks to him, "Now, you piece of shit, you shall feel my wrath!"

Isolde plunges her staff into the fiery crown of the evil lord. Upon impact, Abaddon's hanging body explodes, sending a shock wave so intense it can be felt beyond the Palace of the Rising Sun and out into the Southern Ocean. All life on Pangea suddenly comes to a stop.

The clouds, which have covered the supercontinent, begin to disperse. The storm, which has persisted since the beginning of time over the Black Mountains, begins to stop, and for the first time in the history of the world, the evil mountains are not covered in storm clouds. The dwarf sun shines on the mountain tops for the first time.

The Centaurs in their mountain top village gaze at a sight they have never seen before—the scarlet rays bringing warmth to the air and the ground below their hooves.

{The Fourth Age gives way to a new era and a new beginning.}

The battle happening on the plains comes to a halt as all the participants stop and gaze at the turret, then all becomes silent. Isolde then stands erect. She holds her staff above her head. The end of the staff begins to glow orange. She gazes down at the battlefield and points the end of her staff at her enemies and a flame shoots out of its end, aiming directly at the Malakai and Neanderthals clustered together. A ball of fire, with the intensity of the dwarf sun, incinerates thousands of the soldiers of evil, burning them to a crisp where they stand.

The remnants of Abaddon's army, who have survived, begin to flee the battlefield to run for their lives. A cheer of victory is given by the soldiers of Pangea, as the battle has been won and tyranny has been defeated.

Battered and cut, Philo and Turak lean upon each another to hold each other up. Philo looks toward Turak, then gazes up at the dwarf sun. He then says to his companion, "Looks like the Season of Awakening may be early this time."

Both laugh and hug one another, happy to be alive and still breathing Pangean air.

CHAPTER XXIV

The Aftermath

As the dust settles over the plains of battle, the dead, which number in the thousands, lie scattered across the battlefield. Their blood and guts permeate into the ground, spreading the fluids they gave their lives for and absorbing deep into the ground below the field of battle. Much of their blood lies on top of the white snow in a dark red canvas.

Isolde, still standing on the jut on top of the turret, calls loudly, so all on the battlefield can hear her plea, for she knows what lies ahead. "Quickly, leave the battlefield, head for the hills, or into the castle, for another massacre will soon follow!"

The soldiers look from one to another, for they know not what she refers to, but they will listen to her plea. Quickly, the warriors begin to follow her instructions, for they will not question the slayer of Abaddon the Destroyer.

"We cannot leave the dead to just lie there and rot," Quill states to Isolde.

"They will not rot, my prince, for they will be consumed," Isolde answers him.

"Consumed, by who?" Galgaliel interjects.

Isolde turns to the Centaur. "Galgaliel, it's not by who but by what. You shall see," Isolde answers.

Most of the soldiers who have survived the war begin to wander off the field of battle. Moments later, the ground begins once again to shake.

A panic can be felt amongst the remaining soldiers. The shaking begins to intensify. Then there is movement below the snow, as the ground begins to surge upward like hills beginning to protrude all over where the battle has just taken place.

Many mounds surge upward at a terrifying pace, injecting fear into the souls of all who are witnessing this phenomenon.

Then the top of the mounds burst open like a volcano's pyroclastic explosion. Blood ants begin to explode out of the calderas, sending gasps throughout the ranks. The survivors watching this carnage cower in fear, as the thirty-centimeter insects cover the battlefield with their presence as they begin to consume the remains of the dead. Pieces of flesh are torn and consumed on the spot by the insects. The ground darkens even more with the blood of the freshly killed warriors of both sides oozing out of their bodies with each bite of the large ants.

Isolde turns to her comrades. "There is nothing we can do to stop what is happening. Nature is taking its course."

Queen Lazuli and Aveline have landed the pterodactyls on the walls on top of the castle. They dismount the beasts and walk toward Isolde and her companions. The remaining kings have also entered the turret and are now all standing together high above the plains, watching the consumption by the ants in disgust.

The ants forage until the twilight begins to fade and the dimindark begins to rise over the battlefield. The insects then return en masse to the calderas from whence they came. The battlefield is now quiet. The only remnants of the warriors who gave their lives in battle are their skeletons, picked clean of their flesh and lying in their own blood, for their guts have also been eaten as the blood ants are not picky with what they will eat.

"Your majesties, we need to burn the entire battlefield to cleanse it of all that has happened upon it, and to give final rest to our honored dead so their souls may have a chance to rise up to the Spirit World," Isolde pleads to the monarchs.

The kings and the queen agree.

Oil is then spread throughout the battlefield by the remaining soldiers of the five kingdoms covering the skeletons and the grasses.

Isolde, Giselle, Aveline, and Ursula then walk down to the battlefield and bless all who have given their lives in battle, both friend and foe, for they were all brave in their actions and all are deserving of the proper respect by all.

The sorceresses call on Limrath, the Gatekeeper of the Spirit World, and the Ancient of Days to open to gates for the fallen heroes so their souls can enjoy everlasting life in peace and solitude together with their loved ones, who have departed before them.

As the battlefield is set ablaze by the remaining army of Pangea, along with the monarchs, they bow their heads in respect. They grieve the loss of their friends and comrades with whom they have fought side by side with.

The massive fire burns throughout the night, sending its flames fifteen meters up into the sky, lighting up the surrounding forest brighter than the dwarf sun would illuminate the world at its pinnacle during the twilight. The remaining warriors gaze upon the burning field, as the souls of the dead are released and ascend to the Spirit World. The wounded are brought inside the castle walls and are attended to by those appointed as healers by their crowns.

Hearths are lit and a sparce amount of food is cooked over them, such as mutton and bison. But the mood is somber, at best, for the grieving for the dead has only just begun.

The kings, the queen, and the sorceresses gather in the great room of the Dark Tower to have a final meal together and to discuss how the world moves on from here.

"This castle is evil, for it will never be exorcised of the darkness that abounds here," Isolde remarks.

"These woods and this fortress will always be controlled by Evil, for this has been its domain since the beginning of time and space," Aveline interjects.

Oriel then appears to the monarchs now gathered, his aura lights up the room with a golden projection that surrounds his spirit.

He bows to the kings and queen. He then turns to Isolde and bows to her specifically, then speaks to all gathered, "Your majesties, my dear ladies of enlightenment, it is with great thanks that you have set the world back on a path of righteousness. We must always be aware of the darkness that lurks in the shadows and will always be ready to show itself again and again, given the chance. Return to your kingdoms ands, build back the life you once had. We shall always be watching out for all that thrives in this world. May the Ancient of Days bless you with the goodness he possesses."

The spirit of Oriel then slowly fades away the room returns to the brightness it was before, lit by the torches placed on its walls.

"Then it is settled. We leave this wretched place and return home at the dawn of twilight, agreed?" remarks King Galen.

All the monarchs agree with his assessment.

"What about the Malakai and Neanderthals who have escaped? They cannot be allowed to ravage the land," King Leo states.

"I will ask Galgaliel and his tribe of Centaurs to chase them down and rid the supercontinent of their presence, for they are nomads whose home is the entire wilderness itself," Isolde states.

"Let the Dark Forest be forbidden to all, only we will need patrols to keep a watchful eye on the goings-on within it so we are not blindsided by something like this again," Queen Lazuli states.

"My patrols from Ravens Rock and Juul will have an envoy specifically designed to patrol within the dark realm," King Galen tells all.

"When the weather breaks and the ice covering the Sea of Storms melts as the Season of Awakening begins to take over the north, I will have part of my armada base themselves in the North Sea for the protection of all," King Baltazar states.

King Galen then stands and holds his cup above his head. "A toast! Let us feast on our agreement to move forward in the protection of our world. May we now live in peace forever. Salute!" King Galen states.

All in the room then stand and touch cups together, as the new agreement of the kingdoms is agreed upon.

Ursula turns to Isolde and asks her, "Where will you go from here, my lady?"

Isolde looks at all in the room as they all wait to hear her response. "Wherever I am needed," she responds.

On the hills surrounding the Dark Tower and in the courtyard of the castle, many of the surviving army surround the hearths, which have cooked the remaining food, to warm themselves from the blistering cold.

Galgaliel and Ormarath reunite after hundreds of seasons apart.

"My dear brother, it is good to see you," Galgaliel says in an excited tone.

"He then spots Lika walking up to the two. "My brother from another mother, Lika! The three of us together again. Like old times, yes?" Galgaliel says.

"Like old times," "Lika responds.

As the three embrace one another, Galgaliel asks the two of the great Centaur lord, "How is Khamael? Is he well?" Galgaliel inquires.

"My brother, he has greatly diminished in is leadership," Ormarath responds

"I am so sorry to hear that. I do wish him well," Galgaliel answers.

"Galgaliel, come back with us. Your brothers and sisters need you," Ormarath asks.

"And we miss your leadership," Lika adds.

"My brothers, the wilderness is my home. There is still more that needs to be done before the world is safe again for wander freely, as there is still evil in this world, and it must be eradicated. My tribe and I are just the ones to do it. One day I will return, I promise," Galgaliel answers.

"Then let us enjoy one another's company one last time," Ormarath surmises.

"I'll drink to that," Galgaliel says laughingly.

The two tribes of Warrows mingle together in the courtyard, as most have not been in contact or have seen one another in many seasons due to the vast distance between the two kingdoms and the number of deadly beasts that inhabit the realm, which make it a treacherous journey to undertake.

The soldiers of the three kingdoms have bonded over their time spent together. The anxiety and apprehension they have once had toward one another has begun to subside due to the amount of respect they have given each other over the long journey and the intense battle they have all fought alongside each other as one army.

Isolde leaves the company of the monarchs and the other sorceresses. She wanders out onto the wall between the turrets. She gazes out at the fires still burning on the plains which has sent the souls of the dead warriors to the Spirit World to eternal rest. She now has a sense of peace within her soul, for she has fulfilled her destiny, so far. She realizes that she is destined to wander the world as she is now one of the Watchers appointed by the Ancient of Days. Unlike the others in which she is now a part of, she is fully flesh and blood and will do her part as one of its protectors as a Tehran without any spirit abilities, for she is the warrior on the front lines who will do battle when called upon. Behind her, she hears a scuffle. She turns to face the commotion. She smiles as she sees her mother standing now in front of her—Elisheba, Queen of the Alicorns.

"Mother, I am so glad to see you," Isolde says with joy, as she embraces her.

"My daughter, I am so proud of you," Elisheba responds to Isolde.

"Thank you, Mother. I do what I was trained to do," Isolde answers her.

"No, my dear, you have always done what is right, always. You follow your heart, as all who do good will always do."

"I miss you, Mother, and I miss my home, though I have not been there since I was a child. It will always be home to me," Isolde contemplates.

"As it should be, my child. But as we grow, we will always carry the memory of who we were. But now it is time for you to make new memories on who you have become. Do you understand, my child?" Elisheba asks.

"I think so," Isolde answers.

"I will always be with you, always. Just call to me, and I will respond," Elisheba says to comfort Isolde. Elisheba continues, "There is comfort in your loneliness and solitude. The comfort that you will defend and come to the aid of all who are in need of your help and guidance."

Isolde looks away out onto the battlefield once again and shakes her head in agreement. "I will do my best to uphold the laws instilled in me by you and the Ancient of Days, I swear," Isolde surmises.

"I know you will. You are my daughter!" Elisheba concludes.

The two embrace one another, as they say their last goodbyes. Elisheba then flaps her long white wings and takes to the air, as she now heads back to the Lemurian Archipelago where she has resided since the beginning of time and space.

As the dawn of a new day rises upon the northland, the dwarf sun peeks its head over the Black Mountains as the armies begin to depart and head back toward their homelands. Isolde watches as Queen Lazuli and Aveline ride atop the pterodactyls with their flock in tow back to the Palace of the Rising Sun. Isolde said her goodbyes to her comrades whom she has spent the better part of the Season of Harvest and the winter season with. She now stands alone once again, ready to take on new adventures to right the wrongs, to heal the sick, to guide the weary, and to carry out the tasks asked of her by the creator of all life in the universe.

"Where to? Let's head south to Lions Gate," Isolde murmurs to herself. "I miss my little kitten. Red, I'm coming for you."

Holding her staff, she gazes at the path ahead. She takes a deep breath. Then one foot in front of the other, she is off to wander the world once again.

CREATURES, PLACES, AND THINGS

Abaddon – The demon who sits on the left-hand side of *Evil*, appointed by the evil deity to do its bidding to take over the world and send it into shadow, and to also enslave all creatures that dwell on the supercontinent. He dwells in the Dark Tower and commands an army of Shadow Demons, Neanderthals, and Malakai.

Alastair – Warrow king of the Southern Wildwood who rules over the city of Southold. He is cousin to King Leo the Just. He has ruled over the kingdom in the city of Southold for 2.5 million seasons.

Alexandra Emor – Queen of the Northern Realm and wife to King Galen. Mother of Prince Elton and Princess Ella.

Alicorns – White winged horses with its magical white horn protruding from their foreheads. They dwell in the Lemurian Archipelago. They are the messengers of the Ancient of Days, the creator of all things in the universe. Their magic is unseen like anything before. They have the power and the ability to heal, to destroy, and to foresee the future. They have the stamina to circle the globe in a single flight without resting. They are a blessing given from the Ancient of Days to the world.

Aimsworth – A sergeant in the army of the Northern Realm who is in charge of the troops in the fortress of Ravens Rock on the border of the Dark Forest and the Sea of Storms.

Amolo – A Wiki scout, arthropod, and companion of Isolde, Philo, and Turak.

Ancient of Days – The creator of the universe representing all that is good and pure. He has given birth to all life in all its forms to thrive and has given all species the ability to spread its seeds throughout the world, even beyond the supercontinent and onto the smaller islands scattered and clustered throughout its oceans. He is the creator of his divine laws which are overseen and enforced by the Watchers.

Andalusians – Tehrans in their primitive form. They were the first of the species to walk upon dry land. Mostly aquatic and hairless, with pale skin and webbed hands and feet who dwell within the Lemurian Archipelago. Their diet consists mostly of fish but are omnivorous, feasting on many aquatic plants and seaweeds, as well.

Antoinette Bourgeois – A sergeant in the Daughters of Shayla, the assassin squad of Queen Lazuli. An expert in hand-to-hand combat and with the use of the long blade.

Antler Bats – Meter-high bats with a wingspan of over two meters long. They swarm in a cauldron of thousands. They are nocturnal and hunt in the dimindark. Their habitat is primarily the tall Redwoods and Oak trees of the Dark Forest, though they do wander into the Wildwood, and along the coast of the Sea of Light from time to time if their food source become scarce in the Dark Forest. They swarm their prey in a feeding frenzy and pick their flesh clean leaving nothing but a skeleton behind.

Apollonia – The Sun God given her powers by the Ancient of Days who assists the Alicorns in their time and need and in their times of war.

Arachnids – Huge spiders measuring three meters round and with silken webs almost thirty meters round; dwell in the canopy throughout the supercontinent and feasts on anything that entangles within their webs. They live in large colonies amongst the tree canopy.

Ariel – A Watcher created by the Ancient of Days who watches over all of the firmament on Pangea and beyond, encompassing the entire world including all of the islands scattered throughout the planet. His is to oversee the nourishment giving forth from the land to replenish all that grows on it. He also has the land heal itself by allowing all that grows on it to give forth the nutriments to do so.

Artemis of Mandrake – A dwarf that was set free from slavery by Queen Lazuli because of his ability to breed and train Lambo ponies, an almost instinct breed of horses used only by the Daughters of Shayla. He dwells in the valleys between the peaks of the Corona Mountains in seclusion on his breeding farm.

Atmosphere of the Planet – The atmosphere is highly oxygenated, in which oxygen consists of about 45% of its atmospheric gases, allowing species and many trees to obtain enormous sizes and very long lifespans.

Aurelian Mountains – Mountain range bordering the Forbidden Desert which has a yellowish tint to them. These mountains hold large deposits of sulfur at their core. Its length extends around 11,265 meters, while its narrow width is about 650 meters. Its spires reach heights of 1,219 meters. Its deep valleys encase a forest of dwarf pine trees and thick and treacherous thorn bushes. The dwarf village of Hornsheed is located in their midst by the shore of the Sea of Light.

Aveline – Sorceress of Queen Lazuli who has served her for over three million seasons. She is also her spiritual and military advisor. She has great powers to see into the future and to conjure potions for the queen's desires and to aid her in all aspects of her rule over the Southern Realm.

Baltazar Azumi – King of the Western Realm who rules in the castle of World's End.

Barre – A town in the Southern Realm not far from the Westin Peninsula that consists of about one hundred inhabitants, including about twenty dwarf slaves. The inhabitants are the swordsmiths and forgers of armor for Queen Lazuli's army. They are protected by a squad of twenty-five of Queen Lazuli's soldiers who are stationed just on the outskirts of town.

Beast of a Thousand Legs – A centipede-like creature fifteen meters long and a meter wide and dwells in the caves and the lava tubes below the Dark

Tower. It is rumored to also dwell in the Mines of Mesquite, though that cannot be confirmed as of yet. Thousands of legs and thousands of teeth and its enormous size make this predator a formidable foe.

Billy Zane – A sergeant in King Galen's army and a patrol commander. An expert in the sword and bow and arrow.

Bison – Wild bison roam mostly on the Grassy Plains and the Plains of Auria. They stand almost three meters tall and four meters long. They travel in large packs in the north land. Their primary diet consists of consuming the tall grasses that grow throughout the plains.

Black Lake – Located in the eastern Southern Realm, it is fed by the River of Noir—a river of jet-black water. Its waters are toxic to any and all, except to the evil creatures that dwell in and around it. It is said to be protected by an evil spell created by Evil itself at the beginning of the world's creation, which is the legend that has been passed down from generation to generation. It empties into the Sea of Light, spilling its black waters into its basin, which spreads its toxic waters around the near coast, killing all sea life that swim into its spillage.

Black Mountains – located in the Northern Realm, also known as the Mountains of Evil. Storm clouds have enveloped their peaks since the beginning of the world. Its tallest peak is that of Mt. Hialeah under which the Centaur city of Frostford is located.

Blood Ants – Thirty-centimeter-long insects, burgundy in color that roam below the surface of the supercontinent. They burrow tunnels many, many kilometers long. They are attracted by massive blood losses, and once attracted by the blood, they attack and consume their victims until all that is left are their skeletons. They erupt from underneath the ground by pushing up on the surface, creating a caldera of sorts, similar to a volcano mountain surging upward then erupting.

Cecelia – Half-Tehran half-octopus who dwell in the Sea of Storms. Can be as long as four meters with ten tentacles which protrude from their waist. They feed on the sea life in the Northern Sea. They are all female, except for their king, Horak.

Casabel – Isolde the White Witch's sword, thusly named by the Warrow king, King Leo. It was forged by the Warrows of Wildwind made especially for the sorceress at the beginning of the First Age of Pangea. She has used this sword in the Great Wars to battle against Evil and his disciples.

Centaur – Half horse half Tehran, whose large eyes make up one third of their facial features. Their primary tribe dwells in the caves atop the summits of the Black Mountains within the Dark Forest in the village of Frostford ruled by Lord Khamael. They have resided in Frostford for millions of seasons, though there are a few bands of Centaur warriors that have left the village and now roam the wilderness as nomads who wander throughout the supercontinent.

Centaur Law – Established by the Ancient of Days and entrusted to Lord Khamael to lead the Centaurs and to instill in his tribe to live by its laws. The deity instructed them to dwell in the mountaintops of the Dark Forest to live a solitude life as they are the most unique species on all of Pangea.

Christopher William – Deputy commander in Queen Lazuli's army and a subordinate of General Levi. He is a tactician for the general and a field commander.

Chromium – A very heavy and shiny metal usually forged into thick chains used for restraining prisoners to prevent them from escaping their grasp while imprisoned in the dungeons of the three kingdoms. Used by all kingdoms as a form of mental and physical torture. The metal is mined in the Mines of Mesquite by the slave dwarfs and the Neanderthals of Queen Lazuli, then sold or bartered to the other kingdoms.

Corona Mountains – Mountain range bordering the Southern Ocean in the Southern Realm. It is the home of the dwarf village of Mandrake and the Mines of Mesquite where gold and gems are mined by the dwarfs and the Neanderthals enslaved by Queen Lazuli.

Curly-Haired Brown Bear – Large carnivore who dwells in the Northern Realm of Pangea and flourishes in the Dark Forest. It can grow to about four meters long and can weigh up to about 816.40 kilograms.

Dark Forest – The Forest of Evil situated in the northernmost part of the Northern Realm boarding the Sea of Storms where the Malakai and Neanderthals dominate the Realm, along with many other foul creatures; uninhabited by Tehrans due to the evil nature of this forest where the evil lords dominate its rule.

Dark Tower – The citadel located in the Dark Forest once dominated by Naamah, also known as the Necromancer, then dominated by Abaddon the Destroyer. It is the castle of Evil of the supercontinent. It sits near the Sea of Storms on the northern coast of the supercontinent. Two wars have been fought on the plains surrounding the citadel.

Daughters of Shayla – Queen Lazuli's secret assassins. Trained to be ninja warriors who kill on the orders of the queen. They are a secret band of twelve assassins. They ride the nearly extinct Lambo ponies and are the only ones on the supercontinent to have and use them.

Delphina – Daughter of Queen Lazuli who dwells with the queen in the Palace of the Rising Sun. She is twenty-two full seasons in age and is thin and beautiful, just like her mother.

Dokka – Thirty-centimeter-tall creatures who live throughout the supercontinent. They have flat heads, large eyes, and speak in a high-pitched squeaky voice. They live primarily underground. The largest colony is in the Dark Forest near the Sea of Storms in the caves below the mountains, but the species is spread over the entire supercontinent and their existence has never been recorded before in history, until now.

Dimindark – Referred to as the night, as it is so dark and dim.

Dwarfs – Slaves throughout the supercontinent, primarily held in slavery by the three Tehran kingdoms and have been in their captivity for millions of seasons throughout history, though there are some free dwarfs in villages scattered around the supercontinent. They have large eyes which cover about a third of their facile features. They stand about a meter high and are thick in stature, with a work ethic that is unmatched in all of Pangea which is perfect for mining for gems and gold, which is their primary function as slaves.

Elephant Mice – thirty-eight-centimeter-long rodents that live throughout the supercontinent and the islands scattered throughout the planet. They are solitary in nature and are carnivores that feed primarily on insects and small mammals.

Ella – Princess, daughter of King Galen and Queen Alexandra; three full seasons of age.

Elton – Prince, son of King Galen and Queen Alexandra. He is in his teenage seasons.

Frida – A Lambo pony ridden by Josie, a Daughter of Shayla assassin.

Frostford – The Centaur city located in the cave clusters near the summit of Mt. Hialeah in the Black Mountains. The city sits above the storm clouds which have plagued the mountain range since the beginning of time. The Centaurs have occupied the city since after the Great War of the Second Age as directed so by the Ancient of Days.

Forbidden Desert – Located in the southeast corner of the supercontinent. It is many thousands of square miles of arid desert where temperatures can reach 335.9 kelvins. It boasts only a few oases located within it. It is the home of the louse worms and the giant serpent and many other horrid creatures that live above and below its sands. It has become a hideaway for exiled Tehrans and dwarfs. This desert is avoided by all creatures of all species, for many who have entered it have never been seen again. Its badlands are full of quicksand, which is spread through its barriers, and its sand dunes can reach heights of 22.86 meters.

Galen Emor – King of the Northern Realm who presides in the castle of Lions Gate which sits at the summit of Mt. Gyphon.

Galgaliel – A Centaur lord who departed the city of Frostford to wander the wilds of Pangea hundreds of thousands of seasons ago. He leads a tribe of thirty Centaur warriors who search for new adventures throughout the supercontinent. He is a protector of the meek with the tribe that he commands. He is a sheriff against evil beings the likes of the Malakai and the Neanderthals and any such creatures that threaten the righteous on the supercontinent.

Great Meteor Crater – Located in the Dark Forest ten kilometers west of the Dark Tower which impacted toward the end of the Second Age. It is said that Naamah the Necromancer came upon it in its wake. Its depth has not been recorded through time. It is said that it extends into the Underworld, which is Evil's domain, and that all things evil and sinister emerge from it.

Great Western Road – The highway that goes the width of the supercontinent which passes through Lions Gate, then through the fortress of Juul on the border of the Dark Forest and the Sea of Light. It then heads south and ends at the town of Oium on the Sea of Light. The highway is 29,913 kilometers long.

Green Sea Whales – Ten-meter-long whales. They inhabit the warmer waters of the Neptune Sea. They are jade green in color with white underbellies who feed on small fish who swarm the open ocean. They travel in pods, with up to twenty whales in each family pod.

Giant Serpent – A large snakelike serpent which inhabits the Wildwood in the warmer months and lives year-round in the Forbidden Desert and throughout the Southern Realm, especially in the Corona Mountains. The largest serpent ever recorded was in the Forbidden Desert and was said to be seventy-five meters long and over two meters wide. They hunt in stealth and are known as the Silent Death, for they strike their victims in silence and with lightning speed. They consume their victims whole.

Giant Mole Rats – These meter-long rats have tails twice the length of their bodies. They dwell in the Dark Forest and live in long and multitiered burrows. A colony of a thousand individual rats is not uncommon. They are omnivores but prefer rotted flesh of other animals such as Tehrans. They will eat their prey until their bones are picked clean of any and all flesh.

Giselle – A sorceress in King Galen's kingdom. She is the king's spiritual and military advisor and has been so for over two million seasons. She has served his father before him in the same capacity. She has the ability to concoct spells and to see into the future. Her instincts protect the kingdom from its adversaries. She, through her powers, has the ability to control the minds of the weak and to destroy cities. She is neither good nor evil; she is whatever she needs to be to achieve her goals.

Gobi – King of the Dokka, who dwell in the caves under the Black Mountains, and a guide to Isolde and her companions who led them through the catacombs and into the Dark Tower.

Going to the Sea Road – The road that leads through the Westin Peninsula and terminates at the Palace of the Rising Sun.

Goliath Frogs – These large frogs can reach thirty centimeters in length and weigh as much as 0.91 kilograms. They are located throughout the supercontinent, with their largest concentration located within Wildwood, especially in the Gully of Longmire.

Grassy Plains – Part of the Northern Realm where it borders Wildwood. It extends into the Western Realm where it is known as the Plains of Auria and extinguishes itself at the Neptune Sea. It is the summer territory of the plains raptor, while the bison, northern elk and many species of deer call it home and dwell there in every season. It is mostly treeless and encompasses many hills which can reach heights of twenty-two meters. Its tall grasses are the staple of food for many herbivore species and can reach a meter in height.

Great Meteor Crater – Formed by a large meteor impact toward the end of the Second Age which is said to have brought the evil Naamah with it to the supercontinent. Legends have said it was directed to the planet by Evil itself. Its impact created a hole ten kilometers wide, and its end has never been explored for its depth is unknown. What else resides within it is still a mystery to all the inhabitants of the supercontinent. They will never enter its depths, for legends have said it is the entrance to the Underworld, the evilest place on the planet.

Gully of Longmire – This gully is in the northern tip of Wildwood close to the Grassy Plains. It is a secluded gully with entrances hidden and known only to a few. Its center is adorned with a thorn wall, which is dense and treacherous; thus, almost impassable. It has a running river of fresh water flowing through its core. At its deepest point, it is a hundred meters deep, and its paths are adjacent to its canyon walls whose incline is very narrow and steep.

Mt. Gyphon – The mountain reaches 3,657.6 meters into the sky at its highest point. The city of Lions Gate sits at its base with its ten thousand inhabitants. The castle of Lions Gate sits at its summit. The mountain sits ten kilometers from the boundary of the Dark Forest, separated by the Grassy Plains.

Halgar – Sergeant at arms in Galgaliel's tribe who is in command of the tribe as the War of the Fourth Age begins.

Hamal – The Watcher of the Waters created by the Ancient of Days to oversee all of the oceans, lakes, and rivers on Pangea, plus all water that encompass the entire world; to feed it with life-giving oxygen to promote the reproduction and long lives of all sea life—all but the Black Lake which is Evil's domain that is encompassed by an evil spell.

Hanna – General Harlee Antonia's Lambo pony.

Holgren River – Its headwaters enter the supercontinent from the Sea of Storms as it runs directly alongside the fortress of Ravens Rock. About midway, it intersects with Snake River, where it widens as its waters become full of rapids and extremely turbulent. Its basin empties into the Neptune Sea. It stretches a total of about 11,000 kilometers throughout its length.

HornsHead – Dwarf village of free dwarfs located in the Aurelian Mountain chain where its ending spires are situated on the coast of the supercontinent on the Sea of light. It is a fishing and mining village, mining sulfur for use as a wick for lamps. Their sailors fish the sea to feed the village inhabitants. It is a village with a population of about sixty dwarfs who live in cottages similar in size and shape which are found in the town Mandrake.

Horned Eagle – Large predator two meters in height, with a wingspan of four meters. Brown in color, they can be found roaming the entire world.

They nest on the outer islands scattered throughout the world. They are a cousin of the ivory eagles, who are the royal messenger birds of the three kingdoms. They have a horn which protrudes 16.24 centimeters from the top of their heads which is how they got their name.

Horak – The Cecelian king who rules over the Cecelia; created by Evil itself to originally rule and scathe over all of the oceans. Horak rules over his all-female Cecelia, who serve him and his sinister will, as he is directed to by Evil itself to carry out his dastardly deeds over any and all that sail the Northern Seas. As legends have been handed down from generation to generation, it has been told, as the continents converged, Horak was directed by the evil deity to rule over the Sea of Storms only as his ambassador to the frozen north and as his reward for his faithful service.

Isabella Island – Located off the southeastern coast of Pangea. The waters surrounding the island are some of the most predatorial waters on the planet. They are the breeding grounds of the megalodon shark and the Mosasaurus. Ships sailing close to the island are generally never seen nor heard from again. It is the birthplace of Ursula the Sorceress who is in the service of King Baltazar.

Isolde – The White Witch. A Tehran sorceress of great powers. Sired by Limrath the Gatekeeper to the Spirit World and head of the Watcher Order created by the Ancient of Days. She was given birth by Mira, Limrath's eternal companion, and was one of the original Watchers who, alongside Limrath, oversaw the entire order. Isolde was born before the First Age of Pangea before the continents converged to form a single land mass. She was given to Elisheba, Queen of the Alicorns, to be raised by her and to be instilled in Alicorn Law and the ways of the Ancient of Days. She was raised on the Lemurian Archipelago in the Sea of Light. At about a thousand full seasons of age, she came to the new world to roam as a nomad sorceress to help the meek and the less fortunate and to instill the goodness of the Ancient of Days on the world.

Issa – A Warrow sergeant at arms of the Southern Wildwood attached to Lucic's squad. An expert in the bow and arrow.

Ivory Eagles – The messenger birds of the three kingdoms. Ivory white in color, standing two meters tall with a wingspan of four meters. Highly intelligent and responsive to Tehran commands, they have been domesticated by the Tehran kingdoms for thousands of generations. They are the cousins of the horned eagles.

Jilly – A Tehran assassin in the Daughters of Shayla. An expert in the use of the sword and the bow and arrow.

Juul – A fortress of the Northern Realm under the rule of King Galen. It borders the Dark Forest to the north and the Sea of Light to its east. It is a border fortress, and its soldiers patrol along the edge of the Dark Forest, keeping the foul beasts that try to leave the dark land at bay.

Khamael – Lord of the Centaurs and ruler of the city of Frostford, located on the summit of Mt. Hialeah in the Black Mountains chain. He was appointed by the Ancient of Days to create Centaur Law and to have created a Centaur army to enforce it. A hero of the Great War of the Second Age, he is revered by Centaurs and Tehrans alike. He is now aged, rumored to be around four million seasons old.

Knuckle Buster – Prince Quill's draft horse which stands twenty-eight hands high and weights 1,814.37 kilograms. He is jet-black in color with silver eyes. He is considered the fastest and most powerful draft horse in the Northern Realm.

Kronosaurus – An alligator type of aquatic dinosaur approximately 33.86 meters in length with flippers that can reach more than three meters, allowing it to swim at exceedingly fast speeds in the water. It roams the warm waters of Pangea in both oceans. They challenge the megalodon for the top of the food chain in the ocean. They prey on anything smaller than themselves and can eat as much as 1,360 kilograms of food in one meal.

Krug – A Warrow lieutenant in the service of King Leo in the city of Wildwind. He and his squad are the first responders in reacting to any intruders or predators who enter the city of Wildwind uninvited. He is also an assassin in the king's court authorized to hunt down and kill any enemies of the crown.

Lambo Ponies – An almost extinct species of horse, with about only forty Lambos known to exist in all of Pangea. Jet-black in color and standing around nineteen hands high. They are bred and trained by Artemis the dwarf in his secret ranch located in the Corona Mountains. They are ridden only by the Daughters of Shayla who have the only stock outside of Artemis known to exist. They are the swiftest known animals on the supercontinent.

Lazuli – Queen of the Southern Realm who resides in the Palace of the Rising Sun. She has ruled over the Southern Realm for over 2.5 million seasons. She is the daughter of the Late Queen Ina, who was the keeper of the sacred scrolls, and mother to Princess Delphina.

Lemuria (Lemurian Archipelago) – Located in the Sea of Light one thousand kilometers off the eastern coast of Pangea. It illuminates a golden glow which can be seen from hundreds of kilometers away. Its glow lights up the sky both in the twilight and in the dimindark. It is a cluster of about fifty islands and is home to the Alicorns, the white winged horses with their unicorn white horn, as well as the Andalusians, the primitive species of Tehrans. It is a magical place with fruit, nut, and palm trees of every variety. The water's temperature stays a constant 299.8 kelvins because of its location near the equator and the magic given off by these islands. Isolde the Sorceress grew up on Tiffany Island and was raised here throughout her youth.

Levi Wult – General and commander of the army of the Southern Realm who answers only to Queen Lazuli. He has been in her service as commander of her armies for five thousand seasons.

Liam Collinsworth – A lieutenant in Queen Lazuli's army and commander of the squad which oversee the town of Mandrake in the Corona Mountains. He is also in command of the mining of gold and gems by the enslaved dwarfs and Neanderthals in the Mines of Mesquite. He has been in the queen's service for 500 seasons.

Lika – A Centaur scout and warrior who serves under Lieutenant Ormarath, a Centaur commander. He is an expert with the sword, as well as the bow and arrow. He is based out of the Centaur city of Frostford in the Black Mountains.

Limrath – The first and most powerful Watcher created by the Ancient of Days at the beginning of time and space. He is the Gatekeeper to the Spirit World and the sire of Isolde the White Witch.

Longboats – Are 6.1 meters long and two meters wide with a single sail, which stands 7.6 meters high. They are used by the sailors of Ravens Rock in the service of King Galen to navigate the waters of the Sea of Storms. They are used primarily as a patrol boat to patrol the shoreline of the Dark Forest and do not wander into the deep ocean.

Louse Worms – twenty-five-meter-long worms with a thick outer skin that keeps the moisture they absorb to stay within their five-meter round bodies. They live under the Forbidden Desert located on the southeastern tip of Pangea. They have thousands of needle-like teeth a meter long which are hollow. They puncture the bodies of their prey and absorb their inners by turning them into a liquid by excreting acid that turns their inners to mush. Vibrations in the sand caused by movements on the surface attract them to their prey.

Lucic – A Warrow commander of the Southern Wildwood who serves under King Alastair out of the Warrow city of Southold. He is a traveling companion to Isolde. He is an expert with the sword but is considered, along with Philo, the best with the bow and arrow in all of Southold.

Mali – A Warrow warrior in Lucic's squad. He is an expert with the bow and arrow.

Mammoth Cave Bear – A huge brown bear 7.6 meters long and weighing two thousand kilograms. They have giant teeth twenty-five centimeters long. They dwell primarily in the Dark Forest and in the White Mountains.

Megalodon – King of the seas. The twenty-seven-meter-long killer shark roams the warm waters of all oceans. It is usually found in the deep waters or around the many clusters of islands scattered throughout the planet, though they do seem to breed in two prominent places, Isabella Island and the Umbrella Islands.

Mines of Mesquite – Located in the Corona Mountains, gems and gold are mined here by the dwarfs and Neanderthals enslaved by Queen Lazuli. The mines are located just outside the town of Mandrake where the slaves have lived for millions of seasons.

Mira – The second Watcher created by the Ancient of Days who, along with Limrath, is also a Gatekeeper to the Spirit World. She is Limrath's concubine, and the mother of Isolde the White Witch.

Marauders of the Sea – Pirates that live in bands and usually occupy multiple ships in their brigade. They sail on both oceans and raid many ships to rob them of their wares. They have been known to settle on the many islands off both coasts of the supercontinent to avoid conflict with the three kingdoms. They are the anarchists who live by their own rules where robbery and murder are their way of life.

Mt. Hialeah – The tallest peak in the Black Mountains standing about 4,429.6 meters above the Grassy Plains. Centaur Village of Frostford is located around its summit.

Mosasaurus – A giant aquatic reptile with the appearance of a crocodile with flippers as long as two meters and as wide as a meter. It lives in the warm waters of the Neptune Sea. It can reach twenty meters in length and weigh up to fourteen thousand kilograms. It travels in pods of up to twenty or more individuals and attack their prey in groups by separating their victim from others in their pod.

Nina – An assassin attached to the Daughters of Shayla. An expert in the spear and bow and arrow. She specializes in the strangulation of their enemies.

Norbit – King Galen's swiftest ivory messenger eagle.

Northern Elk – They dwell on the Grassy Plains and on the Plains of Auria in the Northern and Western Realms. They stand five meters tall and seven meters long. Their antlers spread three meters wide and have many points and can weigh as much as 22.68 kilograms.

Northport – The most northern city in all of Pangea located on the tip of the Oolong Peninsula. It is a frozen city year-round. It is primarily a fishing and hunting village with around seventy-five Tehran inhabitants. They fish the Sea of Storms and hunt in the White Mountains to feed and clothe themselves. They are an independent village not attached to any kingdom and govern themselves, but they are not recognized by any other kingdom or king, so they live under the radar as they are isolated in their existence.

Oium – A small village of about forty Tehran inhabitants located on the eastern coast in the Southern Realm. It is a fishing village that also raises mutton for consumption.

Oolong Peninsula – The Peninsula is 12,346 kilometers long, located in the northern part of the Western Realm. The village of Northport is the only inhabited colony on the entire peninsula. The White Mountains are found in its center, running the length of the entire peninsula in which they can reach heights of 3,048 meters. This peninsula is a free land. Even though it sits in the Northern and Western Realm, it is not governed by any kingdom due to its geographical distance to World's End and the rest of the other kingdoms.

Ormarath – A Centaur commander based out of the Centaur city of Frostford on the summit of Mt. Hialeah in the Black Mountains. He is the brother of Galgaliel, the Centaur lord. Ormarath commands the Centaur army under Lord Khamael.

Palace of the Rising Sun – Located on the tip of the Westin Peninsula, it is the ruling palace of the Southern Realm and home to its ruler, Queen Lazuli. It is also a mausoleum of the queen's ancestors who are interned in the catacombs located below the castle, which are now scorpion infested.

Pendulum – An ancient method of torture and death used in the early days of civilization by the three kingdoms of Tehrans. In Pangea's Second Age, it was agreed upon by all the kingdoms to ban its use as it was deemed unnecessary and barbaric. Only Evil still uses it to torture and kill his enemies, usually in a public forum to keep his enslaved in line out of fear and intimidation.

Philo – A Warrow warrior of the city of Wildwind and a member of the King's Guard who protect King Leo the Just. He is an expert archer and a master of the sword. He is also a companion of Isolde the White Witch.

Plains of Auria – The Plains of Auria is an extension of the Grassy Plains which extend as far as the coast of the Western Realm. It was named so by the kings of old. It hosts many species which thrive on it, such as the northern elk and the plains bison. Its grasses are a meter tall or higher. It is flatter than the Grassy Plains with few hills scattered throughout its range but has a higher concentration of tree clusters scattered throughout.

Plains Raptors – Thirty-eight-centimeter-tall raptors. In the Summer Season, they will migrate as far north as the Grassy Plains, though they will head south as the Season of Harvest approaches to settle the winter months in the Southern Wildwood. They travel in herds of up to a hundred individuals. They are vivacious in appetite and will pursue prey of any size and stature for many kilometers as they attack in mass numbers.

Pangea – Supercontinent where most life exists on the planet. It is 41,322.1 kilometers long and 29,113.419 kilometers wide. It encompasses all terrains, including forests, deserts, mountains, and plains. It is a harsh and unforgiving world.

Plains Bison – A four-meter-tall mammal who dwells primarily on the Grassy Plains, as well as on the Plains of Auria. They travel in herds of up to twenty-five thousand individuals. They are herbivores whose primary food source is the tall grasses of both plains. They are a favorite food of Tehrans, Warrows, and Centaurs. Their hide is used by the latter species as clothing and shelter, especially in the winter season.

Plesiosaur – A long-necked aquatic reptile which inhabits the warm waters near the equator of the world's oceans. It can grow as long as thirty meters and weigh as much as 45,359 kilograms. Its neck is slim and can extend to as long as ten meters. It hunts in pods of up to thirty individuals and feed on smaller sea creatures that swim the oceans.

Pouched Squirrels – These twenty-centimeter-long rodents are marsupials. They are herbivores who feed exclusively on the nuts of the oak trees. They are found in the Wildwood as well as the Dark Forest.

Prince Quill – Brother of King Galen and commander of the armies of the Northern Realm.

Red – A baby saber-toothed panther adopted by Isolde after the killing of her mother.

Red-Tailed Deer – Black in color with a bright red tail. They stand two meters tall and roam the Grassy Plains and the Plains of Auria. This species travels in herds of up to fifty deer per herd.

Revealing Spell – A spell spoken in the Warrow language of Wathra. This spell reveals the secret staircases which go between the Warrow villages high in the treetops of Wildwood to the forest floor. The staircases are invisible; only the revealing spell can make them appear. This spell is known only to the Warrows, thus only a few outside the Warrow race know the spell and where the staircases are located.

Ringo – Ivy Denali's Lambo steed.

Rising Ceremony – A common ceremony conducted by the Tehrans, Centaurs, and Warrows. Though each species has their own version, the deceased are placed on a bed of wood, then set afire so the soul can be released from the deceased body and ascend to the Spirit World. The ascending souls can be observed by the onlookers who set them afire as their body releases them.

River of Noir – located in the eastern Southern Realm. It is a toxic river which is filled by the noxious waters of the Black Lake. Its basin empties into the Sea of Light, the eastern ocean. It's a lengthy river flowing 1,287.4 kilometers. Its fumes are as toxic as the vapor generated by the Black Lake itself.

Roland March – Sergeant in Queen Lazuli's army and second in command over the troops, dwarfs, and the Neanderthals, overseeing the mining in the Mines of Mesquite.

Ronin – A town in the Southern Realm under Queen Lazuli's rule which borders the Southern Wildwood. Its western boundary is located on the Snake River. It boasts around 250 inhabitants. It is a farming village who till the land of the King's Playground, which is the largest agricultural area on the supercontinent. A large variety of vegetables and fruits are grown in this fertile soil and exported to the other realms.

Royal Armada – Attached to the kingdom of World's End of the Western Realm. This armada is under the command of Prince Vale. This navy's primary duty is to patrol the coast of the Western Realm with Twenty-five ships of many sizes, from small patrol boats to large ocean crossing vessels. All are made of redwood cut from the edge of the Western Wildwood, then shipped by wagon to the city of World's End where they are all constructed.

Saber-Toothed Panther – Large wild cat, jet-black in color. Two and a half meters in length and can weigh up to 249.14 kilograms. Their large fangs can be as long as 25.4 centimeters in length. They range from the Northern Wildwood south throughout the entire Southern Realm.

Sally – An assassin in the Daughters of Shayla. An expert in closed quarters combat and of the bow and arrow.

Samael – The largest and most feared pterodactyl in all of Pangea. He is the alpha male of a flock of twenty pterodactyls. He and his flock are loyal subjects of Queen Lazuli, who will ride upon his back to venture over the supercontinent.

Saltire Cross – Also known as an X cross. A means of crucifixion used by the kingdoms and the agents of Evil to torture and murder their enemies. Usually done en masse.

Scorpions – Giant in size averaging four meters in length. Black and orange in color, with claws almost a meter long. They dwell and thrive in a damp and moist environment, such as in the catacombs of the Palace of the Rising Sun and the Dark Tower. They live in large colonies of sizes unknown. They very rarely venture on to the planet's surface, but if they do, it is only in the midst of the dimindark to search for food.

Sea of Palms Road or Way – A well-traveled road lined with many varieties of palm trees. It commences at the intersection of the Going to the Sea Road and extends to the town of Mandrake in the Corona Mountains. It is a trade route where gems and gold are transported to the Palace of the Rising Sun.

Sea of Storms – Also known as a wasteland of water and ice. The Arctic Ocean, which freezes over in the winter season, is home to the Cecelia and many other beasts that thrive in the frozen zone above the artic circle. The Season of Summer never touches this far north, as it is in a frozen state as far back as recorded time.

Seasons – Since many species live very long lives, some as many as five million years, time is measured not in years but in seasons. Parts of the planet do have four seasons depending what latitude one is located at.

Shadow Ravens – Large birds which can grow up to almost a meter in length. They are carnivorous, feeding on small vermin. They are found through the entire supercontinent and on the cluster of island chains scattered throughout the plant.

Shadow Demons – Also known as the Jinn-do, created by Evil after being cast out of the Spirit World by his brother the Ancient of Days. Created by the dust of the rancid soil of the Dark Forest. They are almost Tehran in appearance and size, though jet-black in color with orange eyes, and wings in the shape of bats wings. They are the conjurers of evil spells and can change the weather in an instant and are the ones who control the lightning.

Shanti – A Warrow warrior of the Southern Wildwood, attached to Lucic's squad, He is an expert in use of the sword, as well as the bow and arrow, and is an assassin.

Shirley – An assassin in the Daughters of Shayla. She is also an expert in the bow and arrow and the spear.

Sombrero Galaxy – One of the earliest galaxies created by the Ancient of Days at the beginning of time and space. This galaxy was created an estimated 13.5 billion years ago.

Snake River – The longest river in all Pangea intersecting from Holgren River, flowing and emptying into the Southern Ocean some eighteen thousand kilometers long. The river varies in size, from a running brook near the town of Ronin to a raging river as its intersection with Holgren River where it is three kilometers wide. Wildlife will have a tendency to congregate near it as it is the main source of drinking water for many wild beasts that roam free throughout the land.

Southern Highway – The longest road in all Pangea. It begins at the southern tip of the Southern Realm by the Palace of the Rising Sun known there as the Going to the Sea Road. It terminates at the intersection of the Great Western Road near the citadel of World's End, extending some nineteen thousand kilometers.

Southold – Warrow city located in the Southern Wildwood. It is home of the golden-haired Warrow clan, and it is ruled by King Alastair. It was built before the First Age of Pangea of the hardwood of redwoods. It is an ornate city with many carvings and ornate houses. The city sits on top of the canopy of the redwood trees some two hundred meters above the forest floor. There is no census of its population, though it is thought to be in the thousands, which includes a large population of Wiki who live alongside the Warrows.

Spell of Invisibility – Cast only by Isolde the White Witch to make one invisible and free of scent which will allow the receiver of the spell to move unseen by any and all, though it is rumored that it has no effect on Evil itself, as the deity has much of the powers as the Ancient of Days.

Sundance – A Lambo pony ridden by Jilly, an assassin in the Daughters of Shayla.

Sword Shark – A large predator twelve meters in length with a swordlike double-edged protrusion jutting almost two meters from its snout. They are solitary sharks that roam the warm waters of the oceans throughout the world.

Skol Sevverson – The commander in charge of the fortress of Ravens Rock on the border of the Northern Realm and the Dark Forest.

Savage Hornbills – Large predator parrots that dwell in the Dark Forest and along the coast of the Sea of Light. They are carnivorous in nature and attack unsuspectingly from above their victims and feed on their carcasses in midair, dropping their body parts to the ground as they fly and consume their prey.

Tehrans – The dominant species on Pangea. Males stand as tall as four meters; females almost three meters. Their large eyes that make up one third of their facial features, as with most species on Pangea, allows them to see clearly in the duskiness of the twilight and the extreme bleakness of the dimindark.

Tomb of Eternal Light – Sacred tomb where the ancestors of King Galen are encrypted. These souls have not completed the Rising Ceremony for fear that Evil will capture their souls as they ascend unto the Spirit World and condemn their souls to the Underworld.

Trig – A Warrow warrior of the Southern Wildwood in the company and command of Lucic.

Turak – A Warrow commander of the King's Guard. He oversees the procession who protects the Warrow king, Leo the Just. He is also an expert of the sword and the bow and arrow. He is a top Warrow scout and assassin, and a companion of Isolde.

Twin Rivers Bridge – The bridge that spans both the Holgren and Snake Rivers which is part of the Great Western Road. It is in a close proximity to the fortress of Ravens Rock.

Umbrella Islands – Located about one thousand kilometers off the western coast of Pangea. The islands get their name from their configuration. It is the original home of Queen Lazuli's clan. It is also home to a few nomadic tribes and marauders, who are pirates, whose tribes are scattered through the numerous islands.

Ursula – Sorceress of King Baltazar of the Western Realm. She was born on Isle of Isabella off the coast of the Southern Realm. She is the king's spiritual and military advisor. She was taught the ways of magic through Oriel, head of the Order of the Watchers, who has a fascination toward her.

Valley of Lost Souls – The valley cut between the Black Mountains that leads directly to the Dark Tower. It is a narrow valley abounding with many caves which reach high into the sides of its steep spires. It is home to many, many arachnids and cave bears. The Wolfen live in the higher caves cut into the mountain sides. It is a treacherous valley to try to travel through. Many have not lived to talk the tales of their adventure through it.

Vale Azumi – Son of King Baltazar and prince of the Western Realm. Vale is the general of the kingdom's armies and the naval armada.

Warling – An infant or Warrow child under ten full seasons of age.

Wathra – The Warrow language spoken only between Warrows to one another. Isolde is the only outsider to speak and understand their language.

Warrows – The meter-tall elves who dwell in the two Warrow cities within Wildwood. The jet-black-haired Warrows dwell in the northern city of Wildwind, while the golden-haired race dwells in the southern city of Southold. They are masters of the bow and arrow and forgers of swords made of pure gold. Their language is known as Wathra. Their young, who are under ten full seasons of age, are known as Warlings.

Westin Peninsula – Located in the Southern Realm. On its tip lies the Palace of the Rising Sun, home of Queen Lazuli. It is a flat piece of land that juts out like a jetty into the Southern Ocean, dotted with many species of clustering sets palm trees throughout its range.

White Mountains – The mountain range which stretches the entire length of the Oolong Peninsula. They can reach heights of 3,048 meters.

Wiki – Winged Arthropods who dwell alongside the Warrows in both Warrow cities. Wiki are the scouts of the Warrows and their trusted companions.

Wildwind – The Warrow city established before the First Age of Pangea. Home of the black-haired Warrow clan. The city rests upon the canopy of the giant redwood trees some 200 meters above the forest floor and is ruled by King Leo the Just. Its walkways and houses with its wood carving are as ornate as one will ever see. It stretches upon the canopy as far as one's large eyes can observe.

Wildwood – The untamed forest located in the center of Pangea. It is a dense forest with towering redwood trees and brambles as sharp as megalodon's teeth. It abounds with many, many beasts ranging from dinosaurs to large bears, to giant serpents to saber-toothed panthers. Many who enter this realm never live to talk about it. It is the home of the race of Warrows and the Wiki.

William Fry – Captain of the armies of the Northern Realm who operate out of the castle of Lions Gate. He is the commander of the two fortresses of Ravens Rock and Juul.

Wolfen – Large black wild wolves with orange eyes. They stand two meters tall and three meters long. They roam the northern latitudes of Pangea, especially on both Plains and the Oolong Peninsula. Prince Vale has domesticated a pack of them and has been breeding their kind for thousands of seasons. They are the prince's constant companions, especially in battle.